THE COMPLETE STENCILING HANDBOOK

THE COMPLETE STENCILING HANDBOOK

SANDRA BUCKINGHAM

PHOTOGRAPHY BY BERNARD CLARK

FIREFLY BOOKS

A FIREFLY BOOK

Published by Firefly Books Ltd. 2002

First Printing 2002

Publisher Cataloging-in-Publication Data (U.S.)

Buckingham, Sandra.
  The complete stenciling handbook / Sandra Buckingham. – 1st ed.
[288] p. : col. ill. , photos. ; cm.
Includes index.
Summary: Guide to stenciling including basics, techniques, materials, finishes, borders, floorcloths, projection stenciling and stenciling on wood, paper, fabric and glass.
ISBN 1-55209-638-6
1. Stencil work. 2. Stencils and stencil cutting. I. Title.
745.73   21   CIP   NK8654.B835   2002

National Library of Canada Cataloguing in Publication Data

Buckingham, Sandra, 1944 –
  The complete stenciling handbook / Sandra Buckingham.

Includes index.
ISBN 1-55209-638-6

1. Stencil work. I. Title.

NK8654.B79 2002   745.7'3   C2002-930458-7

Published in the United States in 2002 by
Firefly Books (U.S.) Inc.
P.O. Box 1338, Ellicott Station
Buffalo, New York 14205

Published in Canada in 2002 by
Firefly Books Ltd.
3680 Victoria Park Avenue
Willowdale, Ontario M2H 3K1

All original photography by Bernard Clark, with the exception of the photographs on the following pages, which were taken by Sandra Buckingham: 56, 166 (top left and right), 167 (right), 170, 199.

Produced by
Bookmakers Press Inc.
12 Pine Street
Kingston, Ontario K7K 1W1
(613) 549-4347
tcread@sympatico.ca

Design by
Janice McLean

Printed and bound in Canada by
Friesens
Altona, Manitoba

Printed on acid-free paper

The Publisher acknowledges the financial support of the Government of Canada through the Book Publishing Industry Development Program for its publishing activities.

FOR MY SISTER, LINDA BUCKINGHAM

Foreword

The Complete Stenciling Handbook is my fourth book on stenciling. Most nonstencilers cannot imagine there is that much to say about such a simple subject. After all, a stencil is a tool you come across in kindergarten. I tell skeptics that I'm just good at making short stories long. But in fact, stenciling is a craft that is forever changing, in part because of the proliferation of new materials and in part because of the creativity of those who find the stencil a versatile tool.

PORTRAIT OF A YOUNG ARTIST

PHOTOGRAPH OF SANDRA BUCKINGHAM BY A.W. BUCKINGHAM

Throughout the 14 years I have been writing and even through an ownership change of my publisher, I have had the extraordinary good fortune to work with the same production team—a small, close-knit group of talented women based in Kingston, Ontario. They have weathered the many stresses and uncertainties of the publishing industry and have become like a second family for many of their writers.

Right after *Stencilling on a Grand Scale* was completed in 1997, we were devastated by the untimely death of our book designer, Linda Menyes. We had been scheduled to start work on the handbook that fall, but without Linda, none of us felt up to it. So we shelved the project for a few years.

Janice McLean has since joined the team at Bookmakers Press as designer and has overseen photography, organized material and crafted photos, illustrations and words together into this beautiful package. Tracy Read is the patient editor who has orchestrated the whole process. She and Susan Dickinson also reworked my writing, correcting grammar and spelling and ensuring that it met the demands of the design. Catherine DeLury and Mary Patton proofread the text, and Mary also produced the index. Photographer Bernard Clark and his assistant David Kennedy worked long, long hours with Janice and me, capturing the how-to images as well as the finished-project photographs. Thank you, all of you, for doing such a great job.

I have to thank many people for their support while I worked on this book. First, by a large margin, is my family: thanks to my home team, husband Carl Walters and sons Will and Dan, for patiently putting up with my work as it overflowed from my studio and took over many other rooms in the house; to my computer techies Will, Dan and nephew Kirk Savage; to standby assistants sister Linda Buckingham and niece Dana Savage; and to my cheering squad, my mom Pat Shore and my brother Bill Buckingham. Thank you also to Susan Dickinson for my home away from home in Yarker, a small village outside Kingston, and to Terence Dickinson for making sure I knew how to operate the most important equipment in the house (after all, how can you work effectively without satellite TV and stereo?).

Many people gave me technical advice for parts of this book. I owe special thanks to Mike Townsend of Golden Artist Colors, Robert Anderson of ArtTek Studios (technical consultant to Liquitex Acrylic Products), Brian Pfaff of Briste Group International, Scott Small of LeafTek, Rebecca Parsons of Rebecca E. Parsons Studios Inc. and Anne Babcock of Maiwa Handprints Ltd.

I am dedicating this book to my steadfast stenciling partner and best friend, my sister Linda Buckingham. She is also the author of three books of her own (*Projection Stenciling*, *Beautiful Boat Crafts* and *Projection Art for Kids*).

The two of us discovered stenciling in the early 1980s—Linda on the east coast of the United States, I on the west coast of Canada. While she was cocooned in the kitschy pineapples of Cape Cod, I was trying to convince Vancouverites that stenciling was not a process for printing the school newsletter. However, I did have more time to practice the craft, because she was at sea most of the time. Literally at sea—she was living on a sailboat, cruising the high seas with her husband and two young children. When she eventually returned to Vancouver and dry land, we joined forces to create Buckingham Stencils Inc., designing and wholesaling our own line of laser-cut stencils. Almost 10 years later, we sold the business so that we could concentrate on the fun part, designing and writing. I don't know whether I would have lasted the course with this book without our daily phone calls. Linda gave me encouragement, advice and technical help—and the means to procrastinate for the length of a chat.

— *Sandra Buckingham*

Contents

Chapter 1

BEFORE YOU START

In its most basic form, a stencil is a very simple tool: a template that allows a precise shape to be easily painted on a surface and the exact pattern to be repeated wherever and as often as you wish. Templates made of tin, leather, paper and other materials have long been used by people all over the world to create painted decoration. For hundreds of years, the methods employed by stencilers changed very little—one would apply a small amount of paint through the opening in a template, stipple it out evenly, lift the template and move on.

Twentieth-century technology changed many things, and sooner or later, it was bound to affect even the humbler crafts, such as decorative painting. True, painters still climb ladders, dip their brushes into cans of paint and wipe stained hands on their overalls, but they have a dizzying array of specialty materials and tools from which to choose. It doesn't matter that few of these products were developed specifically for stenciling; like most creative people, stencilers

are always on the lookout for new ideas to adapt to their own uses.

Although this project began as an updated revision of my book *Stencilling: A Harrowsmith Guide*, I soon realized that the whole field of stenciling has changed so much that a mere revision wasn't going to be enough. So I decided, instead, to start from scratch and adopt more of a textbook approach to the subject. This would allow me to include not just the nitty-gritty of how to use a stencil but also enough information on materials and related issues to make this a useful reference book and sourcebook. I have tried to organize the subject matter so that both beginner and expert can find what they need without having to sift through sections which may not be relevant to them at the time.

The Complete Stenciling Handbook is not the place to look for creative inspiration in the form of finished rooms and projects. Rather, it is meant to be a source of methods that can be applied wherever inspiration leads. There are

bound to be some new materials I have overlooked and some traditional methods I have missed, and for that, I apologize. The range of topics here was already large enough that by the time I started working on the final chapters, I had trouble remembering what I had covered in the initial ones. We finally had to draw that line in the sand and finish the book.

For all the topics touched on that are not directly concerned with stenciling itself, my comments are necessarily abbreviated and should be considered more of a nudge in the right direction than a comprehensive treatment. For more information on these topics, please see Further Reading.

If you find this chapter hard to wade through, skim over it, picking out whatever information you need for the time being, and jump right into the good stuff by grabbing your paints and trying out some of the methods described in subsequent chapters. Just remember that the information is here whenever you need it as a reference.

Tools, Equipment, Materials

It's tempting for the casual stenciler to focus on the wonderful array of commercial stencils offered through stores and mail-order catalogs and to give short shrift to surface preparation and choice of the actual products to be applied. All you're really interested in is getting started, getting finished and admiring the end result.

However, the past few years have seen an incredible growth in the number and variety of paint products and tools available to both professional painters and do-it-yourselfers. The choices are no longer as simple as they once were, and the creative possibilities offered by different mediums are too good to pass by without at least some consideration.

It's easy to feel bewildered when faced with aisles of products calling out to be bought, each brand claiming subtle advantages over its competitors. The lack of a standard well-defined terminology makes things even more confusing. I hope that this chapter will provide a basic understanding of the products so that you'll know what properties to look for and be able to make informed choices. At the very least, it should help you ask intelligent questions of product suppliers.

I have tried to make sure that what I have written was up-to-date at the time of printing. However, paint technology and creative methods for applying paint continue to evolve quickly—so much so that this chapter may well be ready for an update before the printer's ink is dry.

Wherever product-label information differs from that suggested in this book, please assume the label is correct and follow the instructions for that particular product.

STENCILS CAN BE CUT FROM MANY DIFFERENT MATERIALS, CLEAR OR OPAQUE

STENCILS

In one form or another, stencils have been used for ages as tools for decorating walls, floors, furniture and textiles. In terms of the design, manufacture and use of this tool, traditional stenciling as most of us know it remained basically unchanged throughout the world for centuries.

■ Stencils were once made of materials such as leather, shellacked or oiled card stock and thin metal sheets. For a long time, they were all hand-cut; later, die-cut templates were manufactured for wider distribution. Most stencils incorporated ties, or bridges, either as part of the design or, more often, as a necessity to ensure stability. After the pattern was stenciled in paint on a wall, the painter might go back over the work with a fine brush, filling in the blanks left by the ties. Subsequent innovations included the use of very fine iron or brass wires to replace the ties. The design would be entirely cut out, then the wire ties would be fixed to the stencil with glue or wax. These ties were thin enough that they did not block the paint, so the resulting image was free of the gaps produced by normal ties.

■ Stencils were held in place with stencil pins. Stencil brushes were generally large so that the stencil could be covered quickly. If different colors were to be applied to the same stencil, however, the painter would use smaller brushes to keep the colors distinct. Masks might also be used to cover up various openings in the stencil and thus protect the colors.

After dipping the brush in paint and distributing the color evenly on the surface of the brush, the painter would dab the brush over the whole stencil. Then the brush would be gently pounced over the paint to even out the application.

Stencils had to be removed with great care, because the paint used in older times dried slowly. This made it easy to smudge the work when lifting the stencil.

By the 1920s, airbrushes were being used with stencils, allowing a subtler blending of colors. Airbrushes were particularly useful for printing wallpaper and textiles.

The first big innovation in centuries arrived a few decades ago, with the introduction of transparent stencils made of plastic films, such as acetate and polyester (Mylar). Transparency made it much easier to position the stencil and to line up overlays. The advent of laser cutting allowed for more detail and precision in the designs. Laser cutters are directed by computers from digital translations of the designs, which also means that editing patterns or sizing them up or down is dead easy and that an entire collection can be stored as computer discs instead of bulky metal dies.

Today, most quality commercial stencils used for interior decoration are laser-cut from Mylar sheets of various thicknesses, 5 mils and 7 mils being the most common. Less expensive stencils for the hobby market might be made of different plastics, or even cardboard, cut by die or chemical methods. There is also a market for very small stencils cut from metal sheets. Homemade stencils are hand-cut from materials such as Mylar, cardboard, vinyl and freezer paper.

WOOD, GLASS, PAPER AND PLASTIC CAN ALL BE STENCILED

SURFACES FOR STENCILING

Stencils can be used on just about any surface to which paint will stick and a stencil can be fitted. An ideal surface is flat, relatively smooth and not too glossy. It doesn't really matter whether it's plaster, wood, tile, plastic or metal, as long as it has been prepped with a primer meant for that type of material or the material itself will take the paint without priming. A good primer means that all of these surfaces can be treated more or less the same as far as basecoating and stenciling are concerned. A few materials, like fabric or glass, may need special attention, but such surfaces are discussed in their own chapters.

Surfaces that are not flat can also be stenciled, depending on how "not flat" they are. A stencil can be wrapped around a cylindrical lamp shade, for example, but not around a spherical vase, because the stencil won't bend in two directions at once. However, it may be possible to stencil tiny flower buds on that vase if the stencil for an individual bud is small compared with the curvature of the vase.

Rough surfaces, such as stucco or cedar planks, can also be stenciled, as long as you don't mind a somewhat primitive look to the print. Because the stencil cannot cling to all the contours of a rough surface, the edges of any stenciled image won't be as crisp as on a smooth surface. For applications like this, it's better to use rather simple motifs, since elaborate details will be lost.

Glossy surfaces are difficult to stencil because the paint does not stick well (it tends to slide around under brush or roller action instead of staying put). This can be circumvented by deglossing with sandpaper or with an agent like TSP (trisodium phosphate), available at hardware stores, then stenciling and finally restoring the sheen by applying a glossy sealer. Another approach is to cover the glossy surface with an appropriate primer, apply a low-sheen basecoat, then stencil and finish with a clear sealer of the desired sheen. Some shiny surfaces such as glass can be worked as is with specialty paints.

It feels quite different to stencil on surfaces that are more or less absorbent. A flat basecoat grabs the paint and keeps it wherever the stencil brush puts it down, while a shiny coat almost repels it. I like to work on a basecoat with an eggshell sheen—it allows more control than the extremes on either side.

Paints

The more you learn about paints and finishes, it seems, the more there remains to be learned. I don't want to make this and the following sections more complex than necessary, but a basic understanding of the mediums is important to anyone who wants to achieve predictable and consistent results. Knowing more about a medium than simply whether it is "water-based" or "oil-based" can help you manipulate finishes, choose compatible products and avoid nasty surprises.

■ Before moving on to specific types of paint, I'd like to offer two general pieces of advice. Most paint manufacturers have websites and toll-free information lines. Don't be afraid to use them for any questions you may have about specific products—ingredients, instructions or limitations. I cannot emphasize this enough. The technical experts employed by those companies can provide a wealth of information to guide you in choosing appropriate products or to help you solve a problem.

■ Also, unless you are familiar and comfortable with your paint systems, try to use products made by the same company for any given project. This isn't always possible, particularly with specialty products. But if it is, then potential compatibility issues can be minimized. And if there should be a problem, the help-line expert for the glaze manufacturer can't shift the blame to the paint manufacturer, and vice versa.

LATEX PAINTS

Paint technology has been geared toward producing water-based replacements for most of the old oil-based products. Water-based coatings come in different sheens and are long-lasting, resilient and strongly adhesive. They dry fast, have little smell and clean up with water.

■ I use water-based paints and finishes for almost everything, including floors, kitchen cabinets and concrete surfaces, with excellent results. There are a few exceptions to my water-based rule: I use oil-based varnish for many wood projects and pigmented shellac or an oil-based primer for sealing and priming surfaces such as MDF (medium-density fiberboard), wood or paper.

■ All paints are made up of a pigment, a binder and a solvent. The pigment is a colored powder that does not dissolve. It can be organic, inorganic, natural or synthetic. It has little or no ability to adhere to a surface on its own. This is where the binder comes in—it is the glue that sticks the pigment to a surface and dries to form a protective film.

The binder in so-called water-based paints is, technically, a polymer emulsion, which simply means a stabilized suspension of really small plastic beads in water. The generic name for all such paints is latex. (In Great Britain, the word "emulsion" is used instead.) This label is very general and includes artist, hobby and house paints. Acrylic paint is a particular type of latex paint in which the plastic beads are made of acrylic resin.

NOTE: To recap—all latex paints are made up of pigment (the color), an emulsion of tiny polymer resin droplets in water (the binder) and a small amount of a solvent that evaporates more slowly than water. As the water evaporates, the resin particles fuse together, trapping the pigment in a hard, flexible film. At the same time, the solvent softens the outer coating of the droplets sufficiently that they interlock, and as the solvent evaporates, the linked droplets form a continuous, irreversible film.

■ Latex paint dries quickly to the touch (it's dry when the water has evaporated), but it hasn't "cured" until the solvent has evaporated. Because the solvent is encased by the dried paint film, which slows its rate of evaporation, curing can take considerably longer—days, or even weeks, depending on conditions. This is what causes problems when masking tape or even low-tack tape is used for striping or for securing stencils on a freshly painted and ostensibly "dry" wall. Removing the tape can lift bits of paint off at the same time, because the paint has not finished curing. I think every decorative painter, whether professional or do-it-yourself, has had at least one bad tape experience. The thing is, curing time is variable. It depends on temperature and humidity, and it's not something that can be assessed simply by running your hand over the wall.

■ The specific properties of a cured paint film—such as adhesion, flexibility, hardness—depend on the particular type of resin or plastic used in the binder. Even among paints using the same resin—say, acrylic—there can be variations in properties, depending on the quality and the proportional content of the acrylic used. Properties that relate to color—such as lightfastness—depend on the type and quality of the pigments used.

PAINT ADDITIVES

The properties of latex paint can be manipulated by including one or more specific additives with the basic formula. These may have been added at the factory, but some can be purchased separately, allowing you to customize the coating for your own particular needs. Remember, though, that any additive which does not contain a polymer emulsion (i.e., the glue part of the paint) will have no binding properties and can lower the adhesion and durability of the paint. Be sure to follow label instructions about how much to use. Many additives may have significant effects on the properties of the paint, even though they represent less than 1 percent of the paint composition.

■ Fillers, or extenders, are inexpensive inorganic materials that extend the volume of a coating by acting as a substitute for extra pigment (which is the expensive part of paint). They are the only additives that are used in large volumes. Excessive amounts of filler will lighten the paint color somewhat. If it diminishes the resin component of the paint significantly, then the durability of the coating may suffer. To control cost,

cheaper brands of house paint typically use the highest volume of fillers. Special extenders, available for use with artist acrylics, make it possible to extend the volume of the paint up to 50 percent, with little or no noticeable loss in color intensity. This can result in considerable savings for projects requiring large amounts of paint.

■ Retarders increase the "open" time of paints, causing the paint to dry much more slowly. This makes it easier to blend colors on the work surface and to do detailed brush work. Retarders are often called extenders, perhaps because some extenders can also increase the working time of paint. Whenever you buy an extender,

make sure you know which product you're getting.

■ Flow enhancers improve the flow, absorption and blending of the paint by decreasing its surface tension. They also minimize the appearance of brush marks. On nonabsorbent surfaces, they increase the drying time of the paint as well.

■ A matting agent is added to the binder to control sheen. It may be something like diatomaceous earth, whose particles scatter light reflected by the paint film, thus making the surface appear dull. Any coating with a flat or diminished sheen, whether paint or varnish, should be kept well stirred during application so that the matting agent stays evenly dispersed throughout the container.

HOUSE PAINTS

Latex house paints are made with lower-quality resins and cheaper pigments than are artist-quality acrylics. They also have a lower pigment load and contain extenders to make them spread farther and opaque additives to make them cover better. These are all reasons why there is such a significant price difference between artist acrylics and

latex house paints. Of course, it doesn't mean that house paints are "bad" or that they shouldn't be used for stenciling or other decorative applications. It all depends on the context. If you're painting the Sistine Chapel and want it to last for a thousand years, you should go for broke in terms of paint quality. But if the project at hand is a nursery

mural with purple teddy bears that your child will outgrow in a few years, there's nothing wrong with using house paint, especially if you can pick up some nice mistints from a paint store for next to nothing.

All house-paint brands have different lines of products, each with its own properties. A premium line has more pigment

and higher-quality resins than a budget line. Exterior paint is more tolerant of temperature fluctuations and more resistant to fading than an interior paint. Industrial paint is tougher and designed to adhere to more difficult surfaces. Porch and floor paint is tough and more flexible. Be sure to pick the right product for your needs.

Paints

ARTIST AND HOBBY ACRYLICS

Artist acrylics use a high-grade acrylic resin in the binder emulsion, one that resists UV and remains flexible and nonyellowing. The pigment load is usually as high as possible for a particular pigment. The labels often provide useful information, such as transparency or hiding power, intensity and lightfastness.

Student-grade and so-called hobby acrylics vary in quality from brand to brand. They generally have a lower pigment load than the artist lines and may contain opacifiers or extenders to compensate for this. They generally have a lower tinting strength than their artist counterparts.

■ Acrylic paint dries fast: a thin stenciled film in seconds, a normal painted film in less than an hour. (It does take longer than this to cure, though.) Once cured, acrylic paint is irreversible and water-insoluble, although it can be removed with denatured alcohol, lacquer thinner or acetone. It forms a flexible, stable film that adheres well to both interior and exterior surfaces.

■ Acrylic paint is available in a huge range of colors and in various consistencies. Heavy-bodied acrylics have a thick, buttery consistency and are generally sold in tubes. Less viscous formulations have a smooth, creamy consistency and can be poured from jars or squirted from plastic squeeze bottles. Both can be used for stenciling and glazing applications, although the lower the viscosity, the easier it is to thin and blend with other mediums. On the other hand, thick paints can be used for impasto applications. Most paint companies sell mediums that can be mixed with their paints to alter the viscosity.

■ Viscosity is not a reflection of quality. The thickness of the paint is determined by the makeup of the paint binder, not by the pigment content. For example, compare two ounces of good-quality, medium-viscosity (i.e., "thin") artist acrylic with two ounces of the corresponding high-viscosity (i.e., "thick") artist acrylic. They each have exactly the same amount of pigment. It is simply a myth that thinner paint necessarily has less pigment.

■ In a number of special-effects paints, the standard pigments are replaced or enhanced with mica flakes, dyes or metals. For example, interference paints have coated mica flakes which reflect one color and refract another, giving an effect like that of oil on water.

SOLID OIL PAINTS

Solid oil paints are sold in two formats: as crayon-like sticks and in small pots like lip gloss. The quality of the different brands—in terms of pigment load, and so on—depends on whether they are sold as an art or a craft medium. As always, price is usually a good indicator. Cleanup with the craft version is typically with soap and water, but you will need turpentine with the art version.

◼ Stencilers either love solid oils or hate them, because they have unique properties that impart both advantages and disadvantages. On the plus side, solid oil paints don't spill, and they don't bleed (because they are solid). They blend and shade very easily, because they dry slowly. These qualities alone make them ideal for beginners. The long dry-

ing time means the brushes won't dry out while you answer the phone, and the stencils are easier to clean. It also means that areas of just-stenciled paints can be selectively removed, if desired, to create highlights or add details such as leaf veins.

◼ The colors can be made to look very transparent simply by applying them sparingly, so they work well for adding shadows to stencil work. They can be used in combination with acrylics, where the acrylic is used for opaque coverage first and the oils are used to add shadows or other details. Oils can be applied to many surfaces, including walls, paper, wood and fabric.

◼ The slow-drying characteristic that gives this paint its good qualities can cause some problems—the paint smudges very easily and hence can make

it difficult to work with multiple overlays, unless you apply the paint sparingly and handle the overlays with care. Also, the underside of the stencil should be checked after each print and overlay, and any trace of paint picked up on that side must be cleaned off. The work must be protected from smudges while you are stenciling.

◼ Beware of muddying your colors with solid oils, since the residual paint left on the stencil will blend with any other colors you add (unlike acrylics, which usually dry fast enough to prevent such problems). The best way to avoid undesired color alteration is to wipe the stencil clean after each print.

◼ It is difficult to build up really intense color with solid oils, because the paint is transparent in thin layers and doesn't

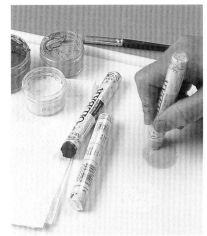

SOLID OILS IN STICK AND POT FORMAT

dry fast enough to allow multiple layers to be built up.

◼ Solid oil paint must be applied with a stencil brush, rather than a roller or an airbrush, and the process is rather slow, so it's not for anyone in a rush.

◼ The product label may recommend spraying a specific clear coat on top for protection.

MASK AREA BEFORE SPRAY PAINTING

SPRAY PAINTS

Some stencilers prefer to use spray paints in pressurized cans. Although the color choice is somewhat limited, these paints can be mixed fairly effectively by simply overspraying one color with another. Spray paints can be used for most of the simpler paint techniques in this book, although I find them rather messy and the fumes noxious. You need very good ventilation and should wear a mask while using them.

◼ Before applying spray paint, mask the area around the stencil with protective paper, because the paint tends to spread out, dispersing in the air in a very fine aerosol, which can cover a fairly wide area. Protect the floor as well, because the droplets that don't reach the surface fall to the ground.

Paints

FABRIC PAINTS AND DYES

Many paints can be used on fabric. Artist and hobby acrylics adhere well to most fabrics without heat-setting, although they get a little stiff when dry. Some paint companies offer flow enhancers that, when mixed with acrylics, help the paint saturate the cloth fibers. Fabric medium does the same thing and helps the fabric remain soft after the paint has dried.

■ For projects that require a lot of paint, little washing and no need for softness, even latex house paint can be used. Applying house paint by roller stenciling (see Chapters 2 and 15) will allow you to zip through decorating yards and yards of curtains in record time and with minimal cost.

■ True fabric paints contain resins that bond to fabric and remain flexible. They may also have flow enhancers to help the paint permeate the fabric. These are the paints to use for consistent results whenever softness is essential—say, for baby clothes or anything worn close to the skin. Most fabric paints require some kind of heat-setting for permanency. This information is always printed on the label.

■ Most fabric paints are quite thick and work perfectly for stenciled application. If you ever need to use something like a silk paint, which is usually too runny and prone to bleeding for stenciling, thicken it by adding a tiny amount of sodium alginate. This powder can be purchased at any shop that sells silk-painting supplies. Do some tests before proceeding with this, however, as the binder is effectively being diluted when the thickener is added, which may cause some trouble with permanency.

■ No matter how fine or supple, fabric paints are all basically alike in that they form a coating which binds to the surface of the cloth. Dyes are completely different, as they form molecular bonds with the fiber itself. There are many types of dye, both natural and synthetic. Each is suitable only for particular types of fiber—silk, cotton, hemp or nylon, for example. Instead of the simple heat-setting needed by fabric paints, dyes usually require steaming or chemical fixing.

Most dyes are extremely fluid and not really suitable as a stencil medium, unless they are thickened with sodium alginate or a proprietary thickener. However, dyes do make excellent background colors over which patterns can be stenciled with fabric paint.

PAINT MEDIUMS

A pure acrylic medium is simply a colorless paint binder. Mixing colored paint with an acrylic medium increases the transparency of the paint without affecting its adhesive qualities, because the proportion of pigment is diluted but the binder remains full strength. Used in combination with a retarder to slow the drying time, a mixture of paint and clear acrylic medium creates a translucent water-based glaze.

■ A gloss medium increases the sheen and enhances the color depth, while a matte medium decreases the sheen. A clear (i.e., colorless) acrylic medium can also be used on its own as a nonreversible protective film to apply over dried stencil work.

■ A number of mediums can alter the characteristics of acrylic paint. For example, an airbrush medium is a premixed blend of acrylic polymer emulsion (binder), water, retarder and flow enhancer. Mixing it with acrylic paint (or other water-soluble paint) renders the paint suitable for airbrushing. Other mediums can be used to thicken paint or to make it iridescent, opaque or transparent. Paint altered with impasto and textural mediums can be used with stencils to create raised motifs with different textures.

■ Mixing a fabric medium with acrylic paint makes the paint easier to use on fabric, allowing it to penetrate the fibers and to dry with a soft hand.

■ Mediums are different from additives in that they contain a binder, just like paint, which means they do not weaken the paint when mixed with it.

GLAZES

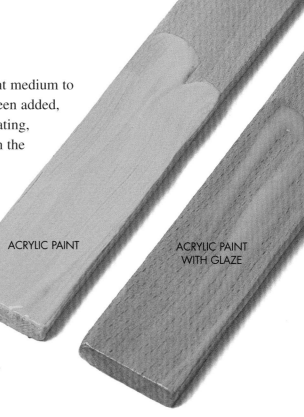

ACRYLIC PAINT

ACRYLIC PAINT WITH GLAZE

A colored glaze is basically a clear paint medium to which a small amount of color has been added, resulting in a translucent or transparent coating, depending on whether the added color is in the form of paint or universal colorant. Glazes can be used on their own as a stenciling medium, wherever less opaque coverage is desired. More generally, glazes are applied over a basecoat as a way of subtly enriching or changing the colors of a wall or a piece of furniture. The finished appearance can be altered by using layers of colored glazes and by manipulating the glazes with various tools. This is called faux finishing.

■ Most glazes are sold untinted. You color them yourself by adding artist acrylics, universal colorants or house paint. Some manufactured glazes are meant to be used with a specific type of colorant, so be sure to read the label before proceeding. Untinted glazes look milky but dry clear.

■ The properties of a glaze can be altered in a number of ways. If the glaze is to be used in a faux finish, it must have a longer open time than a pure paint medium has. Adding a retarder increases the drying time long enough to allow the glaze to be manipulated. Follow the manufacturer's instructions, then experiment to find the right proportion to add for your particular needs. Negative faux techniques (in which glaze is first applied, then removed) require a longer open time—hence more retarder—than do positive faux techniques (in which glaze is manipulated as it is applied). Warm, dry conditions require more retarder than do cool, damp conditions. Note that some manufactured glazes (as opposed to homemade ones) already have a retarder added. Drying times differ from brand to brand, so a test is necessary when changing brands.

■ To make a glaze more transparent, add color in the form of a universal colorant. Except for the dark colors, most house paints contain a mixture of pigments that includes titanium dioxide, which is a very opaque white. Coloring a glaze with house paint that contains titanium white reduces its transparency and renders it translucent instead. Such a glaze produces a dusty effect similar to that of traditional limewashes. Glazes tinted with paint have a shorter open time than those tinted with colorants.

■ If the glaze is not going to be manipulated at all but used only as an even layer of transparent color, tinted acrylic varnish can be used instead of a glazing medium.

Paints

PRIMERS

Picking the right primer is the most important paint choice you'll make, even though you don't actually stencil with it. This is the coating which ensures that the work sticks to the surface. There are primers designed for every type of material—drywall, wood, MDF, metal, glass, laminates, concrete—and they render all these materials essentially the same as far as subsequent coats of paint are concerned. Once the surface has been properly prepared and primed with the right product, it shouldn't matter whether you're working on a tin box or a wood table. The methods and materials for basecoating and stenciling are the same. Your paint dealer can help you select the right primer.

UNIVERSAL COLORANTS

Universal colorants are thick, intensely concentrated liquid pigments used for coloring both oil- and water-based house paints. Available in small tubes as well as large containers and in a limited palette of basic colors, they are used for tinting commercial glazes and for mixing custom colors of latex paint. Pay particular attention to the proportions recommended on the label, because universal colorants on their own do not dry. Adding too much to a glaze or a paint can prevent it from drying properly.

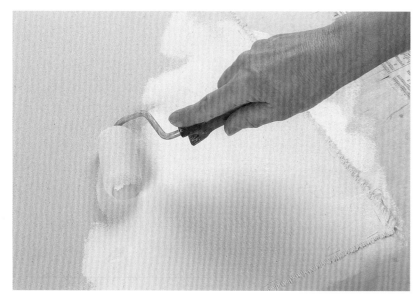

PROPER SURFACE PREPARATION AND THE RIGHT PRIMER ARE PARAMOUNT

Wood Stains

Wood stain can be used to tint a wood surface prior to adding stenciled decoration or used as a stencil medium itself. Unless you understand what type of stain you are using and how it interacts with the wood you are decorating, it is easy to become frustrated with stains. Like paints, stains are made up of colorants, binders and thinners. However, the effect that a specific stain has on a particular wood is not as straightforward as it is with paint; it is determined by the nature of the colorant, the binder and the formulation (i.e., liquid or gel). It is important to understand these components to pick the right stain for the job.

COLORANTS

Stain colorant can be pigment or dye. Pigment is made up of finely ground colored particles of earth or synthetic materials. The particles are solid and do not dissolve in the stain. They are simply held in suspension, which is why pigmented stains must be stirred frequently during use. Most commercial stains are made with pigments.

The pigment particles color wood by lodging in depressions (and in any scratches) in the wood surface. The binder in the stain glues the opaque pigment particles to the surface.

■ Unlike pigment, dye is a molecular color, generally made today from petroleum derivatives. Dissolved in an appropriate solvent, the dye molecules saturate the wood fiber itself with transparent color. They are much more readily absorbed on sections of cross grain, where they can penetrate the wood along its vascular channels. Thus if the wood surface has some areas where the grain is parallel to the surface and other areas where it cuts the surface, applying a dye will result in uneven staining.

■ A dye adheres on its own and needs no binder. It is important, however, that any clear finish coating does not contain the same solvent as the dye, or the solvent may reactivate the dye and move it around as the finish is applied.

BINDERS

All pigment stains need a binder; it's the glue that holds the pigment parti-cles to the wood once the solvent has evaporated. There are four types of binder: oil, varnish, lacquer and water-based. The choice of binder determines how much time is spent wiping off excess stain; it doesn't really affect the ap-pearance of the stain. Lacquer binder cures very fast; varnish and water-based binder cure fairly quickly, and oil binder cures slowly.

■ Stains that are sold as a combined stain and finish have a much higher pro-portion of binder to pigment. Treat these stains more like paint, building up layers rather than wiping off the excess.

GEL STAIN

LIQUID STAIN

SOLVENTS AND THINNERS

Solvents are used to dissolve the dye in a stain. Thinners are used with pigment stains to thin the binder for easy applica-tion. Each dye and each binder has a specific compatible sol-vent or thinner. It might be mineral spirits, lacquer thinner, alcohol, oil, glycol ether or water. Any stain or finish that contains water (as solvent or thinner) presents a problem in that the water causes the wood fibers to swell (it "raises the grain"). This makes the wood feel rough to the touch after drying, even when it has been sanded before wetting.

■ The only solution is to raise the grain deliberately and sand it down before staining. To do this, stop short of the final sand-ing, wipe the surface with water and let it dry overnight. Then lightly sand off the raised grain with fine sandpaper, removing no more than the raised grain.

STAINS AND SEALANTS

Most stains are liquid, but there is a fairly new type called a gel stain, which is much thicker. Gel stains have an additive that resists flow unless mechani-cally disturbed and are the easiest stain products to use with stencils.

Stain can be applied to bare wood or to wood that has been sealed or partially sealed. The effect of a stain is more pro-nounced on bare wood, so to emphasize a beautiful grain (bird's-eye, for instance), this is the route to take.

■ A sealant (sold as wood conditioner) smooths out the crevices that might lodge extra pigment, thus allowing a more even coloration. It also moderates the penetration of a dye stain. It's good for uneven woods, which are prone to splotching, and for wood that has characteristics or flaws you don't wish to emphasize.

■ Woods that do not have a tight grain can be difficult to stencil with a stain be-cause the stain tends to bleed out along the grain. Sealing the wood before stenciling will help prevent this because the sealant fills and blocks the passageways between the wood fibers.

CHOOSING THE RIGHT STAIN

When it comes to choosing a stain, there are no absolute rules—it is very much an aesthetic and therefore personal decision. Your choice should depend on the type of wood, at least for overall staining.

■ Pine varies so much in density, for example, that it takes stain very unevenly. This problem can be reduced by using a gel stain and sealing the wood beforehand. Oak also varies a great deal in density, but it has large pores that take up dye stains quite evenly. Dye stains work best with maple, because it is generally too fine and smooth to accept much pigment.

■ When it comes to stenciling with a stain, you are usually working over a "basecoat" stain that has been applied to the entire surface, so the effect of the particular type of wood is not important. Stenciling is easiest with a gel stain, which has properties similar to those of thick paint.

■ The final consideration when choosing a stain is to make sure it is compatible with the finish coat. If in doubt, consult the experts of the company that makes the product, either by toll-free telephone or by e-mail.

■ If you plan to do more than just the occasional project with wood, you will find it worthwhile to learn more than I have presented here. There are many ex-cellent books available for various levels of expertise.

Clear Finishes

A finish coat is a hard, transparent film that seals and protects the stencil work. It can also unify or alter the final sheen or give greater depth to the colors. Generally, wall stenciling does not require a finish coat, unless a particularly fragile medium has been used or the wall will be subject to a lot of wear and tear. Finish coats are absolutely necessary, however, for anything that goes underfoot (painted floors and floorcloths) and are usually advisable for most furniture.

■ When it comes to finish coatings, there is a lot of confusion among do-it-yourselfers, largely because manufacturers take great liberties when naming their products and are not always specific about the makeup of the products. Water-based finishes are often given the same technical name as their non-water-based counterpart. People use the words shellac, lacquer, varnish and polyurethane interchangeably, even though these finishes have very different chemical compositions and properties.

■ Many finish coatings are designed for use on either stained or natural wood, rather than as a sealer to protect painted surfaces, and some of these finishes may not bond properly with paint. If the label gives instructions for applying the product on wood but says nothing about previously painted surfaces, then it's a safe bet the manufacturer will not recommend that it be used over paint. This doesn't mean it can't be done, just that it might or might not work well. If unsure, call the manufacturer or do some preliminary tests.

■ Many companies do make clear finishes and sealers especially for use on painted surfaces. All the artist- or craft-paint manufacturers provide such products, as do the makers of specialty paint mediums for faux finishing.

■ Most clear finishes or sealers come in a choice of sheen, from flat through glossy. Keep in mind that flat finishes, because of the presence of flatting agents, tend to cloud the depth of dark colors, whereas shinier finishes render them more brilliant.

■ The three finishes I use most are shellac, varnish and water-based. The last one is often popularly referred to as "acrylic varnish," even though it is not truly a varnish.

SHELLAC

Shellac is made up of a natural solid resin dissolved in a solvent (alcohol). Once dried, shellac redissolves upon contact with more solvent. Thus if a second coat is applied after the first has dried, the new coat partially dissolves the first coat, fusing the two layers together. No sanding is needed, so it's easy to touch up damaged spots. Evaporative finishes like this cure from the bottom up, so when the surface is hard, the entire film is hard. Shellac dries extremely fast, with a high gloss that can be buffed to a velvet sheen. It adheres well to many difficult surfaces.

■ Don't confuse transparent shellac with opaque, pigmented shellac. The latter (sold under the trade name BIN™) has a heavy pigment load and is sold as a fast-drying primer for many types of surface, including any that cannot take a water-based product.

■ Clear shellac can be useful in decorative projects as a sealer and as a barrier coat—for example, for quick isolation of reversible (dissolvable) water-based paint or for sealing knots in wood. However, it cannot be used under polyurethane because of adhesion problems. Sometimes, you can get around this by using de-waxed shellac and a good-quality true alkyd varnish or using the shellac as a very thin wash coat, diluted 50/50 with denatured alcohol. Be sure to test the method first. The other problem with shellac is that it is vulnerable to water spots. This can be minimized by waxing the dried shellacked surface.

VARNISH

True varnish is made of a resin cooked in a curing oil to which a thinner and a drier are added. It is a so-called reactive finish, in that it undergoes a chemical change (called cross-linking or polymerization) as the thinner evaporates. The molecules form a network that cannot be broken when thinner is reapplied. In other words, the thinner in a second coat does not soften the first coat once it has cured, and there is no bonding between the coats. This means two things: A topcoat can be manipulated without affecting a dried previous coat; and a first coat must be sanded before adding a second coat, to provide a mechanical bonding between the layers.

■ Varnish cures slowly, from the top down, so it may feel dry but still be vulnerable. It is important to wait for the entire film to dry completely, then sand before adding a fresh coat. Some types of varnish (check the label) have a small window of time shortly after the first application when a second coat can be applied without sanding, because during that period, the thinner is able to soften the surface just enough to allow some cross-linking between the two coats.

■ Varnish is the most durable of the finishes available to the do-it-yourselfer. However, there are many types of varnish, and their properties depend on which resins and oils are used and on the ratio of oil to resin. Alkyd-resin varnish has been a mainstay of the finish industry for most of the past century. Slightly newer is polyurethane resin, the toughest type of varnish. Pure polyurethane finishes are not generally used by the do-it-yourself sector; they come in two parts that must be mixed, like epoxy glue. The finish that is generally sold as polyurethane in paint stores is actually an alkyd varnish modified with polyurethane resin. It cures like an alkyd varnish and is the most popular type of varnish available today. The main disadvantages of varnish are that it cures slowly and yellows over time.

REMOVABLE PICTURE VARNISH

This is a permanent, but removable, final varnish for acrylic and oil paintings. Picture varnish protects the painted surface and allows for removal of surface dirt without damaging the painting underneath. Flexible and nonyellowing, it contains UV inhibitors to protect the colors of the painting, but it is not a really tough finish like alkyd varnish or polyurethane.

WATER-BASED FINISH (ACRYLIC VARNISH)

Water-based finishes are made up of tiny droplets of cured solvent-based finish emulsified in water, along with a small amount of a very slow-evaporating solvent (glycol ether).

■ The product looks milky in the can and doesn't turn transparent until it dries. Water-based finishes cure from the bottom up, and it takes several weeks for maximum bond. Aways follow the label for exact recoating instructions. Generally, you must wait at least a few hours to avoid trapping water in the first coat and making the finish cloudy. The label instructions may offer a window of time wherein you can recoat without sanding, but once the first coat has had more than a day to dry, you must sand to create a mechanical bond between the coats.

■ Among woodworkers, this product is often referred to simply as "water-base." In an effort to make it sound more familiar to consumers, many manufacturers call water-based finishes "varnish" or "polyurethane," even though the finishes have little in common with real varnish or solvent-based polyurethane. Most of these finishes have acrylic in the emulsion, hence the popular name "acrylic varnish," but some have a blend of acrylic and polyurethane. The addition of polyurethane makes the finish tougher but can also render it a little cloudy. This may be a problem if it is used as a protective coating over dark or brightly colored stencil work. Sometimes it's hard to tell from the label exactly what's in the product, but you can call the company to find out the exact properties.

■ Water-based finishes have become very popular because they are scratch-resistant and nonyellowing, have reduced solvent content and require only water cleanup. However, they are not as resistant to heat, water and chemicals as are oil-based varnishes. They also raise the grain of wood, as do all coatings that contain water.

Clear Finishes

APPLICATION

There are two tips to keep in mind when applying all types of finish coats: work dust-free, and use several thin coats instead of one or two heavy ones. Beyond that, each type of finish has its own peculiarities. It is therefore best to read the label and follow the instructions concerning preparation, tools, ambient temperature, application and drying and recoating times.

■ Most finish products are packaged for brush or roller application. A few can be wiped on with a soft cloth. Many are available in aerosol cans, so the finish can be sprayed on smallish projects, which saves having to invest in major spray equipment. Consider a sprayed finish for a really meticulous result without brush marks.

■ Wherever possible, try to avoid options that involve sanding over top of stencil work. Even with a coat or two of protective finish already in place, it is all too easy to rub through and damage the paint. If you must sand, do so very cautiously, and use a fine grit.

■ This stage of the work is worth spending the time and effort to plan and carry out correctly. The finish coat is not something to be slapped on like a piece of punctuation at the end of a sentence. If done properly, it can turn your work into a stunning showpiece; if not, it can ruin the whole thing.

Applicators

A number of different tools work well for applying paint through stencils. Some are better than others for specific situations, but by and large, your choice is a matter of personal preference.

BRUSH

The traditional tool for most kinds of stenciling, a stencil brush looks a bit like an old-fashioned shaving brush, with densely packed bristles trimmed flat and bound into a cylindrical ferrule. Another version is somewhat flattened and has slightly tapered bristles; it is ideal only for a "swirling" application or for linear shading but not for stippling (see Chapter 2).

■ Stencil brushes come in sizes ranging from less than ¼ inch to 1 or 2 inches in diameter and with different types of bristles. Stiff bristles are required for pouncing and softer ones for rubbing or swirling.

ROLLER

High-density foam rollers used with house paint or hobby acrylics are the applicator of choice for covering large stencils quickly. Lap lines can be minimized by choosing a roller with rounded ends and by adding a small amount of retarder to the paint. Do not use soft-foam or nap rollers for stenciling; they hold too much paint and will cause paint to bleed under the stencil.

SPONGE

Cellulose and sea sponges produce stenciled prints with a mottled coloration, which is useful for faux-stone effects. Fine-textured makeup sponges are the best applicators for glass and tile stenciling.

AIRBRUSH

Airbrushes make excellent tools for stenciling, but because of the initial cost of the equipment and compressor, they are used more by professional artists than by do-it-yourself stencilers. You must also be somewhat mechanically adept when it comes to operation and maintenance, but if that's not a problem, an airbrush can be a valuable stenciling tool. It allows for very fast, even coverage of large designs and lets you build up opaque coverage more quickly than with a brush or roller. When it comes to shading and hand embellishment of stenciled images, an airbrush offers the ultimate in control. The best way to find out whether this is your dream tool or not is to sign up for a course with an airbrush stenciler. In addition to the hands-on learning, you will get valuable information on the different brands and types of airbrush and compressor. Some are easier to use than others; some require more or less maintenance.

■ For the hobbyist or amateur stenciler, it makes more sense, dollarwise, to stick with low-tech brushes and rollers. But to get an inexpensive flavor of airbrushing, buy a can of pressurized propellant to power an airbrush, instead of relying on an expensive compressor. Going the cheap route won't necessarily be faster than using a stencil brush, however, because a good proportion of time is spent switching color jars and cleaning out the hose with each switch. When blending a variety of colors with each stencil, this can prove cumbersome. Professionals, on the other hand, typically work with more than one hose and airbrush at a time, all connected to the same compressor.

■ I am not including airbrush instructions in this book, because it would be directed at a rather more select group of painters than I want to address here. This book is primarily meant for the do-it-yourself enthusiast, and as such, it veers away from large investments wherever possible. However, anything I describe that uses a stencil brush or roller can be done equally well (if not better) with an airbrush, and airbrush artists should have no trouble adapting the methods.

Miscellaneous Equipment

Stenciling does not require much in the way of specialized accessories, and if you dabble in paint already, you probably have just about everything you need. Here is a list of items that I find useful.

■ Palette tray: This is a reusable flat plastic surface with a slightly raised edge. I find it indispensable for roller stenciling, for mixing small amounts of paint colors and for working paint into stencil brushes. To make a substitute tray, line an old, rimmed cookie sheet with freezer paper.

■ Putty knife or palette knife: A collection of different sizes is useful for roller stenciling, impasto stenciling and blending colors on the palette tray.

■ Artist's brushes: A small selection of various sizes and shapes is handy for adding freehand details to stencil work.

■ Paper towels: These are essential for offloading paint and for cleaning up the occasional mess. Old bath towels make a good recyclable substitute.

■ Stencil adhesive: This low-tack glue comes as a spray and is used to hold stencils in place, to keep unstable stencil parts from shifting while the paint is being applied and to hold masks in place. Always apply it in a well-ventilated area (outdoors is best). Lightly spray the back of the stencil or mask, and let it dry before using. Sometimes adhesive leaves a residue on the surface. Small spots can be removed from hard surfaces or paper with a soft art eraser. Residue can be wiped off larger areas with a soft cloth dampened with paint thinner, as long as the stenciling was done with water-based paints.

■ Low-tack painters' tape: Use this for guidelines on a wall, for masking stripes, for holding stencils in place and as a surface for removable registration marks.

■ Plastic misting bottle, filled with water: This is my favorite accessory for keeping paints and stencil rollers from drying out.

■ Small plastic squeeze bottles with very fine tips: Filled with paint, these allow you to outline stenciled motifs with a fine line, to add details such as veins to a leaf and to write words of script.

■ If you plan to cut your own stencils, you also need a knife (X-acto or craft), spare blades, a cutting mat and stencil material. A heat cutter (similar to a fine soldering iron) is also useful, especially for cutting heavy Mylar or cutting highly irregular lines.

■ Pencils, ruler, eraser: These basic drawing materials are handy for a variety of uses.

■ Zip-lock sandwich or snack bags: Keep stencil rollers from drying out during short breaks by zipping them in individual plastic bags. The snack-sized bags are also useful for storing individual oil-based solid paint sticks. This keeps the colors from contaminating one another and from smudging other surfaces.

■ Putty adhesive, sold as Fun-Tak or Easy-Tak, is useful for anchoring strings used as guidelines. Test it beforehand to make sure it doesn't leave marks on the wall.

Color

Oh, my, what a subject! When you come right down to it, this is what painting is all about. The rest is really just technical stuff—getting paint to stick, manipulating it into shapes, and so on. It does help to be adept with technique, but in the end, it is color that speaks to the soul. For stenciling to look exceptional, you must know something about color.

Few amateur painters are color experts, but this is really where you should start. It's easy to learn the physics of why a leaf looks green, but that sort of knowledge is far too theoretical to be much help when you open your box of paints and look at a blank canvas.

COLOR WHEEL

To understand color, the first thing you must do is make or buy a color wheel. The second thing you must do is read a good book on color (I've listed some in Further Reading). Even better, take a course. The third thing you must do is get out your paints and start playing with color in some organized fashion—say, by doing exercises proposed in your color book. Many of these exercises can be useful references to check back on, so keep them in a file or journal.

You can become as academic as you wish about color, but if you're serious about it, you want that knowledge to become instinctive. That's not going to happen just by reading; it will come only by watching two colors change as you press a palette knife into that creamy lump of ultramarine and drag it into a smear of burnt sienna.

1 A color wheel organizes the 12 primary, secondary and tertiary colors of artist's pigment colors, placing them in conventional positions around the circumference of a circle. There are three so-called primary colors: red, yellow and blue. They are called primary because they cannot be produced by mixing any other colors. These three colors are always situated on the color wheel with yellow at the top (12 o'clock), blue at 4 o'clock and red at 8 o'clock.

2 Mixing two primary colors produces a secondary color. There are only three combinations of primary colors, so that means three secondary colors. Green is at 2 o'clock, midway between the yellow and blue that produce it when mixed. Violet is at 6 o'clock, halfway between blue and red. Orange is at 10 o'clock, right between red and yellow.

3 The six tertiary colors come from mixing the primaries with the secondaries adjacent to them. For example, yellow-green = yellow + green; blue-green = blue + green; and so on. The names make it easy. A complete color wheel is made up of all 12 colors: three primaries, three secondaries and six tertiaries. If you join the primaries with straight lines, you get an equilateral triangle—the primary triad. If you join the secondaries, you get another triangle —the secondary triad.

■ The color opposite any given color on the color wheel is called its complement, or complementary color. For example, the complement of yellow is violet, the complement of green is red, and so on. Complements have special properties, which we'll get to later. It's a good idea to become familiar enough with the color wheel that you can name a color's complement without picking up a wheel and figuring it out.

This is all pretty straightforward so far, but where color theory really gets interesting is when you start asking, "Okay, I've got five different yellows in my paintbox. Which one is the primary?"

There isn't any answer to that, except maybe, "It depends." You can pick any one of many primary triads, as long as each of the colors making up the triads is compatible—similar in transparency, intensity and tinting strength. Each choice of primaries will produce a color palette with completely different characteristics and personality: delicate or intense, opaque or transparent, earthy or clear.

Color

PROPERTIES OF COLOR

The first three terms used to describe color are hue, intensity and value. Hue is the most obvious characteristic—it identifies a color by name: red, orange, yellow, green, and so on. The choice of hues determines the psychological reaction of the viewer; it conveys the mood. Hue is a very general term—for example, there are *lots* of reds. To be specific, include the pigment name or the hue and brand names.

■ A very general, but useful, classification divides hues into warm (reds, yellows) and cool (blues, greens). This classification is entirely relative; for example, it can be used to describe a range of one basic hue such as red. Warm reds would be those closer to yellow on the color wheel (orange-reds), whereas cool reds would be those with a bluish cast.

In practical terms, the brain interprets colors in such a way that warm colors appear to come to the forefront of the painted surface, while cool colors seem to recede. Thus your paint effects can be reinforced with a judicious choice of colors or diminished with a poor choice. Since warm colors seem warmer when contrasted with cool colors, and vice versa, make that poppy in your stenciled mural pop right out by painting it orange and putting something blue or purple or green right next to it.

The second characteristic of a color is the relative intensity of its hue, whether it is bright or dull. High intensity means pure and bright; low intensity means grayed and dull. Any color can be made progressively duller, or less intense, by neutralizing it with other colors. Generally, the biggest decline in intensity occurs when you mix in a second color that is distant on the color wheel —and the most distant is the complementary color.

■ For example, if a bright yellow makes you feel as if someone is running fingernails down a chalkboard, try mixing in a tiny bit of violet. Or if the yellow has already been applied to the surface, let it dry and then overcoat it with a faint, transparent purple glaze. The intensity of a bright color can also be lessened by mixing in some black or gray or an earth color. There is no way to increase the intensity. What you start with is the brightest it's going to get.

By varying the intensity of a given hue, you can also differentiate contrasting areas within the same hue. For example, rendering different planes of an image in different intensities of the same hue creates a three-dimensional impression. Manipulating the intensity of the hues can also reinforce the foreground/background structure of the painting (or stenciling), because the more intense colors will move to the fore. A color can also be made to appear more intense by placing it on or near a duller rendition of the same hue.

The third characteristic of color is value, which can be best described by imagining a colored picture printed in black and white. Areas that appear lighter are higher in value. Areas that appear darker, whether by virtue of the original hue or because they are in shadow, are lower in value. Yellows are highest in value, violets lowest.

TINT

The value of a color can be made higher (or lighter) by adding white. The lighter color is called a tint. Colors can be made darker by adding black or a darker colorant in the same general hue. Such a color is called a shade of the original hue. Both tints and shades tend to reduce the intensity of a color.

HUE

SHADE

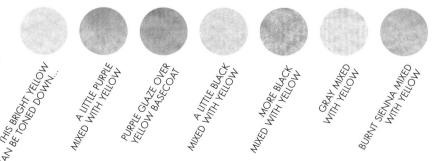

THIS BRIGHT YELLOW CAN BE TONED DOWN... A LITTLE PURPLE MIXED WITH YELLOW PURPLE GLAZE OVER YELLOW BASECOAT A LITTLE BLACK MIXED WITH YELLOW MORE BLACK MIXED WITH YELLOW GRAY MIXED WITH YELLOW BURNT SIENNA MIXED WITH YELLOW

COLOR MIXING

Mixing two colors together alters all three properties—hue, intensity and value. The one property that is most problematic to the untrained amateur is intensity. For example, most stencilers know from using single-layer stencils that mixing two complementary colors produces a color so dull, it's usually called "mud." However, many of us also find that we can avoid obvious complements and still end up with dull colors whenever we try our hand at mixing. It's no wonder that hobby acrylics, with their vast choices of premixed colors, are so popular with amateur painters. They let you venture from your standard palette without the hit-or-miss results of mixing your own.

THE MECHANICS OF MIXING

A couple of things will help keep your mixed colors lively: one lies in the mixing technique itself and the other in your choice of colors. First, avoid overmixing. Instead of mixing two colors beforehand, try to leave a bit of each showing. Apply one directly to the wall, then the other, and mix them slightly, right on the wall. Or premix them lightly on the brush as you pick up each color from the palette.

■ The former method is probably easier for stencilers, because of the need to offload the brush. Pick up some blue, and stencil part of a leaf, leaving a few gaps, or "holidays." Then, with the same brush, pick up a green and finish the leaf. Or pick up the two colors at once on the same brush, as long as the offloading doesn't cause them to mix completely.

SPLIT-PRIMARY MIXING

A large range of intermediate colors can be created by mixing combinations of the three primary colors. The easiest way to retain control over the intensity of the color mixtures is to use a so-called split-primary mixing system. This system is based on the fact that adding even a little complementary color to any given color always lowers the intensity of that color.

BRIGHT COLORS

To keep mixed colors bright, don't add any hint of complementary colors. In your paintbox, you probably have more than one yellow, more than one red and more than one blue. In other words, you have a choice of colors that can be used as primaries, some warm, some cool.

1 Suppose you mix a green, using a warm yellow and a warm blue. The yellow and the blue both have a slight bias toward red (that's what makes them "warm"). In other words, they each contain the smallest amount of red. However, red is the complement of green, so the resulting mixed green contains a hint of its own complement. Hence it will be a dull green.

2 Now mix a green from a cool yellow and a cool blue. This time, none of the colors has any hint of red, so the resulting green is clear and intense.

WARM BLUE AND WARM YELLOW MAKE A DULL GREEN

COOL BLUE AND COOL YELLOW MAKE A BRIGHT GREEN

Color

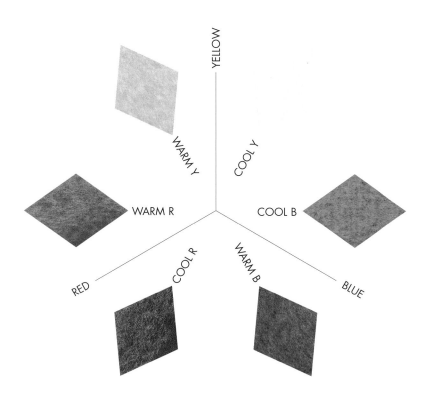

WARM Y + COOL B   COOL Y + WARM B   WARM Y + WARM B

COOL B + COOL R   WARM B + WARM R   COOL B +WARM R

COOL Y + WARM R   COOL Y + COOL R   WARM Y + COOL R

A VARIETY OF DULL COLORS CAN BE MADE BY JUMPING SECTOR LINES; TOP: GREENS; CENTER: PURPLES; BOTTOM: ORANGES

Creating your own colors is a challenge, and it's easy for a novice to get mixed up. Here's where the color wheel comes to the rescue.

1 Start with a plain white circle, and draw three spoke lines radiating from the center to 12 o'clock, 4 o'clock and 8 o'clock, dividing the circle into three sectors.

2 For each primary, pick two colors from your paintbox, one warm, one cool. Starting at the 12 o'clock position, paint a spot of warm yellow to the left of the line, cool yellow to the right. Move to 4 o'clock, and put cool blue above the line, warm blue below. At 8 o'clock, put warm red above the line and cool red below.

3 Now, whenever you want a bright mixture, pick all the colors from the same sector (i.e., the same slice of the pie). Do not cross any spoke lines.

■ To get bright secondary colors, mix yellow and blue from the same sector, blue and red from the same sector, red and yellow from the same sector.

■ For the tertiaries, again stay within each sector (cool yellow and green to get yellow-green, and so on). As long as you don't cross any lines, you'll avoid adding any hint of a complement and always get bright colors.

BRIGHT SECONDARY COLORS ARE MIXED FROM WITHIN SECTORS

DULL COLORS

Don't be put off by the connotation of the word "dull." When referring to colors, it doesn't mean "boring" but, rather, "lower intensity." Dull is for calm, subdued effects, for contrasting brightness, for shadows and shading, for making images recede. It is the counterpoint to bright.

■ The fallback method for producing dull colors is to knock back the intensity by adding grays or blacks straight from the jar. However, by using split primary mixing, beautiful low-intensity hues of any degree can be created, including a whole range of colorful neutrals. This is achieved by starting to cross those sector lines, which allows measured amounts of complementary color to be added to the mix.

COLOR HARMONY

Choosing colors is the hardest part of any decorative project. Color schemes are so personal, they defy regulated selection. It's like trying to use formal decision-theory paradigms for picking a new job or deciding whether to have children—it doesn't really matter what the analytical, calculated outcome is, you always feel most comfortable going with your gut feeling.

■ Nevertheless, there are certain guidelines, certain theoretically pleasing combinations of color, that can help you get started. But don't hesitate to experiment once you reach the starting point. If pulling in some color outside the formal scheme lifts the whole thing out of "correct but boring," then go with it. Often, you will know right away that you don't like something but may not be sure how to fix it. That's where an understanding of color schemes can help.

■ A number of "official" color schemes are considered harmonious. The simplest is a monochromatic scheme, which uses variations in the value and intensity of a single color. An analogous scheme includes colors that are adjacent to each other on the color wheel. Each scheme has its own unique characteristics in terms of energy, intensity and harmony. A good color book will describe and explain them all, and it's worthwhile checking them out, even if you use them only as points of departure.

STENCILED COLOR

The big difference between stenciling and other forms of decorative painting, besides the fact that a template is used, is that the layers of color are extremely thin. A vestige of background color almost always filters through the film of stenciled color. Knowing this, you should tailor your stenciling colors so that the background enhances them. It will help you avoid nasty surprises, such as an unexpected drop in intensity from the layering of two complementary colors.

■ Then there will be times when you *want* to lower the intensity. A border segment may look great stenciled on a sample board but overwhelming when running all around the room. That

boldness can be neutralized by going over it with a complementary or near-complementary glaze.

■ An understanding of color theory will let you choose the colors for a single-overlay stencil so that the blended parts are still lively. It will save time and trouble with stenciled murals and produce a better result.

■ Most stencilers tend to fall back on a few ready-mixed colors like Payne's gray or raw umber for shading and shadows. Once you start experimenting with mixing low-intensity colors and colorful neutrals, you can make your shading and trompe l'oeil much more interesting.

Backgrounds

A simple faux finish on the wall, even for the background of a border strip, can enhance the look of the most basic stenciling. However, this is not intended to be a book on faux. Its focus is stenciling, and I don't want to lose sight of that along the seductive and multi-branching trails of faux finishing.

I have used a few simple methods for basecoats in this book, and you can teach yourself similar finishes with the help of books listed in Further Reading.

If you're not the experimental type, take a short class from a local paint store. As with all techniques, the more you practice, the better the results, so once you get started, decorate the laundry room and the bedroom closet before tackling the living room.

All faux finishes involve some kind of manipulation. In so-called positive finishes, the manipulation is in the way the paint or glaze is applied; rolling paint on a wall with a twisted rag, for example, so that the folds and creases of the rag show up in the paint coat. With a "negative," or "subtractive," finish, the manipulation happens when portions of a previously applied coat of colored glaze are removed. Here, a slow-drying glaze rather than paint is required, because paint dries too quickly to be removed and is typically too opaque to work with these methods. Positive techniques can usually be done competently by one person, but most negative methods work much better with two people, one applying the glaze and the other following behind manipulating it.

It is very important to keep moldings and trim well masked while working on the walls. The most elegant finish will look shabby if glazes spill over onto the trim. And work on one wall at a time, taping the edges of adjacent walls so that the corners stay clean.

LET'S GET STENCILING!

This chapter has covered a lot of technical information. You don't have to memorize Chapter 1 to become a great stenciler—no one is going to quiz you on the composition of latex paint or the makeup of the color wheel. Stenciling is easy, fun and an enormously satisfying craft to master. All you need is practice, enthusiasm and a little imagination.

Chapter 2

THE BASICS OF STENCILING

For those readers who are true beginners, this is your most important chapter. Here, you will learn how to cut your own stencils and make successful prints using a variety of tools and paints. You'll find examples of different kinds of stencils and learn about overlays and how to use stencils and masks in combination. Because even experts make mistakes, we also look at some common problems and how to fix them. Finally, no treatment of the basics would be complete without a discussion about the cleanup and care of stencil tools.

You will get the most out of this chapter if you assemble a few supplies and follow along with some of the examples by practice-stenciling on paper. There's no need to try out all types of paint or to spend a lot of money. Start with what you already have on hand —house paint and a homemade stencil are just fine. Set yourself an easy goal, such as turning a plain sheet of kraft paper into decorative holiday wrap. The more you practice, the better you'll get. Stenciling is an easy craft, so it's not difficult to become adept at it.

Cutting a Stencil

You don't need to learn how to cut a stencil to become a good stenciler. There are thousands of commercial stencils marketed by dozens of companies, and if you stick to these, you can simply skip this section. If you do become an avid stenciler, however, sooner or later, you'll want something just a little different, and you'll have to cut your own. But rest easy, it's not difficult.

■ As for stencil patterns, you'll probably start with ones you find in books or magazines. A good source is Dover Publications, which publishes many excellent stencil-pattern books, covering a wide range of designs from historical to contemporary.

■ Once you get hooked on stenciling, you'll see design possibilities everywhere and patterns in all sorts of everyday images. Start with silhouettes, then gradually move on to more complicated patterns. In the sections that follow, you'll see how elements of a design can be built up with stencils, and this will help you understand how to create your own images.

■ No matter what kind of stencil material you use (opaque or transparent) or what kind of tool (knife or heat cutter), there are a couple of general guidelines to keep in mind when cutting a stencil. The most important rule is to make sure you can see what you are doing. Obviously, the lighting must be good, and if you wear glasses, your prescription must be up-to-date. This may sound silly, but many beginners don't realize how long it has been since their last eye exam until they try to cut a stencil.

■ To achieve better control, always cut toward yourself. Rotate your work as you go so that it is properly oriented. Make long, smooth cuts, including bends and curves, without lifting the cutting tool. To make sharp points, use a knife and make two separate cuts that intersect ever so slightly at the point. Always cut the small stuff first, as well as the inside edge of curved shapes such as vines and scrolls. Wherever you have fine bridges, cut away from the bridge; then if you slip, you won't cut through the bridge.

■ If you cut stencils with a knife, the blade must be very sharp. Be prepared to replace or sharpen it as soon as it ceases to cut smoothly. I use a small Olfa utility knife that has strips of snap-off blades with the same sharp-angled tips as a No. 11 X-acto blade. These blades are inexpensive, and a fresh blade is always just a snap away (which means I don't have to try to remember where I put the package of spares).

■ For a cutting surface, use a piece of plate or tempered glass (with the edges taped), a self-healing cutting mat (for knife cutting only) or a piece of dense cardboard.

■ If you make a miscut, patch the cut on both sides with clear tape and recut that part of the pattern.

Cutting a Stencil

OPAQUE STENCILS

1 Spray the back of a paper pattern with stencil adhesive, and stick it onto a sheet of stencil material, such as cardboard, opaque plastic or freezer paper (shown here). Working on a protected surface, carefully cut along the pattern lines with a sharp craft knife, cutting through both the stencil and the pattern.

2 Peel off the pattern.

3 When using a very thin material, such as freezer paper, you can cut multiple copies at one time by stacking pieces that have been sprayed on the back with adhesive (to prevent them from slipping).

CUT ALONG PATTERN LINES THROUGH BOTH PATTERN AND STENCIL

PEEL OFF PATTERN TO REVEAL STENCIL (BROWN FREEZER PAPER)

TRANSPARENT STENCILS

Stencils can be hand-cut from various types of clear film, including polyester, vinyl, acetate and overhead projection film. These materials are all slightly different—some are tinted, frosted or self-adhesive, some are easier to cut or more flexible. Every stenciler has a favorite, but 5-mil polyester film is probably the most widely used. It is tough, impervious to most chemicals and very resistant to tearing and stretching. Film thicker than 5-mil is hard to cut with a knife; film thinner than 5-mil is very easy to cut but not robust enough for heavy use or large stencils.

Most people outside the plastics industry refer to polyester film as Mylar. Although the name is a registered trademark belonging to the product's inventor, DuPont, it has been adopted as a generic term. "Mylar" now usually refers to polyester films in general (which are manufactured by any number of companies), and I use the term in the same broad sense throughout this book.

1 Before starting, hold the stencil film in the air by one edge, and look at it in profile to see whether it's curved. Some types of film, especially those sold in rolls, never lose their curvature, but you can use this to your advantage by making the concave side the underside of the stencil. Simply place the cut edges so that they always curve in toward the surface being stenciled, thus ensuring good contact. This way, there will be less chance of bleeding or of bristles slipping under the stencil.

2 Lightly spray the underside of the stencil film with low-tack adhesive, and smooth it over a photocopy of the pattern, which is visible through the stencil film.

3 Use a permanent felt-tip pen to transfer all registration marks now (so that you don't forget later).

4 For designs requiring multiple overlays, all overlays should be drawn on the same pattern. This will ensure good registration. (For a more complete description of overlays and registration, see Overlays, starting on page 48.)

5 The pattern will likely fall apart as you cut and remove several overlays, so use multiple photocopies of the same pattern.

6 For transparent films, you have two choices for a cutting tool: a knife (X-acto or utility) or a heat cutter.

KNIFE

Place the stencil film with the pattern underneath it on a cutting mat, a piece of tempered glass or a piece of firm cardboard (*not* corrugated). With a very sharp craft knife, carefully cut the stencil along the pattern lines. The pattern may or may not end up getting cut, which is why you use a photocopy so that the original can be preserved.

CUT ALONG PATTERN VISIBLE BENEATH STENCIL FILM

LIFT FINISHED STENCIL

HEAT CUTTER

Heat cutters for stencils look like miniature soldering irons, and they get extremely hot. Keep the point sharp: From time to time, refine the point and remove corrosion with a fine file.

1 Preheat the heat cutter. Attach the stencil film on top of the pattern as previously described.

2 Place the stencil film and paper pattern on a piece of firm cardboard or a piece of safety glass (not a cutting mat).

3 Holding the heat cutter like a pencil, trace along the lines of the pattern with the hot tip. As you move the tip along, it will melt a line in the film. It is vital to keep the tip moving at a steady rate so that the cut line will remain an even width. If you hesitate, you will melt a wide hole in the film.

NOTE: Often, a small amount of melted plastic builds up along the edge of the cut line, but this will not stop you from getting a good print with the stencil. The melted cut lines are not quite as smooth and perfect as knife-cut lines, but for most purposes, these stencils are just fine in terms of the quality of the prints you can make from them.

■ Since you don't have to exert any pressure, heat cutting is easier on the fingers than knife cutting, and it is much easier for very convoluted cutting. However, it is sometimes more difficult to do long, smooth curves, because the cutter can melt in any direction if your motions are not firm and swift. A knife, on the other hand, tends to stay generally in its track, making smooth curves relatively easy. I sometimes use both knife and heat cutter on the same stencil, employing the former for straight lines, smooth curves and sharp points and the latter for small curves, small holes and wiggles.

■ Do not use a heat cutter for any stencil that will be used to make impasto prints (see Chapter 4).

WHEN USING A HEAT CUTTER, BE CONFIDENT AND KEEP IT MOVING

Making a Basic Print

When it comes to stenciling, there's one cardinal rule: Use the least amount of paint possible while working. Start with a dry applicator (brush, roller or sponge), and keep as little paint on it as you can and still produce a print.

The magic word is "offload," as in offloading, or removing, all excess paint from your brush or stencil roller before touching it to a stencil. This is why stenciling is often called a "dry brush" technique. Offloading is important, because paint has a tendency to creep, or "bleed," under the edges of the stencil, which results in a blurry print. (We'll deal with the exceptions to this rule in later chapters.) For now, all you need to remember is that if your stenciling tends to bleed, then either you are using too much paint or your applicator was damp at the outset.

It's a common misconception that the problem of bleeding can be avoided by using abundant spray glue and making sure the stencil adheres closely to the surface. All this does is leave residual spray glue on the surface. In fact, it might even make the problem worse. Technically, bleeding is caused by capillary action—the spontaneous movement of liquids through narrow channels such as sponges, capillary tubes and the vascular structures of plants. It is caused by forces of attraction between the molecules of the liquid and the walls of the channel and by forces among the liquid molecules themselves. The narrower the channel, the stronger the forces. Ironically, the closer the bond between your stencil and the wall, the more likely it is that the paint will bleed, since a film of sprayed-on stencil adhesive is only a layer of spread-out droplets, not a solid wall at all.

There are only a few ways to make a basic stencil print, depending on the tool and type of paint you use. As long as you can learn to make a clean print with either brush or roller, then there won't be much in this book that you won't be able to do. When boiled down to its essentials, stenciling is really very simple.

WORK PAINT INTO BRISTLES

OFFLOAD EXCESS PAINT

TO STIPPLE, TAP BRUSH STRAIGHT UP...

BRUSH AND LIQUID PAINT

1 Use heavy paper or poster board for a practice surface. Anchor your stencil in place with low-tack tape or spray glue.

2 Place a dollop of paint onto a palette tray or plate. Use artist acrylic, hobby acrylic, fabric paint or latex house paint. Start with a completely dry stencil brush. Pick up a very small amount of paint on the end of the brush. On a clear part of your palette, work this paint thoroughly and evenly into the ends of the bristles by rubbing the brush in firm circles.

3 Now offload, working the brush in circles on a stack of paper towels to remove all excess paint. The point at which you're ready to proceed is difficult to describe and, while you're learning, is best arrived at by trial and error.

4 There are two techniques for applying paint to a stencil: stippling, or pouncing, and swirling. Most stencilers gravitate to one method or the other and stick with it (as in, "Are you a stippler or a swirler?"). To stipple, hold the brush straight up and down and pounce it over the cutouts in the stencil, using short, hard taps.

5 To swirl, hold the brush straight up and down, and rub it in small circles over the cutouts, pressing lightly at first, in case you have a little too much paint on the brush, then gradually more firmly. Most stencilers work around the edges of a stencil cutout before moving to the center, and many apply more color to the

...AND DOWN; FINISHED PRINT, RIGHT

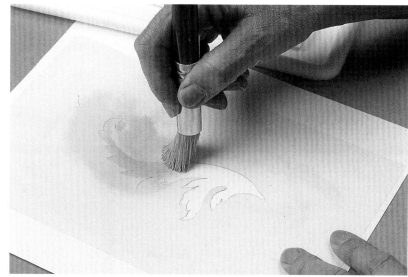

TO SWIRL, KEEP BRUSH VERTICAL AND WORK BRISTLES IN SMALL, FIRM CIRCLES

edges as well. To apply more color, do not make heavier applications, as this could cause bleeding. Rather, make repeated applications, building up the color gradually.

6 The paint always looks darker once the stencil is removed, so lift a corner of the stencil from time to time to see whether you're there yet. When you are happy with the print, remove the stencil. The paint should already be dry to the touch, because it is such a thin film of paint and you're using a type of paint that normally dries fast anyway.

NOTE: Your brush may start to feel dry and leave fainter and fainter impressions before the print is finished. Repeat the procedure for loading and offloading the brush, then resume stenciling. When the brush feels too dry to stencil but still seems to have adequate paint, it needs dampening—*not* wetting, but very slight dampening. To do this, either tap the brush lightly on a damp sponge or use a fine water mister to spritz a light mist of water over the palette (this also helps keep the paint dollop from drying out). Now, without picking up more paint, work the brush in circles on a damp part of the palette. Wipe the brush on a paper towel, and continue stenciling.

■ Some stencilers place a folded piece of damp paper towel at the bottom of a small container (a jar or a plastic yogurt cup). Whenever they are not using the brush, even for a moment or two while moving a stencil, it goes into the container, bristle side down. This keeps the brush from drying out without getting it wet.

LIFT STENCIL; FINISHED PRINT, RIGHT

■ Another way to slow down the rate at which the paint dries on the brush is to work some clear, slow-drying glaze into the brush before you start. Offload any excess onto paper towels, then load the paint as usual. This also makes the brush easier to clean when you're finished.

■ Because you must stencil with a dry brush, you need a separate brush for each color in a given project. You can't simply rinse out your green brush, for instance, and use it right away for red, because the brush will be wet. Once the green brush has been thoroughly washed and completely dried, it can be used for another color, but not before.

Making a Basic Print

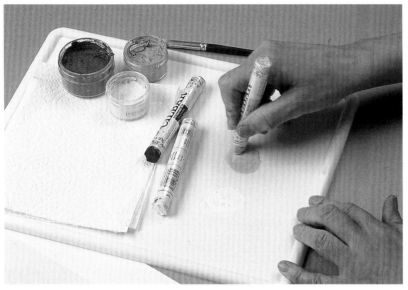

BRUSH AND SOLID OILS

When not being used, solid oil paints form a dry skin on any exposed surface, so before you start, you must peel off the skin. This is easy to do with paint sticks but can get a little messy with the jars. If the skin is thin, it can often be removed with the sticky side of a piece of masking tape. With jar paint that hasn't been used for a while, the skin can be quite tough, and it's easier to skim it off with a butter knife or a sharp spoon. Whatever you do, don't use your fingernail to pierce the skin, or you'll end up with a lot of greasy, hard-to-remove color under your nail.

1 With fresh paint exposed, you are ready to start. Rub a dry stencil brush over the surface of the solid paint (in the jar), picking up a small amount. With paint sticks, hold the stick just like a crayon, and rub it back and forth over your palette until a small amount of paint has been transferred to the surface. Then dab the brush into the paint.

2 Now work the paint into the bristles by swirling the brush on a clean spot on your palette. Wipe the brush on a stack of paper towels to remove any excess and to make sure there are no clumps of paint caught in the bristles. This paint is solid and won't bleed, but if you apply too much at once, it is very likely to smudge when the stencil is removed.

3 Apply the paint to the stencil openings by stippling or swirling, as with liquid paints, and build up the color gradually. Check the print by lifting a corner of the stencil. Reload the brush as necessary.

4 Dampen a folded paper towel with mineral spirits or turpentine, and seal it in a zip-lock bag to minimize evaporation and odor. When the brush seems too dry, open the bag and tap the brush on the towel. Wipe off excess on a dry paper towel.

5 When the print is finished, carefully lift the stencil so as not to smudge the paint. It takes several hours to dry to the touch and may take up to 10 days to cure.

TRANSFER SMALL AMOUNT OF PAINT STICK TO PALETTE

WORK PAINT INTO BRUSH, OFFLOAD, APPLY TO STENCIL; FINISHED PRINT, TOP

SPONGE

Using a sponge with a stencil imparts a certain texture to the print. In Chapters 4 and 11, we will use sea sponges to create stenciled stone effects. In Chapter 13, makeup sponges are used; their soft, fine-grained composition makes them ideal stencil tools for glass surfaces.

1 No matter what type of sponge you use, the first step is to pour several spoonfuls of paint onto a plate or palette—you can pour more than one color into the puddle without mixing them, if you wish.

2 Mist a dry sponge lightly with water. Work the sponge in your hands until the dampness has permeated it and the sponge loses its stiffness. You do not want the sponge wet, merely damp enough to be malleable.

3 Dab the sponge into the paint puddle to pick up some paint.

4 On a fresh spot on the palette, dab the sponge up and down to work the paint into the crevices.

5 Now offload by dabbing onto a stack of paper towels.

6 Sponges (especially sea sponges) tend to retain a lot more paint than a stencil brush does, so be very careful when making your print. Start dabbing lightly over the stencil cutouts, and continue until all areas are more or less filled in. Don't try to make the paint cover solidly, though. Part of the reason for using a sponge is to obtain the spotty imprint of the sponge itself. The print should look somewhat primitive.

PICK UP ONE OR TWO COLORS ON SPONGE, AND OFFLOAD EXCESS

USE VERY LIGHT DABBING MOTION TO APPLY PAINT; FINISHED PRINT, BELOW

Making a Basic Print

PULL OUT THIN FILM OF PAINT

COAT ROLLER WITH PAINT

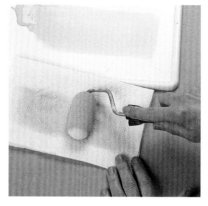

OFFLOAD EXCESS PAINT

ROLL COLOR OVER STENCIL

ROLLER AND LIQUID PAINT

1 Pour a few spoonfuls of paint (latex house paint or liquid acrylic craft paint) onto a flat palette tray or a retired cookie sheet lined with freezer paper.

2 Use a palette knife or spatula to draw out a long, wide, shallow streak of paint from the puddle.

3 Roll a dry high-density foam roller through the paint streak until the entire roller is coated with paint, working it back and forth to distribute the paint evenly. Don't let the roller get into the puddle of paint, though, or it will pick up too much paint on one side.

4 When offloading, make sure the roller has been evenly loaded. Simply run the roller along a stack of paper towels. If the resulting stripe is even, everything's fine. Just continue offloading until you can pull the roller—with no pressure—over the paper without leaving much of a trace. If the offloading stripe is uneven— dark strips alternating with light ones—then you have more paint on one side of the roller than the other. The solution is to reload the roller, making sure you pick up an overly generous amount of paint all round. Work it into the roller, then offload repeatedly until ready.

5 Draw the roller back and forth across all stencil openings, pressing lightly at first. As the roller uses up some of its paint, start pressing a bit harder. Keep the roller as flat as possible; that is, don't try to use just the end of it to fit into one part of the stencil. Roll back and forth willy-nilly, and let the stencil determine where the paint sticks.

6 To blend a second color into a small interior portion of the stencil, you may have to tip the roller and use just the end. If it's done too often or too heavily, however, the foam may tear. Detailed shading can also be added with a brush.

7 Build up the color gradually by making repeated passes with the roller. As with brush stenciling, it's easy to make the print too dark, so lift a corner of the stencil and check it occasionally. When you are satisfied, carefully remove the stencil.

NOTE: Roller stenciling makes it easy to build up large areas of uniform color without the blotching that often characterizes large-scale coverage with stencil brushes. It's also easy to modulate the color. For some variation in intensity, make more passes over some parts of the stencil than others. Sometimes interesting results can be achieved with random shading in a single color. Or you can apply one color with a roller, then blend in small amounts of other colors with a brush.

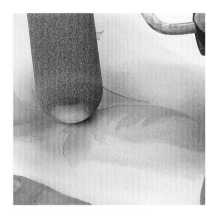

BLEND IN SECOND COLOR

As with stencil brushes, rollers dry out quickly when used with latex paint. Whenever you are not using the roller—even for a few minutes—enclose the foam part in a zip-lock bag to prevent it from drying out.

The roller will still need slight dampening from time to time. One way to do this is to draw the roller over a damp kitchen sponge. Another method is to spritz a fine mist of water droplets over the palette (and over the paint as well, to keep it from drying). Draw the roller through the droplets, roll it back and forth, then roll it over paper towels. This process should merely dampen the roller. If it wets it, then you're using too much water and run the risk of bleeding.

SPRAY AND AIRBRUSH

I'm not a big fan of spray techniques, because I find sprays messy and noxious and I don't like having to wear a mask. Airbrushes are another matter and have been used with stencils for a long time by commercial artists. However, airbrushing is a large enough subject to warrant a book of its own, and I won't be dealing with it here. If you are already an expert with an airbrush, you should be able to use it with almost any of the stenciling techniques discussed in this book.

1 If you stencil with cans of spray paint, the first thing you need to do is protect a fairly large area around the stencil by masking it off with paper, because the spray trajectory is quite wide and not controllable. When stenciling on a wall, you must protect the floor as well, because some of the paint mist will fall to the ground.

2 Start spraying onto the masked area, well away from the stencil opening, and slowly move toward the opening. Keep the spray in motion so that you don't end up blasting one spot. You can control the direction of the spray somewhat by holding a small piece of cardboard in your other hand and using it as a kind of mobile deflector and mask.

3 Build up the color gradually; it is very easy to apply too much. Be particularly sparing with the paint if you plan to add other colors. You want to end up with a nice mixture of color dots, not one color sprayed on top of a dense background.

4 This technique causes greater paint buildup on the stencil than any other method, so be prepared to clean the stencil relatively frequently. Lift the stencil off the finished print very carefully, because the paint is still wet and easily smudged.

USE PIECE OF CARDBOARD TO DIRECT SPRAY

Single Template

Now that you see how easy it is to make a basic stencil print, let's take a look at some different types of stencils. Some are simple cutouts on a single sheet. Others may need multiple templates to complete the print. This section and the three that follow show how the design of the stencil affects both the style of the print and the way in which the stencil is used to make the print.

SINGLE STENCIL, SILHOUETTE

This is as simple as a stencil can get: a single cutout, or silhouette, on a single sheet. Don't ignore it because of its simplicity; in subsequent chapters, you will find many uses for single stencils. It's easy to be seduced by elaborate, many-layered stencils, but more is not necessarily better.

SINGLE STENCIL, FORM SHADOW ONLY

There are several ways to create more detail in a stenciled image. One is to stencil not the entire image but only a shadow of its relief. This is what you would see if the object were illuminated by very strong, oblique lighting. Or do the reverse, and stencil just the high-lighted parts of a three-dimensional image.

BRIDGE

BRIDGE

SINGLE STENCIL, WITH BRIDGES

The simplest way to add detail without extra stencil layers is to use bridges, or ties. These are connective parts of the stencil that translate into gaps in the stenciled print. They serve a structural as well as a decorative purpose by providing stability to the template. For example, the fleur-de-lis motif, above left, would make a very floppy stencil (and would be difficult to paint without using stencil adhesive) were it not for the bridges that separate the horizontal bar from the vertical cutouts.

Bridges also provide a means of making a stencil out of any design that is topologically equivalent to a doughnut. Such a design would normally yield a stencil whose center piece (the "hole") would simply fall out as soon as it was cut. But when a few bridges are built into the design, the hole remains attached to the rest of the stencil, as with this Celtic knot, left. In this case, the bridges also provide a little more detail, such as an indication of which strands are threaded under or over the others.

SINGLE-EDGE STENCIL

I'm not sure whether this should be called a stencil or a mask or something else entirely, but it is a very useful tool. Use the edge of a piece of stencil material —it can be straight or zigzag, curved or torn—to guide your roller or brush. Simply work the tool back and forth along the edge of the stencil, and you're left with a border in which the paint is strong and well defined on one edge and fades away on the other edge. This technique is helpful for creating the impression of texture or a three-dimensional shape within an image and is used frequently in Chapters 3 and 10. It can also be used to add veins to stenciled leaves.

THESE EXAMPLES SHOW BOTH A SINGLE STENCILED EDGE AND THE EFFECT OF PARALLEL, OVERLAPPING STENCILED EDGES

Single Template

VICTORIAN BORDER PRINTED WITH DIRECT, BRIDGED STENCIL

SAME BORDER CONVERTED TO REVERSE STENCIL

FOR THREE-DIMENSIONAL LOOK, BRUSH COLOR ONLY ALONG EDGES OF STENCIL

REVERSE STENCIL

When I polled a group of professional stencilers for an official term to label this kind of stencil, it was pretty much a toss-up between "reverse" and "negative," with a slight edge given to the former. This type of template could be described as a mask made into a stencil. For example, suppose you have a vine pattern to use as a border stencil. Normally, you would cut out all the vine parts on a Mylar sheet (with few bridges), and when you applied the paint, you would get an image of a painted vine.

With a reverse stencil, however, you cut out all the parts that do not belong to the vine, leaving the vine parts attached to the margin of the stencil by a few essential bridges. When you apply paint to this stencil, you create an image in which the background (or so-called negative space) is painted while the vine itself remains the original color of the surface. The image of this vine is not broken by the bridges that characterize the first stencil.

Although reverse stencils are not as common as direct ones, they can be very creative tools, especially if the background (just the strip covered by the stencil) is given a different color—or even a faux treatment—before you begin stenciling (see facing page).

It is not difficult to translate a regular stencil into a reverse one, as shown by this Victorian border, top left. Join up all the bridges in the image and then cut away everything that is not part of the design.

Reverse stencils are an easy way to create a border that looks three-dimensional, bottom left. This works whether the basecoat is flat color or some kind of faux treatment. Instead of stenciling solid color through all the stencil openings, brush transparent color around the edges only. Use just a hint of color on edges that should be highlighted and deeper, wider swaths of color on shadowed edges. If your pattern is highly detailed, you may need to use very small stencil brushes. As a medium, use either solid oils or acrylics mixed with a transparent medium.

REVERSE BORDER STENCIL, PLAIN

WITH COLORED STRIP FOR BASECOAT

WITH CONTRASTING COLOR

IMAGES MADE BY REVERSE STENCILS
OFTEN RESEMBLE BLOCK PRINTS

Overlays

An overlay is simply a second stencil that is laid on top of the image left by the first stencil. It can be used to separate colors, to eliminate bridges and to add details to the original print. The word "overlay" is also commonly used to refer to a single stencil—that is, a one-template design might be called a single-overlay stencil, even though there is, in fact, no overlay. Similarly, a three-piece stencil would be called a three-overlay stencil; in this case, the first stencil to be painted would be the first overlay.

The important thing to learn about working with overlays is how to line each one up with respect to the first print so that the design parts they provide end up in the right places. This is called registration. There are several ways of doing this, depending on whether the stencil is clear or opaque and whether it is die-cut or laser-cut.

CUTOUT REGISTRATION: OPAQUE STENCILS

With opaque stencils, it is usually easiest to make cutouts, partial cutouts or flapped cutouts in the overlay to correspond with certain parts of the image already printed by the first stencil. In this example, the first stencil prints the pepper itself. The overlay (which will print the stem and sepals) has a flap or partial cutout that can be lined up with the body of the pepper. Be careful not to repaint the pepper when painting the overlay. To avoid this, it is helpful if the pepper cutout is a flap that can be folded down once the overlay has been positioned.

FIRST STENCIL IS PEPPER "BODY"

USE CUTOUT TO POSITION OVERLAY

RESULT OF BOTH OVERLAYS

PINHOLE REGISTRATION: OPAQUE STENCILS

Opaque overlays can also be lined up with so-called pinhole, or point, registration, whereby each stencil in the set has two or more tiny cutouts in exactly the same place (typically in the corners).

1 With the first stencil, mark the location of the cutouts directly on the surface to be stenciled (see Note on page 49).

2 Then position subsequent overlays by lining up the corresponding cutouts with the original marks.

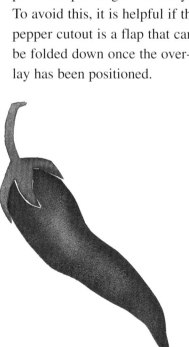

MARK FIRST STENCIL'S PINHOLES

LINE UP OVERLAY WITH PINHOLES

NOTE PINHOLES MARKED ON TAPE

OUTLINE REGISTRATION: TRANSPARENT STENCILS

Transparent commercial stencils all used to be die-cut, and because die-cutting machinery often worked in tandem with printing presses, the registration marks on each overlay were printed outlines of the cutouts on the previous overlay. They didn't have to be cut out, because you could see right through the sheet to line up the outline with the image underneath. This is the easiest method to use for hand-cut stencils.

■ Try to get into the habit of tracing all registration outlines with a permanent felt-tip pen before cutting the overlay. Otherwise, it is easy to forget about it until the stencil has been separated from the pattern—and it is always hard to put it back in exactly the same place.

■ If you transfer outlines to the underside of the stencil, there's no danger of the pen color contaminating the image. Remove top outline with rubbing alcohol.

PINHOLE REGISTRATION: TRANSPARENT STENCILS

Most commercial stencils are now cut by laser. Patterns are digitized and fed into computers that guide the laser heads. Pinhole registration marks (they can be circles, triangles or diamonds) are placed in the corners of each overlay and cut as part of the pattern.

1 As with opaque stencils, mark each registration hole on the surface at the time of painting the first stencil.

2 Then line up these registration marks with the holes on subsequent overlays.

NOTE: To avoid marking the surface, put down pieces of low-tack tape and place the marks on the tape.

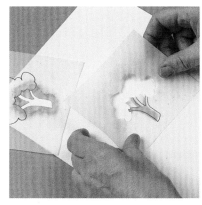

LINE UP SECOND OVERLAY OVER STEM

TRACING OUTLINES ON BOTH OVERLAYS ALLOWS YOU TO STENCIL THEM IN ANY ORDER

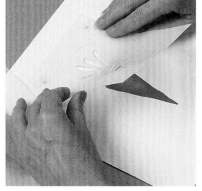

ALIGN CUT TRIANGLES OVER PREVIOUSLY TRACED TRIANGLES

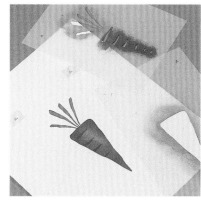

FINISHED PRINT SHOWN WITH BOTH OVERLAYS

When to Use Overlays

COLOR SEPARATION

The simplest stencil has everything cut out on one template. When painting this pear, you can't avoid having some of the pear color falling into the leaf cutouts, and vice versa, unless the leaves are masked off when the pear itself is painted. This overlapping of colors is usually considered a desirable attribute in simple stencils.

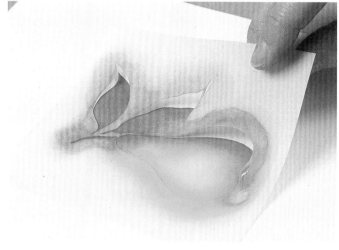

ONE STENCIL FOR PEAR AND LEAVES ALLOWS COLORS TO MINGLE

Sometimes, however, the colors must be kept completely separate, and if the design is complicated, it might not be easy to use a quick mask. In this case, cut one stencil for each color: one for the pear, one for the leaves.

1 Paint the pear first, with a stencil for the pear alone.

2 Remove the stencil, and position the leaf overlay on top of the first print. As long as a water-based paint is used, rather than a solid oil paint, you don't have to worry about smudging, because the first print should already be dry to the touch.

3 Paint the leaves.

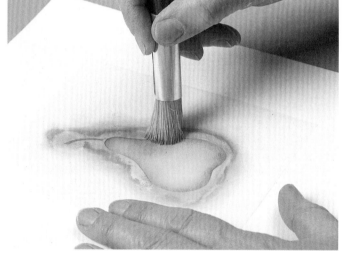

PAINT PEAR

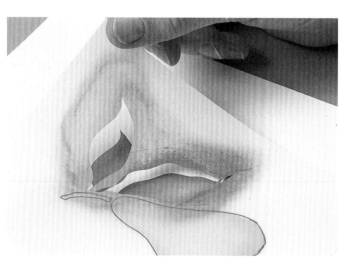

PAINT LEAVES WITH OVERLAY STENCIL

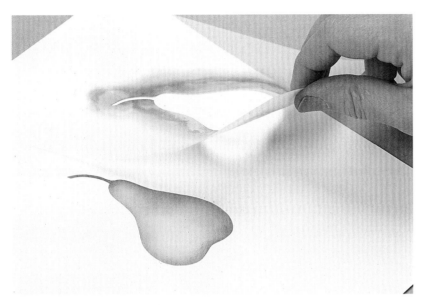

PAINT PEAR WITH FIRST STENCIL

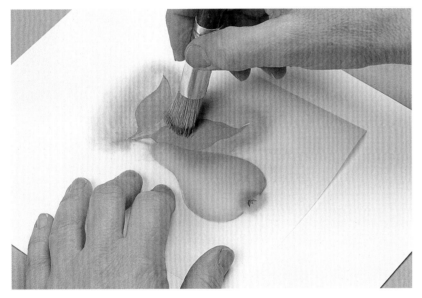

PAINT LEAVES WITH SECOND STENCIL THAT BUTTS TO PEAR AND STEM

OVERLAY TO ELIMINATE BRIDGES

The single-stencil pear print has several gaps in the design, because otherwise, it would be in dough-nut territory; the leaf could not be tucked behind the pear without the bridges that hold the parts of the stencil together. We can get rid of the bridges, and hence the gaps, by putting the leaves on a separate stencil. This is pretty handy in this example, because the same separation works for the colors as well.

When to Use Overlays

FIRST TWO STENCILS CREATE A BRIDGELESS PRINT

THIRD AND FOURTH OVERLAYS ADD DETAILS
DIRECTLY ON TOP OF ORIGINAL PRINT

OVERLAY FOR DETAILS

This example uses extra overlays to provide shading on the body of the pear and on the veins in the leaves. The overlays here actually apply paint right on top of the paint applied with the first stencil. Because stenciled layers of paint are very thin, choose your colors carefully to make sure that the overlay shows up well. This type of overlay gives a different style to the final print. Instead of blended shading on the body of the pear, each stencil is printed uniformly, and it is the shape of the overlay that implies the shape of the fruit.

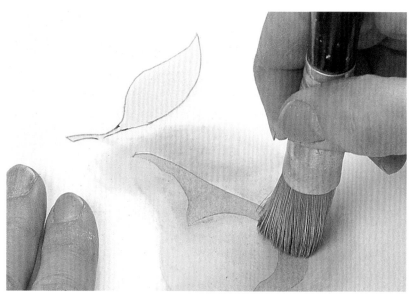

THIRD OVERLAY ADDS SUGGESTION OF DIMENSION TO PEAR

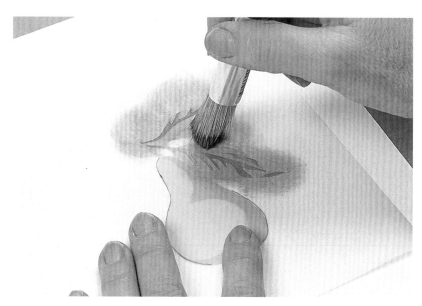

FINAL OVERLAY ADDS VEINS TO LEAVES

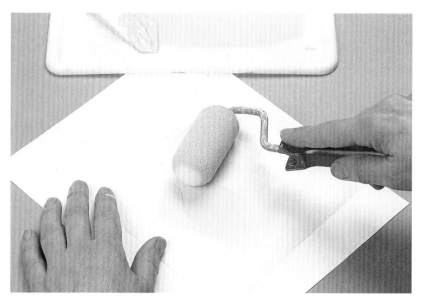

ROLL FLAT BLOCK OF COLOR OVER FIRST STENCIL

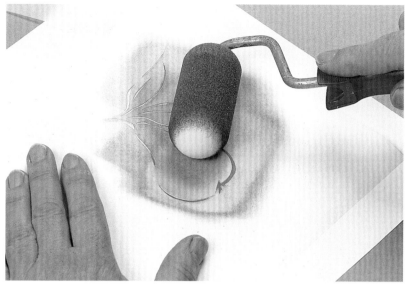

STENCIL OUTLINE OVERLAY IN BOLD COLOR

MISALIGNMENT BETWEEN COLOR BLOCK AND OUTLINE IS DELIBERATE

OVERLAY FOR OUTLINING

Using a stencil that gives just a suggestion of the outline of a shape offers yet another stylistic approach to the motif. It can be used on its own or as an overlay to a rough block of color laid down by a first stencil. Here, the shape of the colored mass is only approximate; it is the linear overlay that gives precise contours.

A slightly different type of outlining was used during the Arts and Crafts Movement of the late 19th century. In this approach, dashed outlines were stenciled in a dark color (and sometimes in gold). Then the design was filled in by hand-coloring with glazes, much like painting in a coloring book. Wiping off selected spots of glaze would highlight parts of the design (see page 115).

Masks

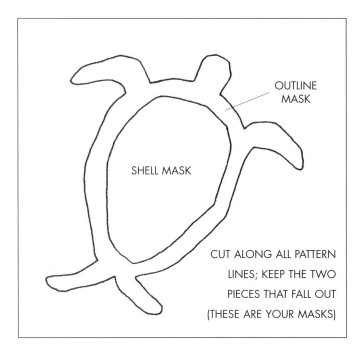

OUTLINE MASK

SHELL MASK

CUT ALONG ALL PATTERN LINES; KEEP THE TWO PIECES THAT FALL OUT (THESE ARE YOUR MASKS)

Masks and stencils are really just two faces of the same thing. Both are templates. A mask usually shields some shape or area from paint, whereas a stencil exposes the shape to paint. With something like an "edge" stencil, mask and stencil are, in fact, one and the same, shielding one side and exposing the other.

The creative possibilities of masks have blossomed with the advent of low-tack adhesive, which lets you secure a mask in place like a sticker, even on a vertical surface, without using pieces of tape that alter the effective shape of the mask. Using such a mask means that finally, the topological equivalents of a doughnut can be stenciled in one pass.

With various stencil/mask combinations, you can add background, create "doughnut" images, overlay details or make overlapping prints. To illustrate all this, let's consider a pattern like this Hawaiian turtle petroglyph.

1 The stencil and masks are made by cutting along all pattern lines. The pieces are then given a light spray of stencil adhesive on the reverse side.

2 There are two mask pieces—one for the center of the shell and the other for an outline of the turtle. When you are not using the masks, keep them taped to the edge of the stencil so that you don't lose them.

3 Now, what can we do with these three pieces? First, create a plain silhouette by using the stencil on its own.

4 Next, with the stencil still in position, replace both masks where they fit in the center of the stencil. Remove the outline mask, leaving a so-called doughnut stencil. Paint this to produce a turtle outline.

BASIC STENCIL PRODUCES PLAIN SILHOUETTE

REMOVE OUTLINE MASK, EXPOSING OUTLINE

PAINT OUTLINE TO CREATE SAMPLE AT RIGHT

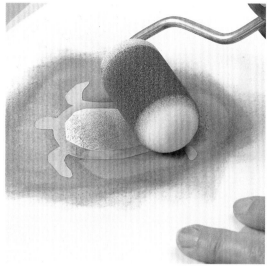

INSERT OUTLINE MASK AND REMOVE CENTER

PAINT CENTER TO CREATE TWO-COLOR TURTLE

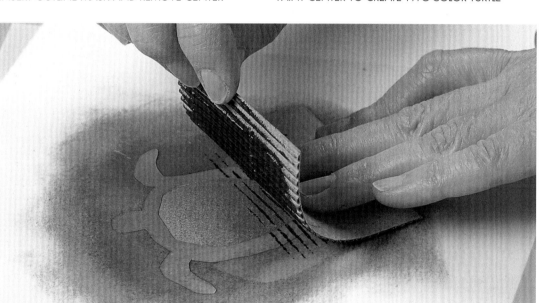

WITH TURTLE SHELL UNCOVERED, APPLY TEXTURE USING CORRUGATED CARDBOARD

5 For a two-color turtle, the traditional approach is to stencil the entire shape in one color, then use an overlay to add a second color over the center of the shell. This works fine when the overlay color is darker or more opaque than the first color. But if the first color is darker—black, for example—it is difficult to make the overlay color bright, as it simply cannot overcome the black basecoat.

The way to solve the problem is to stencil the black outline, as we have al-ready done, using the basic stencil plus the shell mask.

6 Then insert the outline mask, remove the shell mask, and stencil the center of the shell.

7 At the same time, you can further em-bellish the shell, if you wish, as I did here by stamping it with a piece of corru-gated cardboard.

Masks

REUSABLE MASKS

Reusable masks can be easily cut out of paper or Mylar in the same way a stencil is cut. In fact, the cutout piece that falls away from the inside of a stencil can often be used as a mask. Anytime I cut a silhouette stencil, I try to save the inner piece, as it makes a perfect mask. All these little pieces of transparent Mylar are really easy to lose, however, so keep them taped to the original stencil when storing them. It also helps to label them with a permanent felt-tip pen.

■ I usually spray the back of each mask with low-tack adhesive to avoid having pieces of tape disrupt the profile. If I think I may need the mirror image as a mask, I cut two copies of the shape and use the flip side of one.

■ It is often handy to design and cut out an all-purpose mask, or shield, of Mylar. It can incorporate whatever masking shapes you use frequently. For example, its basic shape might be a variation on the standard drafting French curve, perhaps with some round, oval, rectangular or triangular cutouts in the middle. Something like this is very useful for correcting small mistakes and cleaning up edges. It can be adapted to almost any circumstance: Simply hold it in place with one hand, wield your brush or roller with the other, and slide the shield around to follow the needed contour.

■ And don't overlook the possibilities of Post-it Notes for quick, disposable ad hoc shields. They have low-tack adhesive already applied and can be trimmed to shape very quickly with scissors.

LIQUID FRISKET

Liquid frisket, or masking fluid, is the easiest method for finicky one-off shapes, especially where the masking has to be precise. It's like an opaque rubber cement. Spread it over the shape to be masked with a fine brush or, even better, with a special masking tool. When it is dry, stencil right over it. When you no longer need the mask, simply peel the stuff off the surface with an art eraser.

NATURAL MASKS

Don't ignore the world of nature when looking for templates. Fern-work is a decorative technique in which you work exclusively with masks rather than stencils—and the masks are actually real ferns. Start with a walk in the woods or garden to gather a selection of fern fronds. The tougher kinds, like sword ferns and bracken, work better than the more fragile species, like maidenhair ferns.

1 The fronds do not have to be dried, but you should try to flatten them. Place them between paper towels and press under a pile of books, just until they stay flat. Spray the front with stencil adhesive, and let dry.

2 Arrange the fronds, face down, on the surface to be stenciled, and press in place.

Apply paint or stain gently, so as not to tear the ferns. Stippling is probably the least destructive method to use (swirling will cause the ferns to disintegrate). A stencil roller can also be used—carefully. Spraying works too, although you must make sure that every bit of each fern is held tightly to the surface of the work; otherwise, the edges of the prints will be blurred.

3 As soon as you have finished, start to lift off the ferns. Use an X-acto knife to remove any stubborn bits, being careful not to scratch the newly painted surface.

4 This method looks stunning on wood, with a clear or blond stain as the basecoat and a darker stain applied over the ferns. Give it several coats of a clear protective finish to provide a uniform sheen.

APPLY PAINT OR STAIN GENTLY, SO AS NOT TO TEAR FERNS

Layers of Stencils and Masks

You can create a variety of different effects by layering a collection of masks and stencils in different orders. Two examples are shown here, each using a letter stencil, the drop-out piece (or mask) of the letter stencil, a stripe stencil, which is layered to produce a gingham pattern, and a motif (apple or bear) that will be made to appear behind or in front of the corresponding letter of the alphabet. The position of the motif will depend on the manner in which various parts of the ensemble are masked.

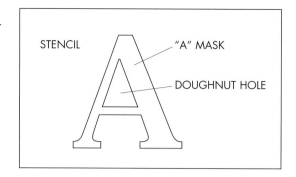

STENCIL   "A" MASK

DOUGHNUT HOLE

1 For the letter "A," position the mask first.

2 Then fit the stencil around the mask, and get the doughnut hole in the center of the letter stuck down in exactly the right place. Now remove the mask.

3 Stencil a basecoat color—here, it's ivory.

4 Leaving the stencil in place, roller stencil horizontal stripes over the basecoat. See Chapter 9 for detailed gingham instructions.

5 Rotate the stripe stencil 90 degrees, and stencil the stripes again.

NOTE: Do not make either set of stripes too dark, because you want the little squares where the stripes overlap to show up darker than the rest.

6 Remove all stencils, and cover up the letter "A" with its mask.

7 Position the apple stencil so that it straddles one leg of the "A," and stencil. Because the mask is protecting the letter, the apple will appear to be behind it.

1 For the second example, stencil the bear first, then cover it up with its mask.

2 Put the "B" stencil on top of the bear mask (first using the "B" mask to position the two doughnut-hole parts of the stencil).

3 Basecoat the letter.

4 Add the gingham pattern as in the first example. In this case, the bear mask protects that area from the letter colors, so the bear appears in front of the letter.

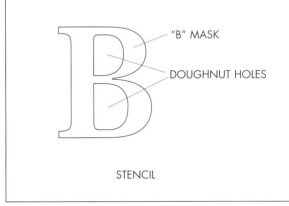

"B" MASK

DOUGHNUT HOLES

STENCIL

Damage Control

It's a rare project that sees everything come off perfectly. Fortunately, there aren't too many things that can go drastically wrong with stenciling, and in any case, most errors are recoverable. Even if they aren't, it's still only paint, and usually, you can paint things out and simply start again. Here's a list of common problems and what to do about them.

BLEEDING

If your stencil prints do not have clean edges—that is, if the paint is bleeding under the stencil—then either there is too much paint on your applicator or your brush or roller was not completely dry when you started. When you stencil, think "dry."

1 Offload as much paint as you can from your brush, sponge or roller before moving to the stencil. This is not the same process as painting a wall.

2 If the print is a real mess, wipe the whole thing off right away using a wet cloth and gentle pressure, so as not to disturb the basecoat. You can do this on most hard surfaces, except for unprimed absorbent ones, which is a good reason for letting a freshly painted wall dry for several days before starting to stencil. A dried but not cured basecoat is likely to be damaged should you wash off a stencil print.

3 If the bleeding is minor, you can repair the damage by shifting the stencil slightly so that the errant wisps of paint are included in the stencil cutout. Simply apply paint (having offloaded thoroughly this time) to the sliver that's exposed by the stencil to cover up the goof.

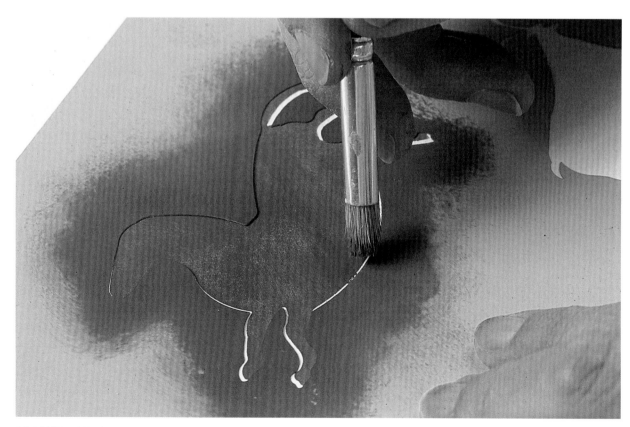

TO REMEDY MINOR BLEEDING, SHIFT STENCIL SLIGHTLY AND APPLY PAINT TO EXPOSED SLIVER

WHEN PAINT ACCUMULATES AROUND CUT EDGES, DETAIL IS LOST

PAINT BUILDUP ON STENCIL

After a number of prints have been made with the same stencil, paint starts to accumulate on the cut edges. At some point, this buildup may cause some of the detail to be lost and may introduce tiny gaps between the elements of different overlays. When this happens, you must either clean the stencil or switch to a fresh one.

Depending on the relative value of your time and the cost of the stencil (factoring in any aversion to stencil cleaning), it might be worthwhile to start with several copies of the same stencil so that you don't have to keep stopping to clean it.

The amount of paint buildup depends on the technique and the type of paint. Solid stencil paints cause less buildup than acrylics, because they don't dry on the stencil right away and can be worked back over the cutouts. Pouncing and rolling cause more buildup than does swirling. Spray paints are the worst, building up very fast because there is no brush action to move the paint from stencil to wall.

COLOR PROBLEMS

So you've finished stenciling, and you stand back to look at the overall effect…and realize the colors aren't right. Short of starting all over again, what can you do? Usually, the problem is that the colors are too bright or that there is too much contrast between the stenciling and the background. The solution to the former is straightforward but somewhat painstaking. Reposition the stencil for each overbright motif, and add a hint of its complementary color. This often works best by mixing up some transparent glaze tinted with the complement and simply stenciling on the glaze.

■ To cut down on the contrast, apply a transparent glaze or wash to the entire wall. For example, if you want to keep a white background, brush on a wash of thinned (with water and retarder) white latex paint, covering both stenciling and wall. If you can play with the background color, then your choice of wash color is pretty broad. You can go with white, pastels, a complement or an aging color such as raw umber. Before starting the wall, do some samples first, just to be sure you won't make things worse.

■ If all else fails and you really can't live with it, paint everything out, get a good night's sleep, and start again. And this time, do a few paper or poster-board samples first. Depending on the colors you've chosen, it may take more than one coat to paint everything out. If this is the case, you might want to use pigmented shellac (BIN™) as the first coat. It can be tinted at your paint store and has excellent hiding power (it will even cover felt-tip-pen marks, which normally bleed through paint alone).

■ Another common problem occurs when stenciling over dark colors. The stenciled color always looks somber, because the dark base color shows through. This is fine if that's the look you're after but not if you are trying for clear, bright hues. The solution is to block the base color by stenciling first with an opaque white. Let this dry, then restencil over top of the white with your chosen colors. However, this causes another problem. Usually, the resulting print has a thin white outline, or halo. To avoid this, mix a little of the final color into the blocking white used for the first stenciled coat. For example, if you want a bright red flower, stencil the blocking coat in a solid pink (opaque white plus a little red). You can also stencil the blocking coat using a dirty stencil— one that has some paint buildup. Then use a perfectly clean stencil for the topcoat. The cutouts on the clean stencil will be just a hair larger than those on the dirty one, and this difference should be enough to prevent the halo.

Cleanup

This is the part of the job nobody likes. Unfortunately, it has to be done, and it's easier if you don't put it off until later. If you get at the paint before it has had a chance to cure, you'll do a much better job of cleaning, with way less effort, and your tools will last a lot longer.

ROLLERS

Foam stencil rollers are easy to ruin if you let them dry out before cleaning them. While you are working, place the rollers in a zip-lock bag whenever you have to stop for even a couple of minutes. Clean them by wetting thoroughly, then working soap and water through the foam with your hand. Squeeze the water out, add more water, and squeeze again until the water runs clear. Rinse thoroughly. Pull the foam head off the handle so that both the foam and the metal axle can dry. Otherwise, the metal will eventually rust.

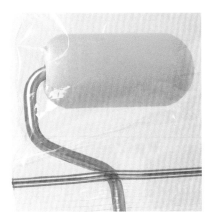

BRUSHES

Water-based paints dry quickly, so if you are working with more than one color, your yellow brush is going to dry out while you're stenciling with the green one. You need a way to keep the "waiting" brushes from drying out, without making them wet. One method is to keep them in a zip-lock bag when not in use. Another is to put them, bristles down, in a cup with a damp paper towel at the bottom. Also, if you're going to take a break, it helps to work a little retarder or slow-drying glaze into the bristles.

1 Once you've finished with a brush for the day, let the bristles soak for a bit in water. You can also soak them in Simple Green or liquid fabric softener (the stuff you use for laundry) or commercial brush cleaner, especially if the bristles have begun to harden.

2 To clean the bristles, rub them in circles on a rough cloth or nail brush, using a dollop of liquid soap, Simple Green, fabric softener or brush cleaner. For tough cleaning, rub the bristles on a Scotch-Brite™ type of pad. These scrub-

bing pads will eventually wear down the bristles, but they do work well.

3 Rinse well, and check the bristles. If they are not completely clean, repeat the scrubbing and rinsing.

4 Squeeze out any excess water with a terry towel, and let dry overnight.

■ I tend to postpone cleaning my brushes and sometimes find myself faced with rock-solid bristles. Some commercial cleaners can take care of this, but the cheapest method is to pour a half-inch of denatured or rubbing alcohol into a jar, add a small squirt of liquid dish soap and let the working end of the brush soak in it until soft. Then clean the bristles as described above. This isn't the best long-term treatment for your brushes, so try to make a habit of cleaning them as soon as possible.

■ Brushes used with solid oil paints should be cleaned according to paint-label instructions—with either soap and water or mineral spirits.

■ Whenever you soak your brushes—whether in water or a cleaning product—don't immerse them beyond the bristles, and keep the soaking time as short as possible. Otherwise, you may damage the metal ferrule or the paint finish on the handle.

■ It's fine to store your brushes upside down (bristles up), but don't dry them this way. It allows water to sit in the ferrule.

SAFETY NOTE: Rags or paper towels used with turpentine or mineral spirits must be handled properly to avoid spontaneous combustion. Soak in a pail of water, dry in a well-ventilated area, or store in a metal fireproof container. Dispose of promptly.

STENCILS

Stencils, like brushes, can be cleaned with ease if the job is done right away and with great difficulty if left until tomorrow or next week. Everyone has favorite tricks for cleaning stencils. Here are mine.

1 As soon as I've finished using a stencil, I put it in the sink and spray it with concentrated Simple Green (which can be purchased at a hardware store). I let that sit for a minute or two, then lay the stencil on a flat surface (in the bottom of the sink or, if the stencil is really big, the bathtub).

2 If it's a delicate stencil, I scrub it with a plastic surgical brush (available from Lee Valley Tools). It's very cheap and effective, and it's soft enough that it doesn't damage the stencil. For more robust stencils that resist cleaning, I sometimes use a nonscratching plastic pad or a foam sanding block.

3 I finish by rinsing thoroughly. If I can't clean up right away, I spray the dirty stencil and seal it in a plastic bag or container until I have time to clean it.

4 With stencils that have somehow missed out on prompt cleaning, I lay them on a flat surface and spray them with denatured or rubbing alcohol.

5 I let them sit for a few minutes, then add a squirt of liquid dish soap and scrub them. Soap makes the paint residue easier to rinse off.

6 I wipe off the goop with a paper towel and rinse. A tough job may take a few iterations.

NOTE: Aggressive cleaning scratches a stencil. Paint then adheres to it better, which makes future cleanings even tougher.

Chapter 3

LIGHT AND SHADOW

For traditional stencil work, you don't usually have to worry about shadow and highlight; you're simply painting a flat decorative pattern. Once you move into the realm of stenciled trompe l'oeil, however, and try to create an image of reality using nothing but paint and a stencil, then shadow and highlight become more important than anything else. This is what expresses the illusion of three-dimensional form. Without a gradation of lightness and darkness, you've got nothing but flat paint.

In the brief description of color in Chapter 1, one of color's three characteristics was defined as *value*—basically, the lightness or darkness of a color. The darkest colors have the lowest value, the lightest the highest value. With painted images, it is the gradation of value, whether abrupt or gradual, that conveys the illusion of three-dimensional shape and volume by expressing the effect of light on the rendered object. This is what most stencilers simply call "shading." Then there is also the simulated shadow, rendered as though cast by the painted image. This adds the final touch that makes the paint seem to move away from the wall. Shadows can be very easy to stencil, and when trying to imitate reality, this is the one step you should not omit.

To illustrate these points, there are two simple shapes on pages 66 and 67—a circle and a polygon—stenciled first in a single flat color. Those same flat shapes can take on the appearance of three-dimensional objects with the addition of different color values, applied either by shading (the circle) or by overlays (the polygon). A stenciled cast shadow reinforces the illusion.

Shadow and Light

DEFINITIONS

When light from a directional source shines on an object, the parts of the object that are directly in the path of the light are *highlighted*. They have the highest value, represented by the lightest of the colors.

Parts of the object that are on the opposite side from the light source are in shadow. The *form shadow* refers to the areas that are shaded by the object itself. They are portrayed with the lowest-value (darkest) colors.

In between highlight and form shadow are the areas of shifting value that define the shape of the object. These transition zones, or *halftones,* must be rendered in tones of shadow and highlight colors. The halftones shift gradually or abruptly, depending on the shape of the object, into the *accents* that represent the darkest spots of the form shadow and the brightest of the highlights.

Because the object is sitting in the path of the light source, it blocks the light and projects a shadow onto the surfaces behind it. This is the transparent *cast shadow*. The shape and size of the cast shadow depend not only on the shape and size of the blocking object but also on the angle of light and the distance of the object from the surface being shaded.

If you are portraying surfaces that are relatively reflective, then there will also be some light reflected back onto the shaded part of the object, within the form shadow. This detail is difficult to capture with stencils and is perhaps more relevant to fine art. However, for trompe l'oeil work that demands a high degree of realism, reflected light could be added freehand with an intermediate value, similar to the darker halftones, although not necessarily the same color.

For painted surfaces that will not be seen close-up, such as a faux crown molding, the highlights and shadows can be exaggerated and simplified. If you are painting ornamentation on a tabletop, however, the gradation of shadow color must be more subtle and transparent, as well as more detailed.

CHOOSING COLORS FOR SHADOW AND HIGHLIGHT

When I started decorative painting as a self-taught do-it-yourselfer, my automatic response to the word "shadow" was the color gray. What I didn't appreciate, as a novice, was the infinite range of colors that could be called gray. Nor did I understand that shadow and highlight colors can reflect in some way the color of the surface on which they are painted.

The three-dimensional illusion of painted forms can be enhanced by using warm colors for highlights and cool colors for form shadows—the cooler a color, the more it tends to recede with respect to the colors around it. Shadow colors can be somewhat transparent, because this makes them subtler and allows color variations and faux texture to show through.

I must confess I'm pretty conservative when it comes to picking shadow colors. I feel comfortable with color schemes in which everything is a lighter or darker version of the same general tones or with an analogous color scheme, where highlight and shadow are simply warmer and cooler versions of my base color. However, whether subtle or dramatic, shadow and highlight colors can provide the visual equivalent of the perfect blend of spices for your work. So experiment with more unusual combinations.

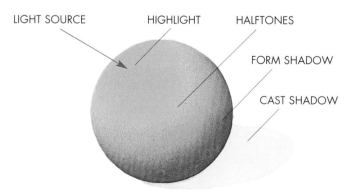

LIGHT SOURCE · HIGHLIGHT · HALFTONES · FORM SHADOW · CAST SHADOW

LIGHT SOURCE

To stencil trompe l'oeil work successfully, you must simulate a consistent light source throughout the room. However, there are normally many sources of light in a room. Sunlight, unless it is strongly filtered, will overwhelm any artificial light. It may enter through more than one window. It also changes direction, intensity and color over the course of the day and varies dramatically with weather and season. During dawn and twilight hours, lighting from sources within the room compete with natural light. At night, there are only the interior lights to consider, but they, too, likely emanate from more than one source within the room. So there are light sources from many directions, made up of different color balances.

Don't drive yourself crazy trying to reconcile a confusion of light sources. First, simplify the situation. Decide where the main source of light will be and the quality of that light. Then impose *that* source on all your trompe l'oeil painting. As long as the final solution reflects a situation that is consistent and not totally illogical, the results will be fine.

When choosing colors for, say, a trompe l'oeil molding, paint a piece of real molding, with simple but strong relief, in the appropriate base color, then move it around near the surface to be painted. Observing the lighted and shaded planes of the molding should give you a good idea of the color range you will need. If you still feel uncomfortable choosing the shadow/highlight colors, however, several craft-paint companies publish tables listing highlight and shade colors to go with their base-coat colors.

Form Shadows

START WITH FLAT BASECOAT

WORK ALONG EDGE

BUILD UP TAPERED FORM SHADOW

USE SMALL BRUSH FOR EMPHASIS

 Shading works best on surfaces with a low sheen.

■ Use opaque acrylic paint or a transparent medium (acrylic glaze or solid oils) for shading. With paint, work with a very dry brush and choose colors that taper gradually in value from that of the basecoat. With a transparent medium, a single shadow color will work over most base colors, because the basecoat shows through. Use transparents over faux finishes and patterned surfaces.

FADING FORM SHADOWS

There's one technique you must learn here, but it's so useful that it is really worth the effort: how to graduate the color application within a stencil or along a straight edge. Try this first with solid oil paints, either stick or pot, because their slow-drying nature makes them very easy to apply in a tapered or graduated fashion. With acrylics, add a little retarder or glaze medium to the paint—both for transparency and for the extra open time that will allow seamless blending and tapering. Don't add much, however, or the brush or roller will keep reactivating the paint and simply move it around (or even remove it) instead of allowing a gradual buildup.

1 For very large-scale shading, use a stencil roller; otherwise, a normal stencil brush or a stencil blending brush works best. Choose the size of the brush according to the sharpness of the contours you are trying to create: small brushes for something highly curved with a sharp gradient to its form shadows;

big brushes for large curvatures and soft shading.

2 Let's try a simple circle template. Start by working the paint along the shaded side of the circle, rubbing the brush in tight little circles right along the very edge of the stencil.

3 Work your way along the perimeter into the transition zones, lightening the brush pressure as you go.

4 When you start on the interior transition area, move the brush in larger, softer circles.

5 Go over the darker areas repeatedly; for the lighter ones, do just one or two passes. It's easy to get too dark too fast, so check the print as you proceed.

6 To emphasize the darkest edge, switch to a small brush and work it along just the very edge of the stencil. Use straight paint with no glaze for this part.

FADING FORM SHADOWS

1 Linear shading is very easy, as long as you don't stipple. With a stencil brush (or roller, depending on the scale), apply the shadow color along the edge of the stencil only, keeping the brush more or less centered over the edge so that a heavier application occurs there.

2 Work the brush back and forth, parallel to the edge of the cutout. Go over it several times, until the shading starts to shape up the way you want it.

3 Now, repeat these steps using a smaller brush and a darker color, to increase the depth of the shading right at the edge. Work the brush back and forth in a linear motion along the Mylar, or work it in tight circles that move along the edge.

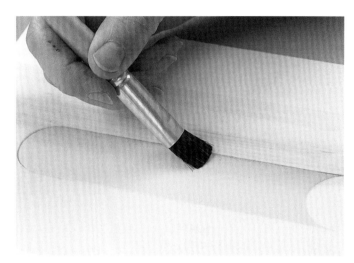

WORK BRUSH BACK AND FORTH PARALLEL TO EDGE OF CUTOUT

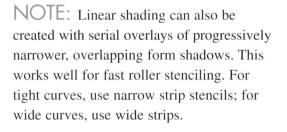

NOTE: Linear shading can also be created with serial overlays of progressively narrower, overlapping form shadows. This works well for fast roller stenciling. For tight curves, use narrow strip stencils; for wide curves, use wide strips.

■ To add a crisp emphasis to the darkest edge, draw a pencil line along that edge before you start shading.

USE DARKER COLOR AND SMALLER BRUSH AT VERY EDGE

Form Shadows

SOLID FORM SHADOWS

Sometimes, an impressive three-dimensional effect can be created with very little effort—a single-overlay stencil, for instance, that reproduces only the shadowed planes of the image. In the fret border below, there is no gradation of shadow at all. It could be stenciled with a roller. It is effective stenciled with transparent glaze on a plain surface or over faux marble.

This technique is also useful for creating narrow ridges in moldings, panels and window frames, instead of having to master the technique of freehand striping.

Rosettes are another good example. If stenciled on a pencil box, rosettes might require overlays or hand-painted detail, but for a crown molding, these single-overlay stencils are perfect. They take a bit of time to design and cut out but only a few seconds to stencil, and from a distance, it's hard to tell they aren't real.

THE POWER OF SHADING

Here's an exercise to practice simple shadows and explore the creative possibilities of directional light, all starting from a simple diamond stencil. A painted illusion of many different three-dimensional shapes can be created depending on how the shadows are layered on that diamond.

To illustrate the power of shading, I masked off half of a stenciled urn (see page 64) and applied graduated circular and linear shading to the other half. The difference is dramatic, the technique simple.

Highlights

Highlights are hard to stencil in a realistic manner. It's often easier to create highlights by leaving areas unpainted, by wiping paint or glaze off or by painting them freehand with a brush. Whether highlights are graded softly or abruptly depends on the type of material being imitated. For example, blended highlights give the impression of a dull surface, whereas sharp, opaque highlights make an object look shiny.

1 I usually start by stenciling a basecoat in the lightest or brightest color.

2 Then I build up the form shadows with deeper values, being careful not to touch the highlight areas. These I simply leave in the basecoat color, as illustrated in this strip of beading. Of course, you could also work the other way, starting with the darkest value and building up the highlighted areas with lighter values. This can be problematic, however, if you want a lot of contrast between light and dark, because stenciled layers of paint tend to be rather transparent, making it difficult to work from dark to light.

3 To make the images look shinier, accent the highlights, making them more focused. For the beading shown here, I placed a dab of white paint in the middle of each highlighted area, using my little finger as an applicator. For a really glossy shine, make the highlights more opaque and sharply defined.

NOTE: An easy way to test the impact of freehand highlights without ruining a carefully stenciled trompe l'oeil vase is to lay a piece of clear Mylar over the image and paint the highlight on the Mylar. If it works, copy the highlight onto the stencil work. If it doesn't, try a different shape or color.

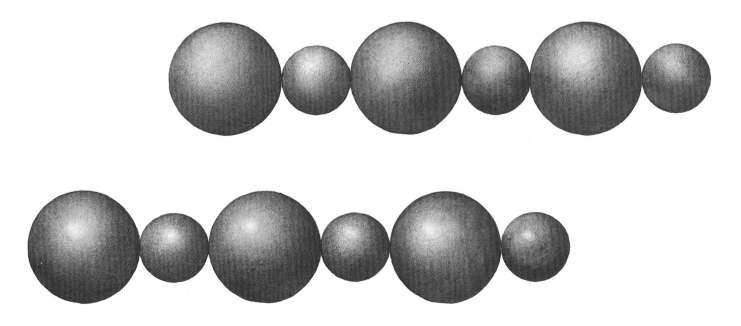

Cast Shadows

Cast shadows can be rendered freehand or by stenciling. The size and shape of the shadow depend on the angle of light and on the distance the shadow is cast. Wherever possible, I prefer a stencil roller to a brush for transparent shadows, as it creates a totally uniform shadow without brush marks or the uneven coloration that often results from stencil brushes.

DROP SHADOW

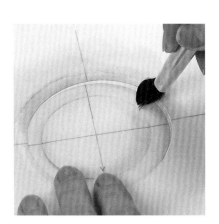 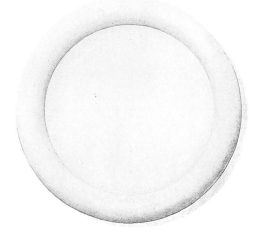

SHIFT STENCIL FOR DROP SHADOW, WHILE KEEPING STENCILED SHAPE MASKED

FREEHAND SHADOW

DROP SHADOW

1 The easiest shadow technique—one that is appropriate for a relatively shallow object placed adjacent and parallel to the surface being shaded—is the drop shadow. Simply shift the stencil slightly down or to one side (or both) of the original stenciled image. The distance shifted could be an eighth of an inch or less for a shallow embossed pattern or up to several inches for a faux curtain hanging against the wall.

2 Once the stencil has been shifted, it opens up gaps adjacent to parts of the painted motif, gaps that are then stenciled with a transparent shadow glaze. If there is a risk of compromising the original motif with the shadow glaze, mask the painted stencil. This is not necessary if the shadow glaze is sufficiently transparent and the object casting the shadow is strongly colored.

The resulting cast shadows imply that the entire stenciled image is the same distance from the shadowed surface. This is perfect for a flat object, such as a button. It may not be appropriate, however, for something like a very "spacious" vine, which in reality would have some branches touching the wall, while others would be projecting some distance away from the wall. In such a case, a freehand shadow is more realistic, because it can be pulled in where the branch touches the wall and spread out where there is a large gap.

FREEHAND OR SEPARATE STENCIL SHADOW

The drop-shadow method cannot be used for any shadow cast onto a surface that is not meant to be parallel to the image. In this case, the shape of the shadow changes completely. Either go freehand or cut a separate shadow stencil. Look how different the image of a circle stencil is when the shadows are altered. Changing the form shadows turns a flat disk into a sphere, and changing the shape of the cast shadows moves the position and angle of the unseen background.

SOFT SHADOWS

All methods for stenciling shadows create hard-edged shadows. Of course, the more transparent the shadow, the less hard it will seem; nevertheless, the edges will be crisp. To soften the edges, add a little more retarder to the shadow glaze. Apply the glaze generously with a stencil roller (don't worry if it bleeds), then immediately lift the stencil and stipple out the glaze with a clean stippling brush, paying particular attention to the edges so that they soften in a uniform fashion. Or stipple the shadow freehand, using a stencil brush but no stencil.

SELF-SHADOW

A shadow cast by an object onto itself is easy to stencil, especially if it is straight-edged. For example, to cast a shadow from the lid of a ginger jar onto its neck, simply keep the original stencil in place and stencil a transparent horizontal stripe immediately below the lid. This example also shows how form shadows, if made transparent enough, can be applied very effectively over a patterned surface.

NOTE: A final word of caution when painting cast shadows. A shadow doesn't exist if there is no surface upon which it can be cast. A stenciled honeysuckle winding over a stone balustrade can cast shadows on itself and on the balusters but not on the sky in between the balusters.

Chapter 4

SPECIAL EFFECTS

Not too long ago, stencils were meant to be used merely as simple templates for applying paint in a very straightforward fashion—one color here, another color there. Before you knew it, you had a perfect pineapple, with green leaves and golden fruit.

Of course, creative people tend to be somewhat experimental. They are not shy about borrowing tools and materials from an unrelated discipline and devising completely nontraditional ways of using them. A decorative painter can find all sorts of promise in the aisles of a well-stocked hardware store: a car-wash mitt, chicken wire, fly screen, a mop, perhaps even an eggbeater. So it's only to be expected that avid stencilers continue to expand the traditional repertoire of their templates.

This chapter describes a range of methods for using paint or other mediums in combination with stencils to produce different effects in the stenciled print. These effects can be applied to subjects described in subsequent chapters, whether it's a simple border, a piece of furniture or an entire wall. Keep in mind that this is not meant to be an exhaustive list of things which can be done with stencils. It's a collection of methods that will give you some idea of the possibilities beyond merely pouncing a color through a hole cut in a piece of Mylar.

Broken Color

The choice of colors and how they are used is probably much more important to the success of painted decoration than is the pattern selection itself. Unless you are replicating historical motifs, you'll find that nothing makes a stenciled print look boring faster than plain separated colors. Even with a monochromatic scheme, things can be livened up considerably by simply varying the color depth and intensity over the stencil. Or introduce a hint of another color or two—say, along a vine or the tip of a leaf—then blend it into the principal color.

The interplay of different colors within a single stencil cutout is termed broken color. It can be applied on various scales, from fine and subtle to broad and harsh, depending on the desired effect. Pile on streaks of solid color, or blend soft drifts of transparent glaze. But keep in mind that when colors are blended, there is the potential for muddy results unless close attention is paid to where you are on the color wheel.

The risk is greatest with slow-drying paints, notably the oil-based paint sticks and solid stencil paints. However, problems can also occur with acrylics, because working a second color over a freshly applied first color can rewet the first, even though that paint may have felt dry to the touch. If retarders are added to the paint or if colored glazes are used to obtain transparent prints, then the issue of muddying the colors is even more important, since the colors are essentially being blended wet on wet as they are applied to the surface.

Broken color is commonly used with single-overlay stencils as a more artistic alternative to the complete separation of colors by masking. Some of the color for one section of the stencil is allowed to spill across stencil bridges into other sections, and vice versa. There are still predominant areas for each color, but there is a sort of blending or overlapping between them. The image remains clear, however, defined by the shape of the bridges. It's rather like crayoning across the lines in a coloring book.

BRUSH-BLENDED

1 When blending acrylic or latex colors through a stencil, a stippling technique often works best. Swirling can sometimes overblend the colors, with potentially muddy results if the colors are complementary.

2 Apply the first color to the selected areas, then fill in the stencil with one or more other colors, using a separate brush for each color and letting the colors overlap to a greater or lesser degree.

NOTE: Because the paint dries very quickly and a dry-brush technique is being used, it is usually relatively easy to keep the colors clean. If you were to look at the resulting print under a magnifying glass, for example (not that you want to get into the habit of doing that!), you would see myriad tiny paint dots of different colors, all intermingled. Each dot is a clear color, but the overall effect that the eye sees is different, because the dots of one color are interspersed with the dots of other colors.

1 When using a swirling method of stenciling, choose the colors carefully, because the brush rubs over previous colors and mixes them with the current color. If using red and green, for instance, you'll end up with brown. There may be times when that comes in

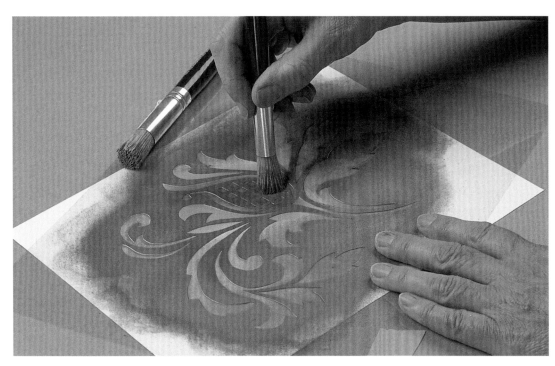

AVOID A MUDDY OUTCOME BY BLENDING FROM GREEN TO YELLOW TO RED

handy—when you blend the red of an apple and the green of its leaf, for example, the stem becomes brown automatically.

2 With repeated prints, the stencil gets more paint built up on the margins, and it becomes harder to keep each color clear, because the brush or roller tends to pick up the other colors sitting on the stencil. If the results start to look muddy, stop and clean the stencil before continuing. Depending on the colors being used, the stencil may have to be cleaned several times before a stretch of border is completed. With slow-drying solid paints, the stencil may even have to be cleaned for every repeat.

NOTE: To minimize cleaning interruptions, start the job with several copies of the same stencil so that you can quickly switch to a fresh one when necessary, then clean them all at the same time.

BRUSH-BLENDED

ROLLER-BLENDED

Color blending can also be done with stencil rollers, especially when you're working on a larger scale. However, because the rollers tend to deposit paint over a large part of the stencil margin, as well as through the openings, there is a greater risk of muddying each roller unless the colors are carefully chosen and anything close to complementary pairs is avoided. The soft yellow and green used for these leaves are a good combination for use with rollers, because they are adjacent to each other on the color wheel.

ROLLER-BLENDED

ROLLER BLENDING WORKS WELL WITH ADJACENT COLORS ON COLOR WHEEL

Broken Color

PATCHY

Here, the painted space appears to be more broken up by color patches, and you don't make as much effort to blend the transition.

1 I started with a uniform print made with a single transparent glaze to ensure crisp and well-defined edges.

2 Next, I used a sea sponge, which is a rather coarse tool, to apply the different colors. A sea sponge distributes a generous amount of paint for stenciling, so be cautious, off-load well, and use a light touch around the edges of the stencil cutouts to avoid bleeding.

NOTE: This background is made up of the same colors as the motif. However, patches of white on the fleurs-de-lis are placed where the background is darker, and darker patches are put over lighter parts. The motif shows up quite strongly, but only because of the way the colors are placed with respect to the background variation.

APPLY PAINT WITH SEA SPONGE

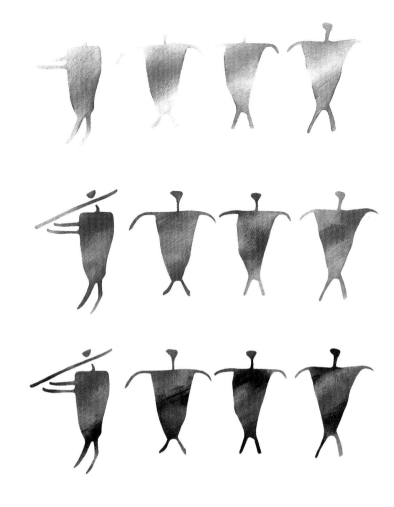

COARSELY BROKEN COLORS STENCILED ON BASE OF SAME COLORS

STREAKED

With this technique, try to avoid blending the colors. Use acrylic paint with no retarder or glaze and a brush loaded with rather more paint than usual, then swipe the paint across the surface. A somewhat stiff, flat artist's brush can be used instead of a stenciling brush. Again, be careful around the edges of the stencil to avoid bleeding. Wherever possible, the brushing motion should sweep from the edge of the stencil toward the middle, rather than the reverse, to lessen the chance of paint being pushed under the stencil.

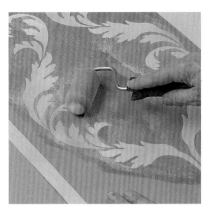
APPLY FIRST COLOR, LEAVING GAPS

BLEND SECOND COLOR INTO GAPS

PAT OFF GLAZE IN PLACES

TRANSPARENT COLORS

Stencil work done in transparent colors looks particularly beautiful over a background that has been prepared with a softly blended faux finish. For the medium, use either tinted acrylic varnish or tinted glaze, in two or three colors that will marry well with the background. Any type of applicator—brush, roller or sponge—can be used.

1 Mix enough medium in each of the colors to more than finish the job.

2 Apply the first color, either randomly or restricted, more or less, to certain parts of the pattern.

3 Apply the remaining colors, blending them to a greater or lesser degree depending on the desired effect. It is not necessary to obtain 100 percent coverage. Allow the glaze to taper away completely in places. This approach has a secondary benefit—you can taper off the stenciling in difficult corners of a wall without its looking like a deliberate omission. A taper can also be used to compensate for mistakes in repeat registration or to fake the matchup between the start and finish of a continuous border.

4 If the coverage seems too heavy in places, remove excess glaze by patting or wiping through the stencil with a barely damp soft cloth.

NOTE: When stenciling with transparent glazes, it is difficult to tell exactly what's been done as long as the stencil is still in place. The color just isn't strong enough. It helps to use tape to hinge the stencil on the wall. The stencil can then be lifted back to gauge the work without moving it. Do this frequently, because it is very easy to make the print too heavy.

Faux Stone

DAUB DIFFERENT COLORS OVER BASECOAT

BLEND AND LIFT COLORS WITH RUBBER BRAYER

ADD A SPATTER OF FINE DOTS IN SEVERAL COLORS

ROUGH STONE

A variety of materials can be imitated with this method simply by changing the color palette. Different sets of three or four colors can imitate granite, weathered concrete, terra-cotta or sandstone. In this example, I used white, ocher, warm brown and terra-cotta, all in acrylic house paint. A different choice of colors will yield a very different look.

1 First, apply an uneven basecoat of ocher with a stencil roller.

2 Then, using a sea sponge, daub on drifting shapes of brown, terra-cotta and white, making no particular effort to blend them. (At this point, it looks pretty awful.)

3 Just as the paint starts to dry, roll over the whole thing with a rubber brayer or a hardened stencil roller (i.e., one that you forgot to wash before the paint dried), exerting just enough pressure to blend the colors slightly.

4 Now roll it over the surface again, this time pressing harder. This should cause more blending and also lift patches of the sponged paint. If it does not, spritz the surface very lightly with water or sprinkle a few drops of water on it with your fingers, wait a few seconds and roll again. The dampened bits should lift off on the brayer.

5 If you wish, spatter fine dots of dark paint (more than one color) at this point. This technique is employed for a variety of examples shown in Chapter 10.

NOTE: Any time a sea sponge is used for stenciling, there's a risk of bleeding. If you can't wipe off a bleed, try shifting the stencil slightly so that it encloses the bleed. Then stipple the exposed gap using a stiff stencil brush and the same colors as before.

■ Some paints on the market mimic the textural effect of rough stone (they contain a dispersion of tiny acrylic beads), but use these only if you're sure you won't tire of the effect. Some of these products may be removed by sanding, others not. The advantage of using straight paint is that it's easy to paint over when it's time to redecorate.

APPLY DRIFTS OF COLOR TO BASECOAT

BLEND COLORS WITH SOFT BRUSH

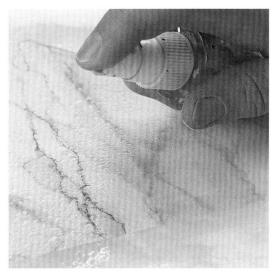

MIST WATERCOLOR PENCIL LINES TO DIFFUSE VEINS

MARBLE

1 Marbleizing usually involves manipulating copious amounts of glaze and paint into drifts of color, so when using stencils, a few modifications are needed to avoid bleeding. This is usually easiest with a very thin stencil, made of something like freezer paper. Fix it to the surface with stencil adhesive, then give it several roller-stenciled basecoats. When dry, this multilayered basecoat will tend to seal the edges of the stencil, leaving you free to inundate the surface with various glazes without the risk of bleeding.

2 Apply drifts of color over the basecoat using a brush, sponge, rag or roller. To extend the open time so that the drifts can be blended into each other, add a little glaze or retarder to the color.

3 Let dry thoroughly. For a more sophisticated look, layer additional drifts of transparent color.

4 Add veins in several layers, bottom ones softened with a badger brush, top ones fine and crisp. Use a fine brush, feather or watercolor pencil for veins.

NOTE: Check Further Reading for titles of books that devote more attention to faux marble.

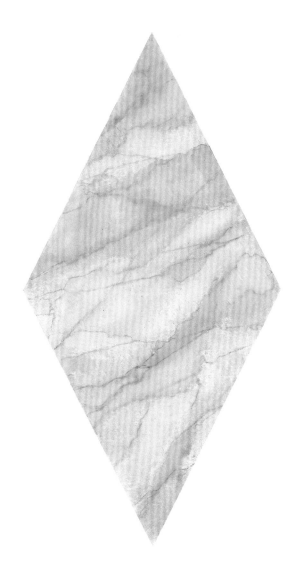

Damask

Damask fabrics originated in the fourth century A.D., in the Syrian capital of Damascus, which lent its name to this distinctive textile. Traditional damasks are reversible monochromatic textiles, originally made of silk. The pattern on these luscious fabrics is produced not by color but by the way in which the threads are woven, giving a different sheen to the motif as compared with the background. The typical designs were formal flowing patterns of stylized leaves, flowers, birds and exotic fruits.

Damask variations may include two colors (rarely more). However, the coloration is derived from thread color rather than printing and is uniform, without shading. Brocade is very similar to damask, except that the designs are raised above the background by an embroidery-like technique employing extra threads.

In its simplest forms, a damask effect is one of the easiest stencil treatments. The idea is to imitate the look of the damask and brocade fabrics that are commonly used as wall coverings in the decorating schemes of the average palace, château or *Schloss* without having the requisite imperial budget. A similar effect can be achieved simply with paint.

■ For the painted version of damask, stencil the motifs with a medium that has the same color but a very different sheen from the basecoat—for example, a gloss paint stenciled over a flat background or a flat medium stenciled over a glossy background. (The terms "flat" and "glossy" are relative as used here; simply ensure there is enough difference in sheen between the background and the stenciling that the finished pattern shows up.) A clear transparent medium, such as acrylic varnish, or a transparent medium with just a hint of color, such as a tinted glaze, can also be used. There are several variations on this basic theme, but they all boil down to single-overlay stencils done in an all-over pattern. The ideal tool for this is the stencil roller; it's fast and provides even coverage.

■ To imitate the look of brocade fabric, make the pattern look slightly embossed by using the embossed-leather method described on page 87. An easy alternative is to use the basic damask method (with a slightly tinted medium) and add freehand accents (highlights and shadow) with a small artist's brush.

Damask

BASIC METHOD

1 The first step is to pick the mediums, making sure there is enough difference in sheen between the basecoat covering the wall and the stenciling medium (acrylic varnish, paint or glaze). If the room lighting tends to be very subtle, the contrast between background and pattern can be enhanced by tinting the stenciling medium so that it is very slightly different from the background. A small amount of interference paint can also be added to the stenciling medium. This will tend to dramatize its reflection of light and provide a changing color shift as well.

2 Since this is an all-over pattern, particular care must be paid to the placement of each motif. (Read Chapter 6 to learn how to set up guidelines that will keep the motifs lined up in true rows and columns.)

3 Pinhole registration is usually easier to work with, because the low visibility of the prints makes it difficult to use outline registration. (I've used outline registration in the example shown here.) Mark vertical and horizontal guidelines on the stencil, and match these up with guidelines on the wall.

4 Position the stencil on the wall, holding it in place with stencil adhesive or low-tack tape or both.

5 Pour a small amount of medium onto a palette tray. In this example, I've used untinted acrylic varnish in a gloss finish. The wall is painted flat.

6 With a spatula, pull out a thin layer of medium from the puddle, and roll a dry roller through it. Work the roller back and forth to ensure even distribution, then offload any excess on a stack of paper towels.

This procedure is basic roller stenciling, as described in Chapter 2. The only difference is that the medium is transparent and colorless, so it is difficult to tell how well or poorly the roller is loaded. For this reason, always make the first couple of passes over the stencil very light, just in case there's too much varnish on the roller. If everything is okay, increase the pressure as needed.

■ Sometimes it can be difficult to see the stencil coverage. It helps to work with strong lighting that is oblique to the surface. This produces the kind of reflection needed to see the prints. Before lifting the stencil, transfer any pinhole registration marks. Don't worry about a minor bleed—it won't be visible once the entire wall has been completed.

NOTE: To help the camera capture this subtle effect, I added a bit of colorant to the clear varnish, hence the pale green on roller and stencil at left.

STENCIL ROLLER IS IDEAL FOR DAMASK

ADJUST STENCILED COLOR TO BACKGROUND

DAMASK WITH WALL REFLECTION

Damask stenciling can be made even more dramatic by imitating the diffuse reflection of light from the wall as a whole. Create the reflection before stenciling by making part of the wall lighter than the rest. This requires a glaze with a very long open time. Tint some of it slightly lighter than the basecoat color and some slightly darker.

1 The lighter part of the wall can be any size or shape that seems appropriate for the room and its light source. One choice is a broad band across the middle of the wall. To do this, divide the wall into three more or less horizontal bands. The top and bottom will be glazed with the darker tint, the middle with the lighter.

2 Working down from the top, use a large roller to apply the darker glaze to the top band, tapering the application near the middle band. Work quickly, making the glaze coat as even as possible. If you have a helper, that person can follow and even out the glaze by stippling or by going over it with a large foam roller.

3 Use a clean roller to apply the lighter glaze to the middle strip, blending the top edge up into the bottom of the darker top strip.

4 Add a little of the darker glaze near the corners of the room. Blend all color merges carefully.

5 Finally, apply dark glaze to the bottom strip, blending the top edge into the bottom of the lighter middle strip.

6 Once the glaze has thoroughly dried, carry on with the stenciling, in the same way as described on the facing page. Because the background is not completely uniform, the stenciling will show up better if it is slightly darker, as well as in a different sheen. Use a transparent stenciling medium that is somewhat deeper than the wall color. Make it lighter or darker depending on what part of the wall is being stenciled. As with the basic damask method, make sure the sheen of the stenciling medium is sufficiently different from that of the wall finish.

Embossed Leather

IMPASTO EMBOSSING

Unlike the method on the facing page, in which the embossed decoration is merely a painted illusion, this technique gives a tactile dimension to the embossing because the motif is stenciled with an impasto medium. Both methods are shown applied to papier-mâché boxes fashioned in the shape of books. Because the lid (or front cover) would be subject to handling, I wanted a tough medium for the impasto embossing and so used a thick ornamental acrylic gesso rather than joint compound or something like it. Before starting either method, I sealed the paper boxes with shellac.

1 The first step is to apply a smooth skim coat of the gesso to the whole surface. (For the "book," I taped off the binding area so that I could paint it separately.)

2 When the skim coat is dry, stencil a raised motif on its surface, using the same medium and following the instructions that begin on page 90. Let dry fully. Sand the motif lightly to smooth its edges.

3 For color, tint some acrylic varnish or sealer in a couple of leather-like hues. Apply with a soft cloth, rubbing it in circles to avoid leaving any application marks. Apply repeat coats until the color is as deep as you want it. Extra color should accumulate around the edges of the raised motif. For really dark leather hues, use tinted gesso for the skim coat and stencil work; finish by rubbing on a darker color.

COLOR SURFACE BY RUBBING IT WITH TINTED SEALER

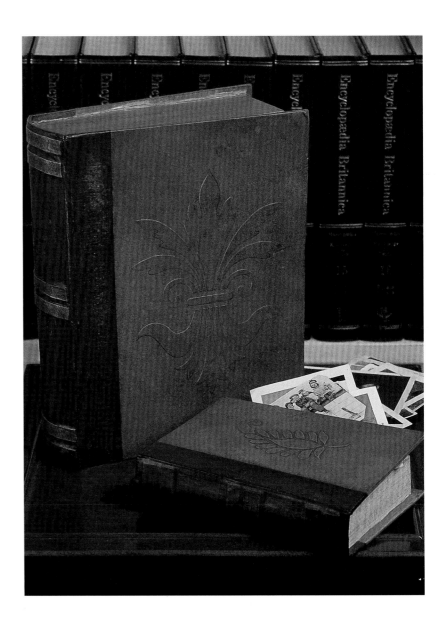

PAINTED EMBOSSING

The basic idea here is to imitate the look of embossed leather by stenciling with transparent glaze to hint at the overall shape of the embossed motifs. Then the dimensional effect of the embossing is simulated by highlighting the edges of the motifs facing the light source and casting a shadow from the trailing edges.

ADDING FREEHAND HIGHLIGHTS

1 The simplest way to get the look of leather for a panel is to start with an easy blended paint finish. For the basecoat, use a light earth color with yellow-ocher overtones in an eggshell finish. For the topcoat, apply a translucent mid-brown glaze with a foam roller. Work the roller until it starts to lift glaze in places, leaving an uneven finish. Let dry. Repeat glazing step if necessary. Another faux-leather treatment is to sponge or brush one or two different brown glazes over the basecoat, then stipple the entire surface to blend them. Let the faux leather dry for at least 24 hours, or long enough that the next step doesn't disturb the finish.

2a There's more than one way to get an embossed look. I've used two methods. For the first, choose two glaze colors, one darker than the background and one lighter.

3a Apply the darker glaze around all the trailing edges of the stencil—that is, all the edges in the shadow of your imagined light source.

4a Apply the lighter one around all the leading, or highlighted, edges.

5a Then use a very soft stencil brush or soft cloth, slightly dampened (not wet!), to work the glaze gently toward the very edge of the stencil so that virtually no glaze remains in the stencil opening itself. The result is a hint of the motif, defined only by a thin leading highlight and a trailing shadow. When it is completely dry, finish with a flat sealer.

2b Another method is to apply a thin layer of the darker glaze to the entire surface. As soon as it is dry to the touch, position the stencil over it.

3b Dampen a clean stencil roller with either a mist of water or a small amount of clear glaze. Offload excess moisture, then run the roller over the entire stencil. After a few seconds, the dampness should have softened the original layer of dark glaze. Keep the stencil in place.

4b With a soft cloth, very gently wipe off the softened glaze from as much of the stencil cutouts as possible. Use a clean stencil brush to work the glaze toward the edges of all cutouts. The motifs should end up outlined by a fine line created by a small buildup of glaze around the edges.

5b Now add subtle freehand highlights with a brush or pencil on the leading parts of the motif, just inside the outline. The easiest way to do this is with the stencil. Position it over the motif, and trace the highlighted edges with a pencil crayon. Finish with a flat sealer.

Impasto Methods

Impasto refers to a painting technique in which the paint itself is thick enough to have form and texture. A similar effect can be achieved with stencils by using a variety of thick mediums, including simple patching compounds and various types of plaster, as well as a number of art products.

This is a very straightforward technique that can yield a wide range of dramatic results, such as the look of anaglypta or Lincrusta wallpaper, a Wedgwood border or fossils embedded in limestone. Instead of normal paint, use a type of plaster (or highly viscous paint). A drywall spatula or putty knife replaces the stencil brush. The result is a three-dimensional image in low relief. The plaster can be tinted beforehand either to match the background or to provide contrasting relief.

■ For the strongest relief, use a thicker stencil—no less than 7 mils, preferably something like 20 mils. The medium always shrinks a little as it dries, so the end result is never as thick as it looks when wet. The thinner 5-mil stencils give a very thin relief, but this may be the best choice for some applications.

■ If using a hand-cut stencil, make sure it was cut with a knife rather than a heat cutter. The surface of the stencil must be perfectly level to get a smooth face when the plaster is applied. Even with a very good heat cutter, there are always some small deposits of melted plastic along the edge of the cuts, and these, being rather uneven in height, cause ridges in the surface of the plaster as the spatula is drawn across the stencil. The only case where this does not matter is when some texture is to be stippled or sponged onto the stenciled plaster.

FOR SMALL PROJECTS, USE A PREMIXED PATCHING COMPOUND OR CRAFT PRODUCT

MATERIALS

■ For interior decoration not subject to wear (a frieze, for example), use an interior joint compound, either ready-mixed or powdered (mix it yourself). There are many brands available at paint and hardware stores. For a small project, just buy a jar of pre-mixed interior patching compound, such as Spackle™. It is very easy to use and can be sanded off whenever you tire of it. Some of the lighter and fluffier compounds do not work well; they tend to pull out of the stencil as the spatula passes over. There are also exterior products—these are tougher and more flexible and can tolerate temperature changes, but they cannot always be sanded off or removed easily. They would be appropriate for relief work on a tabletop.

■ If you may want to remove this decoration at some point in the future, choose a medium that can be scraped, chipped or sanded away.

Or consider applying wallpaper liner to a wall that will be subjected to this treatment. Then it can be removed by taking off the liner.

■ Venetian plaster products can also be used. The viscosity varies from brand to brand. Thinner ones have a silky smooth finish and need more care in application. Venetian plaster produces wonderful "embedded fossils" when used with stencils (see instructions on page 96).

■ There are also various textured coatings that contain tiny acrylic beads. Some of these are thick enough to be used with a stencil. They give a more rustic look than does plaster.

■ Manufacturers of hobby and artist's paints and of faux-finishing mediums have produced a number of so-called dimensional mediums that yield excellent results when used with stencils. Most of these products have an acrylic base and are much more durable than plaster. Some are smooth, and others have various kinds of texture. You can also use high-viscosity paints.

■ Before beginning (in fact, while shopping for the product), read the label carefully, and make sure you understand how the product can be used (indoor/outdoor, durability, etc.), what safety precautions must be taken and whether the product is removable once cured. Most acrylic-based products are labeled as nontoxic. Others may require appropriate ventilation or even dust masks if sanded.

VICTORIAN BORDERS STENCILED WITH TINTED SPACKLE™

Impasto Methods

BASIC IMPASTO METHOD

1 Use a metal spatula or putty knife to apply the medium through the stencil. Pick a width appropriate to the scale of the work; it's easiest if the spatula is as wide as the stencil motif. Before starting, use coarse sandpaper to round off the corners of the spatula. (Some spatulas are manufactured with rounded corners, but many are not.) This will help avoid lap lines. Some people prefer flexible spatulas. Try both and see which works best for you.

2 Use two spatulas: a small one to lift the product from the container and put it onto a larger second spatula for application to the stencil. When loading the second spatula, try to get an even bead of medium along the entire straight edge. Keep refreshing the application spatula as you work so that there is always a line of medium right along the edge.

3 Once the spatula has been loaded, drape a damp cloth over the top of the container to keep the product from drying out. Any peaks or bits around the edge will dry very fast, forming solid nubbins that can ruin the work if they find their way onto the spatula. Whenever the spatula is scraped off to apply a fresh bead, discard the scraped-off medium. Do *not* put it back in the container, as it will contaminate the container with dried bits.

4 Tape the stencil in place to prevent movement. If the stencil has any parts that may tend to shift during use, anchor it with stencil adhesive.

5 Start with the spatula poised at one end of the stencil, angled to the surface. Spread the medium over the stencil slowly and carefully, scraping it level with the Mylar. Try to fill the stencil with one pass.

NOTE: If any bits are missed, go back to the beginning and drag the spatula over the entire stencil a second time. These little bits can't just be patched, because the spatula leaves starting and stopping marks on the surface. Don't overwork it; otherwise, the surface won't be smooth. This is one of those situations where it's much better to leave well enough alone. Reworking it will only make a mess.

6 Lift the stencil carefully and evenly—loose parts of the stencil can easily spring up and over part of the damp medium, causing major damage. It helps to practice this a few times on a sample until you can lift the stencil easily. Rough edges that may appear when the stencil is lifted can be removed with a very light sanding after the medium has dried.

7 Residue builds up fast on the stencil. Try to rinse it off for every repeat. Lay the stencil flat under a small amount of water, and rub it gently with a soft brush, such as a surgeon's brush. It cleans very easily while the medium is still wet. Do this in a plastic pan or tray so that you can decant the water and dispose of the solid residue separately, to prevent it from building up in the plumbing. Work with two stencils and a partner, if possible. Your helper can be cleaning and wiping dry one stencil while you are working with the other.

NOTE: This is one technique where stencil adhesive usually helps, because the stencil must cling to the surface so that the medium does not get forced under it. Even so, there may be the occasional bleed. If it is really bad, scrape the still wet product off for the entire repeat. Wipe the wall clean with a damp towel, and let dry before continuing. A minor problem can sometimes be repaired by scraping up the offending bit while it is still wet, using either a Q-tip or a very small spatula. Often, though, it is better to leave it until dry, then touch it up with background paint rather than trying to remove it.

APPLY BEAD OF PLASTER TO SPATULA

SCRAPE PLASTER OVER STENCIL

CAREFULLY LIFT STENCIL

FINISHED PLASTER SAMPLE

SAME METHOD WITH THICK PAINT

DRAW PAINT QUICKLY ACROSS STENCIL

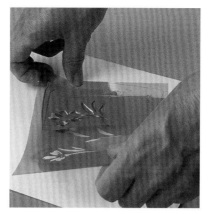

PULL STENCIL TAUT, AND LIFT UP

FINISHED VISCOUS-PAINT SAMPLE

LIGHT RELIEF

1 To stencil a motif in shallow relief, apply the medium only as thick as the stencil. At the same time that you trowel the product across the stencil, make sure the spatula scrapes level with the surface of the stencil, thus removing excess compound. The stencil should end up looking almost clean.

2 You can lift the stencil as soon as you've finished applying the medium.

■ Because the stencil won't be accumulating much medium, it's sometimes possible to stencil a couple of repeats before washing the stencil. However, any little bits that run under the stencil must be wiped off right away, even if the stencil as a whole doesn't need cleaning.

HEAVY RELIEF

1 The easiest and most controllable way to get heavy relief is to use thicker stencils, applying the impasto medium in the same way as for light relief. The relief can also be built up thicker than the stencil. Start by applying the medium as before, then add another layer, building up the medium as thickly as needed. The stencil will be covered with the material. Smooth the surface or texture it with the spatula or other tool.

2 Wait a minute or two, until the medium just starts to set up, then very carefully remove the stencil. Be sure to pull the edges taut, and try to lift it straight up. Lay the dirty stencil flat on some newspapers, scrape off the excess medium, then wash as described on facing page before continuing.

3 Don't worry about any rough edges on the thick motif. Once the product has dried, they will disappear with *very light* sanding. Do *not* force the drying time by using a hair dryer. This may cause the medium to crack.

NOTE: Another way of building up the relief is to apply a second coat after the first has dried. The thickness of the medium shrinks somewhat as it dries, so if the original layer was, say, 7 mils thick, it will be more like 5 mils when dry. Now, place the original 7-mil stencil back over the dried print, pressing it down to an exact fit. Scrape another layer of impasto medium over the stencil, building up the first layer to the thickness of the stencil. This approach is a more efficient use of the medium.

FINISHING

■ Once the medium is completely dry, remove rough bits on the edges with a *light* sanding. Depending on the material used (read the label), the surface may have to be sealed for water protection or before painting. The sealer/primer can be stenciled on, if necessary, but it is easier and more effective to apply it to the entire surface.

■ The easiest way to get color on the relief is to tint the medium beforehand. It is also possible to fit the stencil back in place over a dried motif and add color, but this may create a very narrow halo around the entire motif, because the paint may not cover the edges of the built-up print.

■ A color or faux finish can also be applied to the entire surface, if you wish. Extra color will tend to accumulate along the edges of the relief, an effect that can be enhanced for an antique look.

Plaster Examples

PLASTER WITH PAINT SHADOW

A shadow stenciled in paint can enhance the impasto look. Stencil the motif first with paint, then shift the stencil a fraction of an inch higher and to the leading edge. Now stencil it again with a plaster medium. Only the trailing edge of the painted image will remain visible next to the dimensional image.

RELIEF WITH GLAZE OVERLAY

This scroll border was stenciled first with a plaster medium. It was left to dry completely, then an overlay stencil was used with a transparent raw umber glaze to add the shading. It's a little tricky holding the second stencil in place, because it rests on a surface that is no longer flat but raised along the scroll by the thickness of the plaster.

RELIEF AS OVERLAY

The idea in this example was to capture the look of Wedgwood Jasperware. The silhouette of the Grecian ladies was first stenciled in translucent white over a solid blue background. Each silhouette was then overlaid with a single stencil whose bridges supply all the design details. This overlay was rendered with a white plaster medium. The contrast between the opaque white of the plaster and the translucent white of the paint gives the initial impression of molded plaster. It is especially effective when seen from a distance, as would be the case were it incorporated as part of a frieze.

Textured Examples

MONOCHROMATIC RELIEF WITH TEXTURE

A variation of the impasto method is to stencil motifs in relief on a textured background. Use a smooth medium like plaster, applied roughly, or a gritty, textured one. Many textured mediums are available commercially. Some, produced by art- or craft-supply companies, are better suited to small projects, but many are meant for overall wall coverage. These mediums usually contain either sand or tiny acrylic beads to give them texture, and some are available in a range of colors.

1 First, apply the medium to the entire wall (or to a taped-off frieze band), following the label instructions, with either a spatula, trowel or roller. (This example was done with a roller, and the coverage was purposely left imperfect.) Let dry.

2 Stencil the motifs in relief, either randomly or in ordered repeats, using the spatula method described on pages 90-91. With random elements, the thickness of plaster can also be tapered off as you stencil, just as you would with paint or glaze, so that the motifs seem to be emerging from and receding into the background. Another option is to leave some stencil openings partially filled with medium, either by

doing a partial trowel-over or by using torn paper masks. Remove the stencil carefully.

3 It can take quite a while for the stenciled motifs to dry, so be careful not to ruin one by letting the stencil overlap it too soon. It's best to do widely spaced motifs in the first go-round, then fill in closer ones when the first ones are thoroughly dry.

4 The motifs can be finished, colored and sealed in one step by applying a tinted flat water-based sealer. I like to brush it on loosely, then rub it in with a soft cloth to create some color variation. The color will tend to accumulate more in the recesses and against ridges in the surface.

STENCIL MOTIFS USING THE SPATULA METHOD DESCRIBED ON PAGES 90-91

RUB TINTED FINISH SO THAT COLOR ACCUMULATES IN RIDGES

THIS TECHNIQUE PRODUCES A LOVELY ANCIENT-PLASTER EFFECT

TWO-COLOR TEXTURED RELIEF

Another option is to pretint the medium with different colors for the background and for the stenciling. In this case, I applied the background with a trowel, using two slightly different shades of medium. The medium itself was gritty, and the surface was left slightly rough. After the background had dried overnight, the vine was stenciled with the same medium in a lighter color. The result has an appealing rustic look, with the feel of worn sandstone.

MULTICOLORED TEXTURE

This example was done with a hobby medium that contains colored acrylic beads, which give it a very stonelike look and texture. Several different colors were applied in streaks for the background. The motifs were done in similar colors so that they show up best with the shadows of oblique light, just as petroglyphs would.

Textured Examples

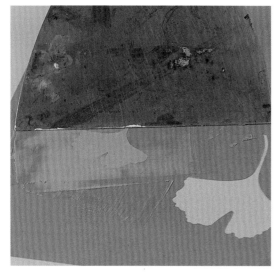

TINT MOTIF PLASTER A SLIGHTLY DIFFERENT COLOR

LET SOME OF THE GINKGO LEAVES BE IMPERFECT

RECOAT BACKGROUND PLASTER (IT DRIES LIGHTER)

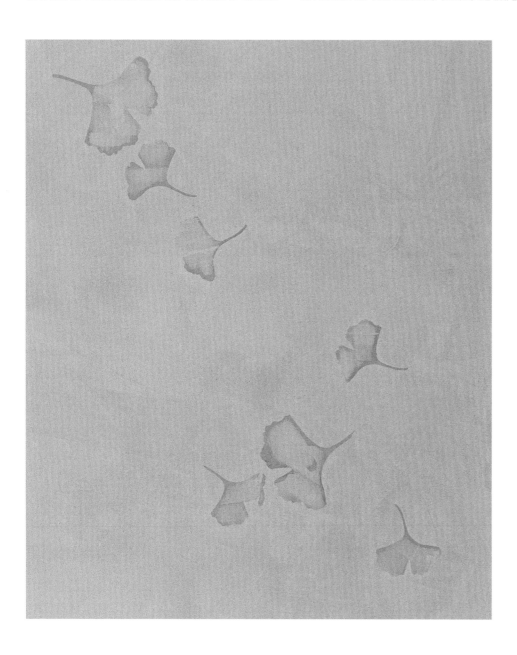

EMBEDDED FOSSIL MOTIFS

1 The effect here is one of fossils embedded in a polished stone surface. Start by applying a very thin layer of tinted Venetian plaster, using a wide metal spatula and following the label instructions. Let this dry.

2 Tint a small amount of plaster in a color that's slightly different from the background color. Use this to stencil fossil-type motifs, such as leaves or shells, randomly over the surface. Use a thin stencil. Let some of the motifs be imperfect—that is, don't completely fill the stencil. Let dry.

3 Give the surface of the stenciled motifs a light sanding.

4 With the original background plaster, apply another layer all over, bringing the surface up to the level of the fossil motifs. Allow plaster to scrape over top of parts of the motifs.

5 Let dry, then sand lightly with very fine grit. Burnish the whole surface according to the directions on the product label.

SCULPTED MOTIFS

1 Fish "fossils" take more time, as each motif requires a little sculpting. After preparing the first layer of Venetian plaster as before, stencil a simple but realistic fish shape in a slightly different color, using a medium-thick stencil (around 7 mils).

2 Working quickly, before the plaster dries, drag a small comb (a cheap plastic one cut into small pieces works well)

through the plaster in the direction of the bones that come out from the spine. Sometimes, this means working in two directions—one from the spine to the belly, another from the spine to the dorsal surface.

3 Do the same thing for the tail and any fins. Don't worry if the dragged plaster spoils the outline somewhat. It will get covered up in the next step. When the plaster is dry, give it a light sanding to remove any rough bits.

4 The starfish were done in a similar way. Use a piece of bamboo skewer, a pencil or an embossing tool to press indentations along the arms.

5 Once the fossils have dried and been sanded to remove excessive ridges caused by the sculpting, apply the final layer of plaster to bring the background layer level with the fossils. Scrape this layer right over the fossils so that it fills in the sculpted crevices, allowing the "bones" to show. Let dry. Sand with very fine paper, if necessary, and burnish.

METALLIC TOPCOAT

This fossil technique is slightly different. It is meant to look as though the stone around the fossils has eroded. The background in this example was applied with a sea sponge and a trowel, using a tinted acrylic plaster medium. Once the background was dry, the shells were stenciled with the same medium. When each motif was almost dry, I laid a metal spatula flat on the motif and compressed it slightly. This caused some of the features to spread out and fill in bridges. When everything was completely dry, the entire surface was finished with a metallic gel coat, applied with a wide spatula.

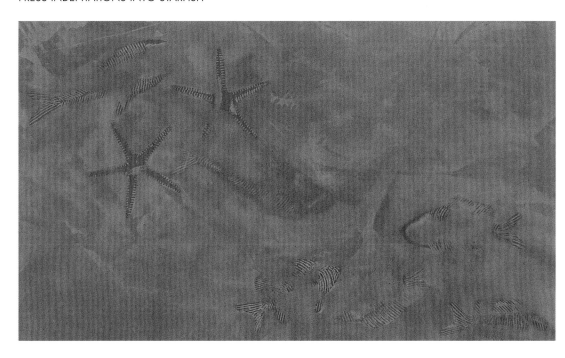

PRESS INDENTATIONS INTO STARFISH

Layered Pattern

It's easy to add a superimposed pattern or the illusion of texture to a stenciled image by layering a thin sheet of screenlike material with a stencil. Many manufactured materials work well, and you'll find good candidates, such as plastic window screens, sheet-metal screens, cheesecloth, lace and paper doilies, just by wandering through a hardware store, a ship chandler or a fabric shop.

The first example shown with this simple rose motif was done by placing a piece of thin plastic screen over the stencil, then stippling on the paint. It is important to tape the screen in place on the stencil so that it will not shift while you are painting. If it does shift, it will ruin the neat, tidy grid that suggests precise needlework. You need a stiff brush and some patience for this, as each section of the motif must be worked repeatedly to build up a good pattern without bleeding.

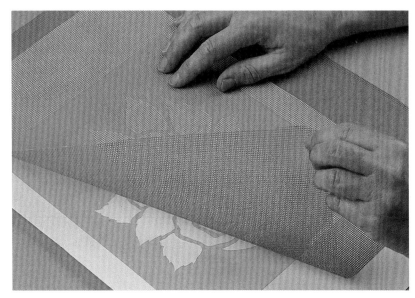

PLACE SCREEN OVER STENCIL AND SECURE WITH TAPE

A STIFF BRUSH AND PATIENCE ARE KEY

NOTE: If you reverse the layer order and place the stencil on top of the screen, you can stencil the screen itself, as long as you use a paint that sticks to the screen material. It shows up surprisingly well on screen doors and window screens.

For a loosely woven effect, use a piece of cheesecloth instead of the screen. First, prepare the cheesecloth, making it stiff so that it can be held in place without moving. To do this, stretch the cheesecloth over a flat surface and anchor it with tape or staples. Coat the entire surface with shellac. I used BIN™, a shellac loaded with white pigment. It dries very

quickly, and once dried, the cheesecloth forms a stiff sheet. Lay it over the stencil, and tape securely. As with the previous example using the plastic screen, stipple or pounce paint through both cheesecloth and stencil with a stiff stencil brush. This treatment is also useful for creating various rustic effects. It gives the border, above right, the look of grasscloth.

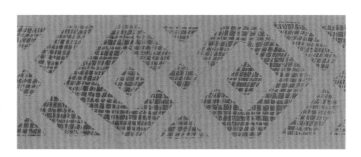

LAYER STIFFENED CHEESECLOTH OVER STENCIL FOR A WOVEN, TEXTURED LOOK

LAYER LACE AND STENCIL, RIGHT, FOR ELABORATELY PATTERNED PRINTS

Combining a piece of lace with a stencil allows a whole range of choices for adding visual texture to your stencil print. As with cheesecloth, this works best when you stiffen the lace with shellac first.

NOTE: To get more than a mere illusion of texture, apply an impasto medium through shellacked lace or cheesecloth, using the method described in the previous section. Unpredictable, but fun!

Heavy Metals

When it comes to creating opulent images, nothing beats a touch of gold. Stenciling with gold or other metallic paint is no different from normal stenciling, but there are other mediums from which to choose as well; many of them are not traditionally used with stencils. These methods are perfect for use with furniture and decorative objects.

COLORS

Whether you use paint, foil, metal leaf or metal powders, there is a huge palette of metallic colors available. Decide first which metallic finish will look best next to the colors it is meant to embellish (or vice versa).

Then, because some metallic treatments provide less than 100 percent coverage, be careful about choosing a base color to go under the metal. Gold looks best over warm colors—deep red, terra-cotta or brown—while cooler greens, blues and grays are more flattering to copper. Silvery metals look good over just about anything. Experiment to find just the right combination. You can apply the base color to the entire surface or stencil the base color, thus confining it to the shape of the motif.

FOR SUBTLE EFFECTS, STENCIL WITH METALLIC GLAZE

GLAZE

If you want just a shimmer of gold, rather than a solid blast, try a translucent golden glaze. Buy it ready-made, or make your own by mixing metallic paint or metallic powder (available at art-supply stores) with a glaze medium or an acrylic varnish. The border shown here was roller stenciled with a commercial gold glaze on top of a linen background treatment. The latter was done with a Venetian red basecoat followed by two dragged coats of the same gold glaze used for the stenciling.

PAINT

The most straightforward approach to a metallic look, as well as the least expensive and the easiest, is to use one of the many water-based gold, silver, bronze or copper paints on the market. Try several brands and several colors within each brand to find the one you like best on your particular base color.

It may be necessary, when stenciling, to apply more than one layer to achieve the depth and richness produced with a thicker freehand application.

You can also make your own metallic paint by mixing bronze powder with varnishes, shellac or even fabric paint. Wear a mask to avoid breathing in the fine powder, then pour some medium into a container, add metallic powder, and stir well. Make only as much as you need at one time. Stir the paint frequently during use, as the powder tends to sink to the bottom.

GOLD PAINT USUALLY REQUIRES SEVERAL COATS

GEL COAT

For a very thick, textured gold, try one of the new thick gold mediums produced by several faux-finish manufacturers. Meant to be used as metallic topcoats applied with a trowel, they are thick enough to be used with stencils, according to the instructions for impasto mediums (see pages 90-91).

TEXTURE OF GOLD GEL MEDIUM IS THICK ENOUGH FOR STENCIL USE

APPLY SIZE OVER STENCILED BASECOAT

SMOOTH FOIL WITH A SOFT CLOTH

FOIL

Gold paint is good enough for many applications, but sometimes you need an extra sparkle that paint just can't deliver. The next step up the scale in terms of cost and effort is a type of polyester foil that is coated with a shiny metallic film (gold-, silver- or copper-colored). When you place the foil on a tacky surface and rub the backing, it transfers the metallic film to the surface.

1 Here's how it works: Stencil your motif in a chosen base color. I've used a warm yellow-green for this ginkgo leaf.

2 Then carefully stencil a coat of water-based adhesive, or size, right on top of the base color. The adhesive looks milky in the jar but dries clear. It's terrible stuff to clean off a brush, and using a cheap brush doesn't give very good results, so I use small makeup sponges to stipple the adhesive through the stencil. This type of sponge is

AFTER RUBBING, PEEL OFF FOIL

very fine and gives quite a uniform application. It's also cheap, so it can simply be discarded after the project is finished.

NOTE: Do *not* use stencil adhesive on the back of the stencil. There is always a chance it will leave the smallest bit of adhesive residue on the surface, and this residue will grab onto the gold foil, marring the work.

3 Once the adhesive has been applied, remove the stencil.

4 When the glue is dry and clear (but still tacky), lay a piece of the foil, dull side down, over the motif.

GOLD FOIL HAS A MUCH STRONGER SHINE THAN PAINT

5 Smooth it out with your fingers or with a soft cloth wadded into a firm ball, and rub firmly all over. You can also try rubbing with various burnishers or with an art eraser. Each type of tool transfers different amounts of gold and leaves different traces. Yet another look can be created by wrinkling the foil as it is applied.

6 After rubbing, peel off the foil, and you're done. The gold coverage is not as perfect as it is with paint, but it has a much stronger shine, and the interplay between gold and basecoat may be just what you need.

7 For the finished example shown above, I rubbed more gold on the stem end of the leaf than over the top part of the leaf. To give an impression of the fine ribbing on the ginkgo leaf, I ran a pencil along the back of the foil, in the general pattern of the ribs. This transferred more color along those lines.

■ For total gold coverage, stencil a layer of gold paint instead of the green, then apply the gold foil on top of the gold paint. The result will be solid gold but of varying intensity and shine.

Heavy Metals

METALLIC LEAF

Once you've used metallic leaf—whether real gold or silver or the less costly substitute metals—it's hard to go back to anything else. Mere paint looks weak and insubstantial by comparison; foil looks cheap and gaudy. Metallic leaf doesn't shine—it glows richly. Yes, it *is* more expensive and more difficult to use, but nothing else looks as good.

Gilding is the technique of decorating objects and moldings with *very* thin sheets (around one ten-thousandth of a millimeter) of gold, silver or other metal. The sheets are fixed in place with an adhesive, or size, and except for the purest gold, they usually need a transparent finish coat to prevent tarnishing. Gold size is available in both water-based and oil-based formulations. Water-based size stays tacky forever, allowing unlimited time to get the metal leaf down. However, to avoid sticky spots on the surface, this means all the sized area must be covered with leaf. If any size is to remain uncovered, use oil-based (it's like varnish), which stays suitably tacky for only a short time before drying completely. There is also a "dry" size; to transfer to a surface, rub on its backing sheet. It is best suited to free-hand designs but can be used with very thin stencils.

Traditionally, metallic leaf is not used with stencils, but that doesn't mean it can't be done. Apply the size through a stencil, and let it reach the tacky stage. Then lay down the leaf over the stenciled size, and burnish with a soft brush. The excess gets brushed away, leaving the gold motif. It's best to stencil a basecoat of a suitable color before adding the size, because it can be very difficult to achieve perfect coverage with the metal leaf. To highlight portions of a stenciled motif with gold leaf, simply apply the size to the desired parts with a fine brush.

It is very important not to use any stencil adhesive on the back of the stencil, in case it leaves residue on the surface. This residue will cause the leaf to stick, and it will be very difficult to remove.

REAL GOLD

Real gold leaf is sold in two different forms: in "books" of small loose sheets inset between sheets of paper and as "patent" sheets, where the leaf is adhered to a backing paper with wax or an electrostatic charge. The latter is a little more expensive than loose leaf but is easier to handle, especially with stencils. Loose leaf works better on carved surfaces, because it can mold itself to the shape.

Gold leaf is produced in various shades of gold. The color depends on many things, from the country of origin to the amount and kind of other metals added to the gold.

The purest and softest gold is 24 karat. A lower karat rating means silver (and possibly other metals) has been added to the gold—the lower the karat, the more silver. Twenty-two karat gold is 90 percent pure gold, 12 karat is 50 percent. Gold of 22 karats or higher will not tarnish, but anything less pure than this needs a clear, protective finish applied to prevent it from tarnishing.

COMPOSITION GOLD

Imitation gold comes in books of loose sheets. The leaves are somewhat thicker than leaves of real gold. Known as faux gold, Dutch leaf or composition gold, this metal leaf is available in a number of colors, each an amalgam of various metals that look like gold. There are also variegated forms, in which the metal has been heat-treated to give it random patterns of bright colors. Composition gold needs a finish coat or sealer to prevent tarnishing.

SILVER

If your sheets of metal leaf measure 4¹⁄₁₆ inches square, then they are made of silver, no matter what the actual color. Silver leaf is chemically dyed to produce a whole range of colors, including bronze, reds, greens and blues. It is mostly available in loose leaves and is somewhat more difficult to use than gold, being more brittle and susceptible to cracking. Like all silver, it tarnishes and so needs a clear finish coat.

PICK UP LEAF FROM BOOKLET

GENTLY PAT LEAF OVER SIZED MOTIF

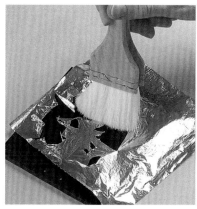

RUB AWAY EXCESS WITH SOFT BRUSH

BRUSH UNTIL MOTIF IS EXPOSED

WORKING WITH METALLIC LEAF

Whether working with real gold leaf, imitation gold or silver, the process is the same. The only difference in application is between loose leaf and patent leaf. Here, I have used composition gold with water-based size to illustrate the use of loose metal leaf, and real gold with oil-based size to show the patent-leaf process.

■ Some stencilers prefer to lift off the stencil after applying the size and before laying down the leaf. This is the best approach when using water-based size, because any minor bleeds (potential tacky spots) will be covered by the leaf.

■ Leaving the stencil in place while laying the leaf can make for cleaner edges, but it means using oil-based size, because if there is any bleeding at all, you want the bleeds to dry without remaining tacky. With this method, you can leave gaps in the leaf, if you want the basecoat to show through, but use a very thin stencil so that the metal leaf can get right into the edges.

■ Any leftover scraps of leaf can be used to patch up missed spots. If they won't stick, apply a little more size to the spot.

■ If you want to add a slight dimension to your gilded motif, stencil it first with an impasto medium (see page 90), then sand the edges lightly and basecoat it before leafing.

LOOSE LEAF

Loose metallic leaf is very thin, very light and extremely susceptible to crinkling and tearing. Keep it covered up until the actual moment of application, because the slightest draft, a sneeze or even a sigh will give it a life of its own. I've used a water-based size for this example.

1 The first step is to stencil an appropriate base color for the motif. When it's dry, stencil a layer of size over the basecoat. Use a makeup sponge and a stippling or pouncing application, taking great care to avoid bleeding. Remove the stencil.

2 When the size has dried to the tacky stage, carefully place a sheet of loose Dutch leaf into position over the stenciled size. You don't get two chances to do this, and leaf tears very easily. Position one edge of the leaf, then slowly lower the rest into place. Once the leaf sticks, it cannot be moved. If you prefer, work with smaller pieces of metal leaf, dabbing them down onto the motif.

3 Use a soft brush to smooth the leaf onto the surface, pouncing lightly to make sure it has adhered completely. Go over it again more firmly. Then rub the brush in a circular sweeping motion to remove the excess leaf—that is, any leaf that extends beyond the motif.

NOTE: It can be difficult to determine when the size has reached the right degree of tackiness. This is something that comes only with practice. If the leaf is applied too soon, the size can work through the pores of the leaf and spoil the shine; if applied too late (particularly with oil-based size), the foil may not adhere properly.

Heavy Metals

APPLY UNDERCOAT AND SIZE

PLACE GOLD ON STENCIL

PAT GOLD INTO STENCIL OPENING

CAREFULLY REMOVE STENCIL

NOTE: Composition gold (see previous example) is tough compared with this real gold, which is gossamer-thin. Anything more than the most delicate touch of the burnishing brush will cause the sheet to disintegrate completely and spoil the sheen of the gold.

PATENT LEAF

Only real gold comes in patent-leaf form. The sheets of gold are lightly stuck to a sheet of waxed paper. The backing means it won't fly away or tear as it is being placed. You can handle it without touching the leaf, because there is a nice margin of waxed paper around the edges. Although more expensive than loose leaf, it might save you money in the end, because it can be cut (carefully) into pieces just the right size for stenciled motifs and thus prevents waste. It is perfect for stenciling.

1 For stencil work, patent gold leaf is applied in the same way as loose metal leaf. First, stencil a base color. Then apply the size (here, oil-based) through the stencil using a stencil brush and a gentle stippling motion. In this example, I'm leaving the stencil in place. Let the size dry to slightly tacky.

2 Lift a sheet of gold leaf, holding it by the margin of the backing paper. Turn it over, and lower it to the surface. Pat the backing paper gently all over with a soft brush.

3 Once the leaf has adhered to the size, carefully lift off the backing paper. Any leaf not stuck to the motif or to the stencil should still be attached to the backing paper. Store it, carefully, between the sheets of the leaf booklet to use for another project or to patch any missed spots.

4 Now, working very gently, tap all over the image with a soft brush. Gradually start brushing with a light circular motion to ensure good adhesion. The leaf will break at the edge of the stencil (especially if the stencil is thick), where it tries to fold into the edge of the cutout. Pick up pieces of scrap gold with tweezers, and pat them along the break line to fill the edge of the cutout.

5 Carefully lift the stencil. Brush the motif once more to make sure any edges lifted with the stencil are secured.

LEAF FLAKES

This beautiful material consists of scraps of metal leaf in plain or mixed colors, including blue, green and red.

1 Apply the size through the stencil by gently pouncing (using a fine-textured makeup sponge for water-based size or a small stencil brush for oil-based size). Remove the stencil. Let the adhesive dry to the right tackiness. This doesn't take long, since it's a very thin layer.

2 Use tweezers to pick up a pinch or two of leaf flakes. Drop them over the motif in a little pile.

3 Tap the flakes into the size, then rub them over the motif with your finger or a soft cloth, working in small circles.

4 Gradually increase the pressure. Keep going until foil pieces cover and adhere to the entire motif. Brush away any excess.

DROP LEAF FLAKES OVER SIZED MOTIF

TAP THE FLAKES INTO THE SIZE WITH SOFT BRUSH

RUB IN CIRCLES TO MAKE FLAKES ADHERE

METALLIC WAX

This medium is basically bronze powder, of one color or another, mixed with clear, solid furniture wax. You can either make your own or buy it ready-made at art- or craft-supply stores. This product is not meant to cover large areas. It is usually applied with a finger, rubbed over frames or small objects to highlight the relief.

Alternatively, use a stencil brush to rub the metallic wax through a template. As with other stenciling mediums, the excess wax must be wiped off the brush before working with the stencil. Apply only a thin layer of wax; otherwise, a ridge of wax may build up around the edge of the motif. If this happens, do not try to fix it on the spot. Instead, let it harden overnight, then carefully scrape away the ridge with an X-acto knife.

Like the oil-based stencil paint sticks and the solid stencil paints, metallic wax smudges very easily. Be careful when removing the stencil and when handling the object before the wax has dried.

Heavy Metals

RUB POWDER OVER THE MOTIF WITH A VELVET PAD

BRONZE POWDER

Bronze powder can be mixed into a medium to create metallic paints, but it can also be applied directly with a stencil. This technique was widely used in the United States during the early 19th century as a means of decorating furniture and accessories, particularly chair backs. From the name, you might assume that these powders are all more or less bronze in color. In fact, they are available in a wide range of colors, from pale gold and red-gold to antique copper, silver and pewter, to name a few. Moreover, they are made up of aluminum, copper and zinc—not a bit of bronze in sight.

NOTE: Wear a dust mask when working with these powders, because they are very fine and powdery; one sneeze, and you'll have metallic dust floating around all day.

1 Start with a fresh coat of oil-based gloss or semigloss varnish (which serves as the size) applied over a very dark basecoat. Cover the entire surface. Oil-based gold size can also be used.

2 When the varnish dries just to the tacky stage, lay down a thin stencil (I use one made of heavy tracing paper). Mask off the rest of the surface to protect it from stray bits of powder, if necessary.

3 Fold a small pad of velvet, or wrap a piece of velvet around your finger. Pick up a small amount of bronze powder on the velvet, and tap it on another piece of cloth to offload excess.

4 Then gently rub the powder into the tacky surface with a sort of circular polishing motion. Work the brightest parts of the stencil design first, then fade away to nothing. The powder is almost always applied in a tapered fashion; solid coverage is rare.

5 When the bronze powder has been applied to your satisfaction, make sure there are no loose grains sitting on the stencil or on the surface being decorated. As soon as the stencil is lifted, those little grains will find their way to some nice clean spot on the background and adhere there.

NOTE: If the varnish gets too dry before you have finished or if you are interrupted before completing the entire surface, let the piece dry, then revarnish and continue stenciling. If you try to revarnish too soon, the stenciled bronze will be picked up and moved around by the varnish brush.

6 When all the stenciling is finished, let it dry completely, after which the surface can be washed gently with soapy water to remove any excess powder.

7 Finally, varnish once more for protection.

■ This example shows a motif common to the 19th century. Make repeated overlapping prints of the same small leaf, arranging the prints to form a circle. For the overlaps to show up properly, it is important to taper the shading quickly, from heavy gold on one side to nothing on the other.

■ For small cutouts, your finger may be too big to create the delicate gradations of gold. In this case, use a "bob" to apply the powder. Fashion a bob by folding a square of velvet over the end of a cotton swab and tying it with thread or dental floss. Most of the historical bronze stenciling of any quality was of composite, or theorem, design. Much like today's "freeform stenciling," a few different stencils for individual leaves or grapes, for example, would be used repeatedly to build up an overall composition of many leaves and bunches of grapes, with the different elements usually overlapping one another.

EMBOSSED METAL

Aluminum, copper and brass foils, packaged for the arts and crafts market, make interesting surfaces for stencil embossing. They are sold in short rolls of a few feet, looking not unlike kitchen foil but of a much heavier gauge. The embossed pieces can be used in a variety of ways—as decorative accents on greeting cards or home accessories or as all-over coverings for small tabletops, boxes or journal covers.

NOTE: Cut metal edges are sharp, so this is not a product for children to use. Safety glasses and gloves are recommended. However, I find it hard to do fine work wearing gloves, so I usually opt for bare hands and a few bandages. You might consider using close-fitting disposable cotton gloves, which will also prevent fingerprints from getting on the metal. Collect and store or safely dispose of all metal trimmings.

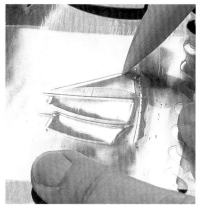 

OUTLINE MOTIF ALONG STENCIL LINES   TURN OVER AND PRESS OUT CENTER

1 Start by cutting a piece of metal foil somewhat larger than needed for the finished piece.

2 Tape it to the back of the stencil, with the motif centered on the piece. Place this, stencil side up, over a firm but cushioned surface, such as a piece of neoprene, a loose stack of newspapers or a cushioned mousepad.

3 Using a pointed wooden tool (embossing tool, sharpened dowel or knitting needle), outline the motif by tracing along the edges of the stencil cutout. Press firmly enough to make a light indentation in the foil. Proceed carefully; it's easy to slip and carve a line across the middle of the cutout.

4 Repeat the tracing a second time to make the indentation slightly deeper.

5 Remove the stencil. Now, to make the design protrude, turn the foil and work from the back, pushing the design out with a more rounded wooden tool. The one I'm using here is part of a set that is sold with the foil, along with an embossing pad to work on.

6 When you have finished embossing, trim the piece to size and glue it in place with a glue gun. Wear gloves for this part, because the hot glue will make the metal very hot to the touch.

7 To increase the durability of heavy embossing (i.e., to make it less vulnerable to being squished), fill the back of the contours with hot glue before mounting. Level the surface of the glue before it hardens.

Distressing

There are many ways to "age" stencil work—some rustic-looking, others more refined. The most direct method is through the original choice of colors, for both the basecoat and the stenciling. Pick subdued background colors that impart a sun-faded look. Then, for the stenciling, stay with a similar value range as the background. A more or less monochromatic scheme of faded hues can be very effective.

There are also several aging treatments that can be applied to the entire painted surface, either before or after stenciling. They range from a simple color wash, which can be easily rubbed over a wall, to the very demanding craquelure, which is best applied to small areas.

MONOCHROMATIC COLOR AGING

An easy way to give your work a timeworn look is to keep it dull and monochromatic. The entire design—here, a honeysuckle border—can be done in shades of a single hue; something that recalls the faded sepia tones of an old family photograph.

NEUTRAL COLOR AGING

One approach is to manipulate the colors so that they stay neutral. Begin by stenciling the entire image in a color that will neutralize the brighter hues you might normally use. In this case, I stenciled the honeysuckle first in burnt sienna. Then I stenciled the greens, yellows and reds on top. Because all single stenciled layers are very thin and therefore somewhat transparent, the burnt sienna shows through the fresher hues and neutralizes them. You can still see color, but it's subdued.

AGED DESIGN

Sometimes the stencil pattern itself can be designed with chips and cracks right from the start, as in this fret border, rendered here with a textured plaster medium over a similar background. Impasto stencil work like this could be further distressed with selective sanding or chipping.

START WITH A WELL-CURED BACKGROUND AND BORDER

WIPE OFF EXCESS GLAZE

COLOR WASH/GLAZE

This is an easy solution to a stenciled wall that looks too fresh and new; it creates a finish that imitates the mellowed patina of a well-aged surface.

1 Before you begin, it is essential that the background and all stenciling have had time to cure; otherwise, the glaze may soften and disturb them.

2 Pick a glaze medium that is very transparent and has a fairly long open time. For a sun-faded look, tint it with white or ivory; for a tea-stained look, tint it with raw umber or a medium earth brown.

3 Tape the edges of the wall to keep the corners neat. Roll very thin layers of glaze over the surface with a foam roller, working the roller in random directions. Use a small brush to stipple the glaze into the corners. Another method is to apply an excess of glaze with a normal roller, then rag it off by pouncing and wiping the surface with clean, lint-free rags.

4 The final result depends, to a certain extent, on the sheen of the original wall surface. The flatter the finish, the more the surface grabs the glaze, resulting in uneven and darker coloration. A semigloss finish, on the other hand, lets the glaze slide around and allows a greater degree of blending.

WHITE GLAZE CREATES A SUN-FADED LOOK

RAW UMBER GLAZE PRODUCES A TEA-STAINED EFFECT

Distressing

SANDING

Selective sanding is an effective aging tool for painted furniture, especially when there are multiple layers of paint in different colors. The object is to wear away the layers of paint (and stenciling) in areas that would have been subject to the most handling—corners, handles, high points of relief and molding, and so on. The surface should not look obviously sanded, so stick to relatively fine grits, or use wet/dry paper and sand it wet.

Walls that have a slight texture can also be sanded back to create an effect similar to worn fresco, particularly if the colors are faded. In this case, do all the work with low-sheen colors—background and stenciling both.

1 Apply one solid base color to the entire wall, then one or two brushed color washes in related colors (not too much contrast).

2 Finish all stenciled decoration, again using faded colors. Give everything a few days to dry completely.

3 Use a pole sander to go over the entire wall lightly, wearing down the high points to reveal the different layers of color. Parts of the stenciling will be rubbed right out.

■ This approach works even better if the walls have a plaster type of finish. Layers of colored plaster can be applied as the basecoat, and there will be more leeway with the sanding.

TEXTURED AGING

This is basically the opposite approach to that of sanding. Instead of removing areas of stenciling by sanding down the plaster, you cover them up by applying thin layers of colored plaster to selected areas.

1 First, create a slightly textured background, using a trowel to apply a plaster or an acrylic medium. The texture can be fairly smooth or randomly broken (use a sponge to break up the wet medium, then knock back the peaks with a trowel). The medium itself can be tinted, or the surface can be glazed after it dries.

2 When the background is dry, stencil borders or freeform compositions using either glazes or paints, depending on whether you want a transparent or an opaque look.

3 Cover up parts of the stenciling with the same colored medium used for the background. The effect should look as though chunks of plaster have simply worn off the wall through the ages, so this means some carefully considered randomness in the way this medium is applied. Alternatively, cover up the parts of the stenciling you are less happy with and leave exposed the parts that please you most.

Use a trowel alone, if you wish, or for a more broken effect, dab on generous patches of medium with a sea sponge, then lightly drag a wide trowel over it. This smooths out the spots of medium and merges some together into larger patches.

SPREAD GLUE OVER SURFACE

APPLY LATEX TOPCOAT

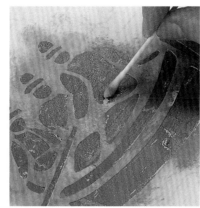
STENCIL, THEN LIFT UP BITS OF PAINT

NOTE: Picking an old historical design such as this Moses Eaton sailor stencil reinforces the timeworn effect.

CRACKLED PAINT

This finish crackles the top coat of a painted surface, allowing the underlying color to show through. It is a rustic look that imitates the effect of years of outdoor weathering. To apply a crackle finish to an entire wall, use one of the brand-name products sold under a number of different house-paint labels, and follow the product instructions. Personally, I think this finish is more appropriate when applied to smaller areas, like pieces of furniture and decorative objects. The method described here is meant for such surfaces.

There are three layers to this finish: a basecoat of acrylic paint, a layer of animal-hide glue or fish glue (or a commercial crackle medium) and a top layer of low-sheen latex paint. The top layer is applied before the glue has completely dried. As the glue finishes drying, it shrinks and causes the top layer to crack. Achieving the right amount and pattern of crackle

is a matter of trial and error. Speeding up the drying process with a hair dryer produces larger cracks, as does a thicker layer of glue. Applying the top layer of paint with a roller, rather than a brush, creates a finer network of cracks. The crackle tends to align itself with the direction of glue application, so a more even crackle is produced when the glue is brushed on in straight lines and a busier, more random crackle when it is brushed on in overlapping crisscross strokes.

1 The first step is to basecoat the surface with the color that is going to show through the cracks. Let it dry overnight. Try to have each surface in a horizontal position, if possible, when working on it. That will mean doing one part at a time and turning the object as necessary.

2 Pour some glue into an open container. If the glue is very thick, stir in just enough water that it can be spread with a brush.

3 Use a medium-sized synthetic paintbrush to spread the glue over the surface in a thin layer (see discussion above on glue application).

4 As soon as the glue starts to get tacky, apply the topcoat of low-sheen latex (the cracking works best with low-quality paint for the topcoat). Use a fresh paintbrush for this, and try to get total coverage in single nonoverlapping brush strokes. Overbrushing just makes a mess. Cracking should start within minutes.

5 If the surface is so large that the glue dries before you've applied all the paint, then work in sections. If just one spot is dry, add more glue and proceed.

6 This finish is not usually suitable for use with stencils themselves and is generally applied as an interesting background for rustic stenciling. Let the finished surface dry for several days, then stencil the decoration (and distress it, if you wish). Seal with a clear acrylic varnish.

Distressing

FAST-DRY COAT OVER SLOW COAT

RUB OIL PAINT INTO CRACKS

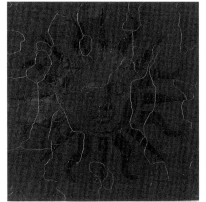

TOP: FINISHED PRINT. ABOVE, LEFT AND RIGHT: OTHER COLOR IDEAS

CRACKLED VARNISH (CRAQUELURE)

Craquelure is a transparent topcoat that imitates the fine cracks of aged porcelain. It does not affect the paint underneath it and can be applied over stencil work to give it an elegant aged look. To produce a craquelure finish, you apply two layers of different transparent coatings, the first slow-drying and the second fast-drying. The first coat continues to dry (and shrink) after the topcoat has completely dried, causing tiny cracks to appear in the topcoat.

The traditional craquelure method uses gold size and gum arabic and can be difficult to master. Commercial kits use their own proprietary products and are available in most craft stores. This is the easiest route to take and the one shown here. Test a few brands to find the look you like. Each one produces a slightly different result—a network of cracks that is more or less dense, more or less regular, thicker or thinner.

1 For this finish, everything must be kept as dust-free as possible. The basecoat and stencil work should have a low sheen so that no sanding is required.

2 The exact instructions may vary slightly from brand to brand, but the first step is to apply an overall, even layer of the slower-drying product. When this dries to a certain stage (the label will say whether it should feel dry or tacky), apply a layer of the faster-drying product on top. The second layer doesn't always like to coat the first one; sometimes it will bead up as soon as it is brushed on. This is called *cissing*. To get rid of it, keep brushing out the second layer whenever it starts to ciss. Eventually, it will stop.

3 As the second layer dries, tiny fissures will appear in the surface. They may not be very visible except in strong oblique lighting. Let the surface dry for several days.

4 Rub a small amount of artist's oil paint (traditionally a dark color like burnt umber) over the surface with a soft rag, then immediately wipe the surface with a clean cloth. Some of the paint will remain, stuck in the fine network of cracks, thus making them visible. When the oil paint has dried, finish the entire surface with oil-based varnish.

■ If you want to try traditional craquelure, the method is very similar. Brush out a thin coat of four-to-eight-hour oil-based gold size. It can be thinned up to 10 percent if necessary. As soon as the size becomes tacky (a subjective judgment that improves with practice), apply a generous layer of liquid gum arabic over top. It will probably start cissing right away.

■ Wait a minute to let some of the water in the gum arabic evaporate, then gently and quickly massage the surface with your fingers. If it cisses again, wait one more minute and try another light massage. This can be done a couple of times. Follow steps 3 and 4 to finish.

NOTE: Another way of dealing with cissing is to rub the tacky size with fuller's earth or fine whiting to absorb the surface oil. Use a soft brush to dust off any excess, then apply the gum arabic.

METALLIC PATINAS

This is my favorite aging technique. It involves putting an oxidizing chemical on top of freshly applied (and still wet) metallic paint. The results are never exactly the same, but they are always dramatic.

This process works only with paints that have real metal particles in them. For these examples, I used products from a single manufacturer (see Sources) to ensure that the chemicals would indeed react with those particular paints. The paints come in a range of metallic finishes and a variety of patina colors. Some of the paints react only with certain patina solutions, so it's important to read the instructions and make sure you have a pair that will work. The products are normally meant to be applied as overall coatings, but they will also work with stencils, as long as the surface is positioned horizontally.

1 Start by stenciling a motif with one of the metallic paints. Keep the paint well stirred while working, because the metallic particles tend to settle fast, and it's those particles which react with the patina solutions. Apply a second stenciled coat to build up the amount of metal.

2 I prefer to remove the stencil at this point, because the patina solutions are very fluid and bleed under it. Start applying the solution right away, before the paint dries. Experiment with different ways of doing this. I dab it on with a round artist's brush so that I can more or less control where it goes, but in a random kind of way. It is also possible to mix patina solution with the metal finish before stenciling, but you have less control over the final result that way.

3 Don't worry if some solution runs off the edge of the motif. It's very transparent. If it shows up at all, you can wipe it off with a damp Q-tip after it has dried.

4 Let the motif dry thoroughly, then apply a clear sealer.

NOTE: The oxidation doesn't always show up right away—you may have to wait for 15 minutes or so to see the effect. Do touch-ups by adding either more paint or more paint plus oxidizing solution. And remember, to have an effect, the solution must be applied while the paint is still damp.

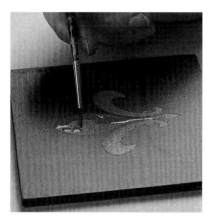

APPLY PATINA SOLUTION

THE EFFECT OF OXIDATION

DIFFERENT COMBINATIONS OF METAL PAINTS AND PATINA SOLUTIONS PRODUCE VERY DIFFERENT PATINA EFFECTS

Outlining

Outlining a stenciled print is an easy way to add a lot of visual interest. There are several tools from which to choose, depending on the effect you want and the amount of money you're willing to spend.

■ Paint pens or paint markers are like felt-tip pens, except they contain water-based paint. They come in several nib widths and a limited number of colors. A paint pen won't run, which makes it a good choice for use on vertical surfaces.

■ For a custom color or a slightly raised dimensional look to the lines, use a fine-tipped squeeze bottle that can be filled with the paint of your choice. This type of bottle can be found in stores that sell silk-painting supplies, as it is often used for applying silk resist. For large amounts of outlining, it might be worthwhile to buy an Air Pen™. Powered by a small air pump and a simple vacuum device, it is like a high-tech version of a squeeze bottle, only easier to control.

I used a squeeze bottle to outline this Indian elephant. There is a slightly raised dimension to the outlining, which makes the gold lines look particularly rich. When outlining, work in an organized fashion, and constantly turn the piece to avoid smudging, as these thick lines take a long time to dry.

Hand-Painting

Adding hand-painted details to stencil work is an effective way of embellishing the work and, at the same time, giving it the look of freehand artistry. With a few strokes of a brush or a pen, you can create simple highlights, shadows, vines, stamens and leaf veins without excessively fussy and numerous overlays. While the examples shown here are limited to brush and pen, any number of tools can be used, such as pastels, Conté crayons, pencils and watercolor pencils.

PEN

If you like doodling, you'll love this kind of embellishment. Here, the tool is a straight pen and the medium is acrylic ink. These inks are available from art-supply stores in a number of opaque and transparent colors. Start with a fairly plain stenciled image, such as this mushroom. Then, using nibs of different widths, add dimension and shading with sets of parallel lines of varying densities.

BRUSH

This approach gives you the freedom to do some hand-painting without requiring the ability to draw. The stencil simply provides an outline, rather like a coloring book. Your role is to take a small artist's brush and a set of acrylic colors and start playing around. No matter what you do, it will end up looking pretty good.

BRUSH AND PEN

When you feel really creative, try combining freehand brush and pen work to embellish a plain stencil, as I've done here with the radish.

STENCILED RADISH

ADDING DETAIL WITH PAINTBRUSH

RADISH WITH BRUSH AND PEN WORK

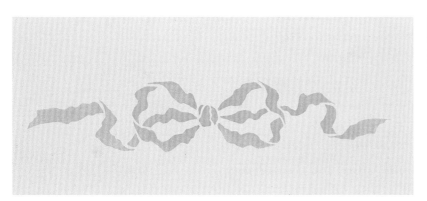

BOW STENCILED WITH SINGLE-OVERLAY TEMPLATE; NOTE BRIDGES

FILL IN BRIDGES

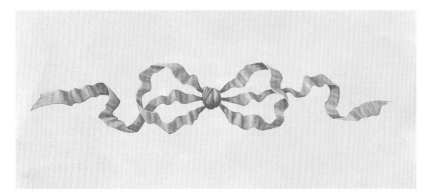

FINISHED BOW WITH FREEHAND SHADOWS AND HIGHLIGHTS

SAMPLE BORDER IN STYLE OF THE ARTS AND CRAFTS MOVEMENT

ROUGH-DRAFT STENCIL

Most of today's stencil work is considered an art or a craft to be used by itself. However, in the past, stencil work was also extensively used as an aid in laying out decoration that would subsequently be finished by hand. In other words, the stenciling was only a preliminary step in the work.

1 With the blue bow, I started with a one-piece, single-layer stencil. Then, using an artist's brush and more of the same paint, I filled in the bridges and added shading, highlights and shadows. The result looks completely hand-painted.

Stencils can also be used to create an outline that will then be hand-painted, as was done during the early 20th century. This is faster than transferring the design by carbon-paper methods. The outline is stenciled as dashed lines, and the outlined areas are filled in by hand with glaze colors. The glazes are then blotted with cheesecloth. Sometimes highlights are wiped out of particular areas.

Chapter 5

TRADITIONAL BORDERS

B order designs are the mainstay of the stenciling industry. They are most often used in the same way as wallpaper borders: as a decorative trim around a room, either at the top of the walls or along a horizontal architectural feature, such as a chair rail or baseboard molding. They can also be used to make decorative vertical stripes that cover a wall or wainscot.

Combined with a matching corner stencil, border stencils become a versatile tool. Use them together to frame windows or doors, to create decorative panels or to edge floorcloths. The corner stencils can even be used as decorative elements on their own, as single motifs or grouped and rotated to make larger, symmetrical motifs. On a smaller scale, borders can be stenciled on furniture and on any number of decorative objects, even stationery and wrapping paper.

No matter how a border is used, the main challenge is to keep the whole thing in a straight line as repeated sections of the pattern are stenciled, whether these are horizontal, vertical or parallel to the edge of a bureau. That means learning to use a guideline and registration marks. Much of this chapter will focus on borders as they are used on walls. However, with a change of scale, the same information is directly relevant to the use of borders on furniture or other surfaces.

Guidelines

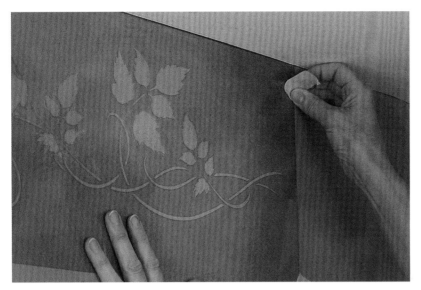

CEILING GUIDELINE: LINE UP STENCIL EDGE WITH CEILING

MEASURED GUIDELINE: LINE UP STENCIL EDGE WITH CHALK LINE ON TAPE

The guideline is what keeps the border level as you work around the room. Sometimes you can get away without marking one by using the ceiling or a chair rail instead. But if a particular design must be oriented precisely, it is better to measure and mark a separate guideline, since something like a ceiling edge may have the odd waver here and there.

1 A guideline should be measured from whatever architectural feature is closest to the border—for instance, the ceiling, the baseboard or the chair rail. In some cases, you may want to use a carpenter's level to help set up a guideline, always bearing in mind that any true horizontal or vertical guideline should be tempered by the possible slope of old walls, floors and ceilings. It doesn't much matter that your border is perfectly horizontal if your 200-year-old ceiling dips to the north. Your brain is more likely to put its faith in the ceiling being level and will judge your truly horizontal border as sloping.

2 The guideline can be marked with tiny pencil dots or by snapping a chalk line or laying out a stretch of painters' tape. Personally, I like to use a snapped chalk line laid over painters' tape. This way, I don't have problems removing either the guideline or the registration marks later, because they're all marked on the tape.

3 I measure the position I want in a couple of places, then with the help of a second person, I stretch a length of wide, low-tack painters' tape across the wall in roughly the right position.

Next, I remeasure each end and snap a chalk line along the tape. To position the stencil, I align any registration holes (see Note below) or the edge of the stencil with the guideline on the tape and mark the holes right on the tape.

NOTE: Many people simply use the edge of the stencil as a general guideline, but keep in mind, it is often just that—a general guideline, rather than a precise one—because the design may not have been cut precisely parallel to the edge of the Mylar. For precision, it is usually more reliable to use whatever guidelines or registration holes are supplied on the stencil itself.

■ A word of warning when using tape on walls: To avoid damaging the surface (by lifting paint or leaving an adhesive residue), always use painters' tape with the lowest tack. This is sold at paint and hardware stores. And when working over a fresh coat of paint, always, *always* give the paint time to *cure* before putting tape of any kind on it. If you are unsure how long this might take, check the label on the paint can. It should give cure times as well as drying times for a particular temperature. Remember also that in very humid conditions, curing takes longer.

Plain tape without any printing on it is best, because all your guideline and registration markings will be immediately visible and won't be competing with company names and logos. Also, the ink on the tape may not be impervious to every type of medium you may use. The last thing you want is to pull back the tape to find the tape logo printed repeatedly on the wall.

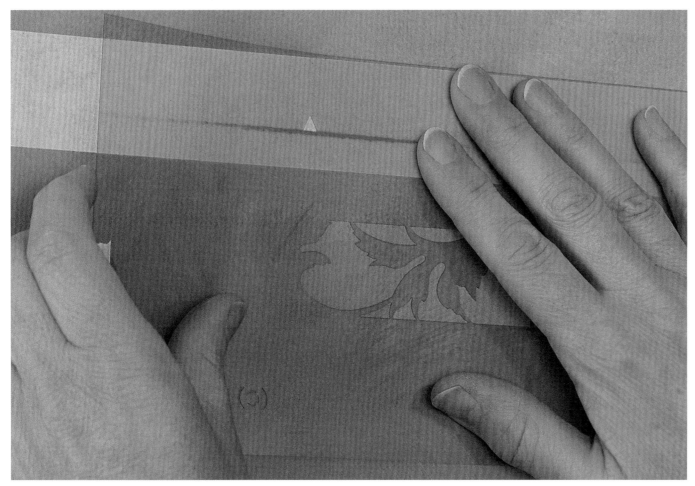

ON SOME COMMERCIAL STENCILS, REGISTRATION HOLES ARE CUT PRECISELY ON AN AXIS PARALLEL TO BORDER;
IN THIS CASE, ALIGN EDGE OF HOLES WITH GUIDELINE

Remove any tape as soon as possible after you have finished work. Slowly pull it straight back on itself rather than out away from the wall. If it resists removal, a few seconds of hot air from a hair dryer will soften the adhesive. The adhesive on tapes has a cure time as well, and if you go much past this time, you may have a problem removing even low-tack tape. If, for any reason, you are going to leave tape on the wall for a fairly long time, check in advance with the various tape companies or with your local sales center to see which product is safest.

Registration

Repeat registration is simply a method of ensuring that adjacent repeats of a border stencil line up correctly with respect to each other. There are several ways of doing this, depending on whether the stencils are opaque or transparent and whether or not the registration needs to be really precise. Some designs are very loosely connected and can stand a fair bit of slack in the way the repeats match up. Others must have each repeat positioned with great accuracy.

OPAQUE STENCILS

Opaque stencils are not very common anymore; transparent ones are simply much easier to use. However, opaque materials are still used for hand-cut stencils (and transparent stencils that aren't cleaned will rapidly become opaque).

The easiest way to line up repeats when using an opaque stencil is to cut out parts of the adjacent repeats at either end of the stencil. It's basically the same as outline registration for transparent stencils. Then line up the cutouts over the corresponding parts of the previously printed repeat.

Sometimes paint can be accidentally applied through a registration cutout. To avoid this, don't cut completely around the registration cutouts. This produces a hinged flap. Fold the flap back to open the cutout when lining up the stencil, then press the flap back in place to mask the cutout before painting.

Remember that while positioning the repeat registration, you must also make sure the stencil lines up against the overall guidelines to keep it straight.

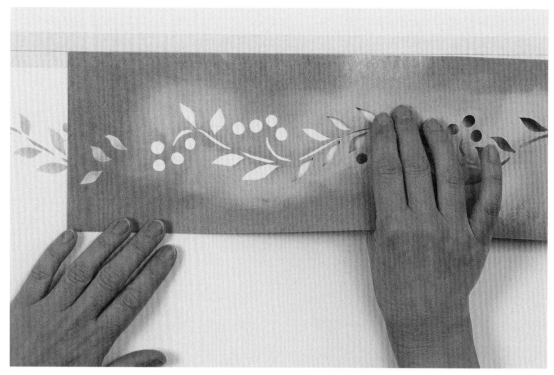

REGISTRATION CUTOUTS ON LEFT SIDE OF STENCIL OVERLAP PREVIOUS PRINT AND LINE UP WITH LEAVES

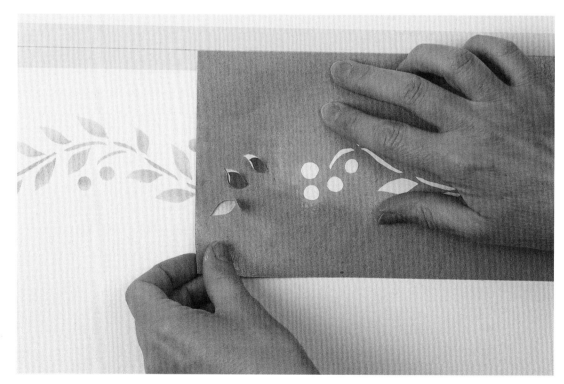

LEAVING FLAPS ON REGISTRATION CUTOUTS PROTECTS PARTS THAT ARE ALREADY PAINTED

TRANSPARENT STENCILS

Virtually all commercial and handmade stencils today are transparent, thanks to the many types of suitable clear film available. Being able to see through the template makes registration easy.

'EYEBALL' REGISTRATION

Many rambling or country-style designs do not require precise registration. In fact, a somewhat uneven repetition may contribute to the overall charm. In such cases, align the edge of the stencil with a guideline, then simply position each repeat on an ad hoc basis, adjusting the spacing "more or less" by eye.

'EYEBALL' REGISTRATION, WITH APPROXIMATE SPACING

OUTLINE, OR OVERLAP, REGISTRATION

Most die-cut and handmade stencils rely on outlines for registration. At either end of the stencil is a printed or cut outline of the trailing cutouts for the adjacent repeat. When shifting the stencil over for the next repeat, overlap and line up these printed or cut outlines onto the corresponding parts that have just been painted. When the top edge of the stencil is lined up along the guideline and the registration outlines are lined up over the appropriate stenciled parts, then the stencil is in the right place for the next repeat. If the registration outlines are cut out rather than printed, be careful not to paint them a second time.

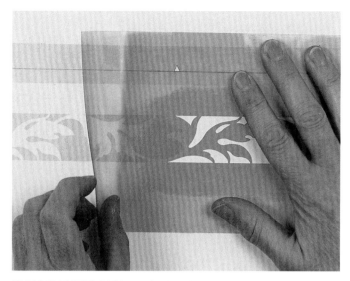

PINHOLE REGISTRATION: TRIANGLE CUTOUT LINES UP OVER TRIANGLE TRACED WITH PENCIL

PINHOLE REGISTRATION

This is used on most laser-cut stencils. The term pinhole is a historical remnant; in fact, there are small triangles, diamonds or circles cut into each end of the Mylar, usually above or below the pattern. Trace these shapes onto the stenciled surface with a pencil before moving the stencil. After shifting the stencil for the next repeat, align the leading trace with the trailing hole. At the same time, of course, the stencil must also align with the guideline. Registration marks are easy to remove if traced onto tape.

OUTLINE, OR OVERLAP, REGISTRATION

Spacing and Corners

When using a border stencil to create a continuous pattern around a room, you always have to face the fact that the length of the wall is probably not going to be an even multiple of the stencil length. There are several ways to deal with this. No matter which method you choose, try to arrange your work so that any potentially awkward meeting or transition points don't end up front and center in the most visible spot in the room. For example, if you know that the start and finish of the border may not accommodate an unbroken repeat of the pattern, place this point in one of the less conspicuous parts of the room—say, behind a door or an armoire—just in case the matchup is not quite seamless.

CONTINUOUS WRAP

Border stencils that are not too fragile can be folded into corners so that the design wraps around the room in a continuous fashion, at least until the end of it comes back to meet the starting point. If it is a simple stencil, consider cutting a copy out of freezer paper, just for use in the corners. Freezer paper can be readily folded into a corner and will adhere there more easily than will a Mylar stencil.

1 Start the border in the most inconspicuous corner of the room. Keep going until you hit the next corner.

2 Corners are rarely true, making it difficult to position a folded stencil so that it lines up perfectly on both sides of

the fold at the same time. The way to handle this is to stencil one side of the corner at a time. To protect the adjacent wall while working on the current one, mask the adjacent side of the corner with painters' tape.

3 Bend the stencil into the corner, paying attention only to lining up the part on the current wall. Tape it securely in place. The rest of the stencil will angle off, but just ignore it. Stencil the current side. Stipple with a brush to get the paint right into the corner.

4 Release the stencil, and remove the masking from the wall. Let the stenciled paint dry (you can use a hair dryer to speed up the process).

5 Now mask the completed side of the corner, and bend the stencil into the corner again, this time lining it up right on the new wall. Tape securely. Apply the paint and continue.

NOTE: With some types of border design, it is possible to get in and out of corners without folding the stencil. Work into the corner as closely as possible (on both sides) without trying to match up the two sides. Then fill in the gap with bits and pieces from the border—for example, with a couple of individual leaves if it's a botanical design. If necessary, cut a small paper stencil with a leaf or two just for this purpose. This is also a useful way to join up the start and finish points of the border once you've worked your way around the entire room.

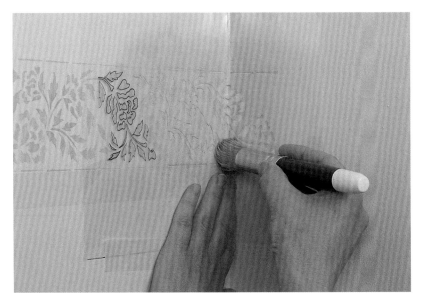

FOLD STENCIL, AND STIPPLE INTO CORNER

FIRST SIDE OF CORNER FINISHED; MOVE TAPE AND REPEAT FOR SECOND SIDE

TRUNCATE ON BOTH SIDES OF CORNER

BROKEN WRAP

This approach avoids the problem of trying to work into a corner with an unwieldy stencil. Simply start the border on each wall slightly short of the corner and finish it short of the next corner, truncating the design with tape. This leaves a small gap in each corner, but it will not look odd if the ends of the border are truncated cleanly and if all the corners are treated the same way. Handling corners this way works best with a border design that is dense with pattern, as opposed to one with a strong and spare undulation.

CORNER PIECE

Sometimes a border that's broken at the corners looks better when used with a coordinated corner piece—a very short stencil piece used to mark the end of a border segment, rather like a period at the end of a sentence. It can be a piece that connects with the end of a border repeat, but more often, it is a kind of stand-alone motif placed adjacent to a truncated section of border, separated by a small gap.

1 Stencil this corner piece at both ends of each wall first, positioning the prints so that each one has the same small gap from its corner.

2 Then fill in the border sections between the corner pieces, truncating the border at each end when you reach the corner piece.

NOTE: There are a few variations on this theme. How well they work depends on how suited your border design is to being segmented. One option, for example, is to place a corner motif in the middle of each wall and stencil symmetrical mirror images of the border running away from it on either side toward the corner.

TRUNCATED BORDER WITH CORNER PIECE

PLANNED SPACING

If your pattern just wouldn't look right without full and complete repeats spaced along the wall, then some advance planning is needed. To check your planned spacing, stencil a long paper strip, and tape it to the wall.

1 First, measure the span of each wall and the length of a single stencil repeat.

2 Calculate equal spacing between repeats so that there will be an integral number of whole repeats across the wall.

3 When positioning the stencil for each print, use your calculated spacing to separate the repeats, ignoring the registration marks. If the spacing looks a little large, use a corner motif midway along the wall or at some other interval to use up some of the excess. This method doesn't work with all designs—you need border segments which look good on their own, with a bit of space around them, rather than a vine or fret that begs to be tightly connected to the next repeat.

Borders as Frames (FOR WINDOWS, DOORS, PANELS, FURNITURE)

Using a border as any kind of frame always requires advance planning to determine how the repeats are going to fit the sides of the frame and how the border can be made to turn the corners. The designs most suitable for frames are those with short repeats, because they are easier to fit into the precise spaces dictated by the size of the frame.

■ No single design will ever fit exactly around a given window, but there are two things that can be adjusted to improve the fit. One, of course, is the spacing between repeats. The other is the size of the margin left between the border and the edge of the window. For example, if the border is positioned an inch from the window moldings instead of half an inch, you gain an extra four inches in the perimeter covered by the border. If it is moved out to an inch and a half, you gain eight inches.

■ There are several standard methods for turning corners, and the choice is determined by factors such as how a particular stencil fits within the span between corners, how good it looks if it has to be truncated, whether it is possible to make the design flow around a corner or whether an exact number of repeats can be fitted between corners.

COMBINATION FRAME

One option is to pick a fairly substantial symmetrical motif designed to be placed in the center of the top edge of the frame—for example, on top of a doorway. Then select a narrow border pattern with a tiny broken repeat. It could be something like dashed lines or some kind of beading. Stencil this border on either side of the central motif to fill up the top edge of the frame, then turn a right angle and continue on down the sides of the frame. Because the repeat is so small and spaced, it can be made to turn a corner practically on a dime.

CARPENTRY CORNERS

Two corner treatments are borrowed from carpentry—mitered and square-cut corners, just as wood is pieced together to make a picture frame.

■ For a mitered corner, mask off the end of a straight segment at a 45-degree angle. Stencil the border until it reaches the tape, and let the tape truncate the pattern at that angle. Remove the tape, then retape at the same 45-degree angle, masking the last portion of the border. Then continue with the border (see illustration on page 125).

■ A square-cut corner is the less sophisticated of the two carpentry corners. Start the border at one corner, and truncate it squarely at the next.

MANIPULATED TURN

Sometimes a vine stencil, especially one with a short repeat, can be manipulated into turning a corner without a noticeable break in the pattern. This may mean stenciling parts of the design out of turn, to force the border around the corner.

CORNER MOTIF

The easiest and most consistently aesthetically pleasing method is to use a special corner stencil, which begins and ends each border segment. Place the corner motifs first, then paint out the stencil repeats in between, truncating them when you reach the corners. Some commercial stencils come with their own corner piece.

INTEGRATED CORNER PIECE

This reverse border also turns with the help of a corner piece, but this one was designed to integrate with the border, rather than truncate it, making it look like a smooth, continuous turn.

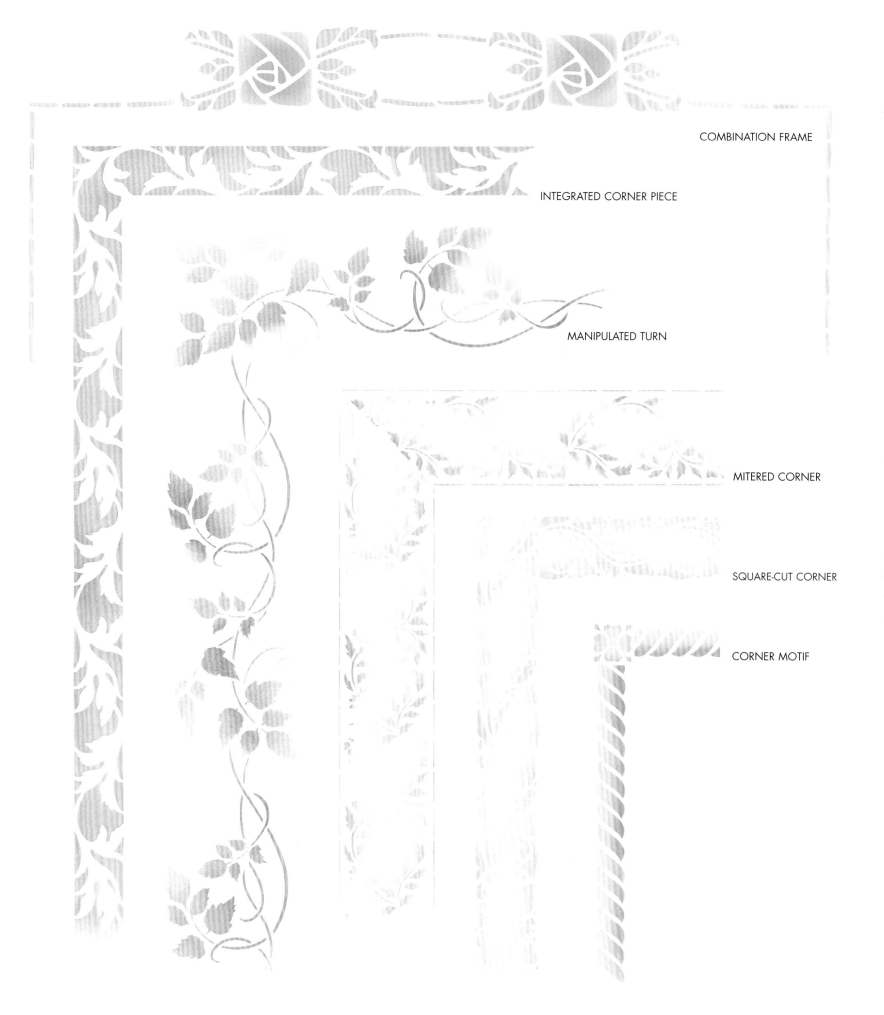

COMBINATION FRAME

INTEGRATED CORNER PIECE

MANIPULATED TURN

MITERED CORNER

SQUARE-CUT CORNER

CORNER MOTIF

Impasto Borders

In Chapter 4, we saw how to use a plaster-like medium with a stencil to create a pattern with a slightly raised relief. This technique can be used to produce interesting borders as well, as long as you make a slight departure from the usual procedure of stenciling one repeat after another.

1 Because plaster takes much longer to dry than paint does, the stencil margin must not overlap a freshly stenciled section when a new repeat is started. The best way to do this is to use pinhole registration and mark the registration points along the entire length of the surface that you plan to stencil prior to starting. Position the first repeat of the stencil, mark the points, move the stencil over, and mark again. Keep going until you reach the end of the wall. You end up with nothing but registration marks on your taped guideline.

2 Now start again at the beginning. Align the stencil with the first set of registration marks, and this time, apply the plaster.

3 Lift the stencil carefully, and clean it.

4 Skip the next repeat position, and place the clean stencil over the registration points for the third repeat. This way, none of the Mylar will touch wet plaster.

5 Continue laying down every other repeat until you finish the end of the span. Wait until the plaster is dry, then go back and fill in the missing segments.

NOTE: For designs that look good with a fair separation between repeats, this procedure is not necessary. Just be sure to trim the margin of the stencil and leave enough spacing so that there is no chance of an overlap. With impasto work, you also want to stay out of corners, so pick a design which can be truncated, use a corner piece, or plan ahead so that the border ends before it reaches the corner.

FIRST PASS: JUST MARK REGISTRATION POINTS

SECOND PASS: STENCIL EVERY OTHER REPEAT. THIRD PASS: FILL IN SKIPPED REPEATS

Creative Borders

Just because you are using a mass-produced stencil to decorate your walls doesn't mean the result has to look like everyone else's. Here are a few simple ideas for getting some extra mileage from your stencil. Once you get started, you'll think of others.

PAINT THE BACKGROUND

For a straight-sided border, consider laying down a background color before stenciling. Mask a strip equal in width to that of the stencil, and paint it. If you use a roller-stenciling technique for this step, there will be no bleeding under the edge of the tape. When the strip is thoroughly dry, stencil the border on top of it. Now you have a two-color border that looks more elaborate than the original. To see an example of this, turn to Chapter 2, page 47. Another option is to use a simple faux finish for the background.

GROUP INDIVIDUAL MOTIFS TO LOOK LIKE A BORDER

COMBINE MOTIFS

The border shown above is merely a grouping of individual shell stencils, accented and tied together by an undulating wave combed into the wall paint before stenciling. Some retarder or slow-drying glaze must be added to the wall paint so that there is still time to run the comb through it after painting enough of the wall to cover the border area.

If the motifs are too large for the width of the border, truncate them. For example, use painters' tape to mask off a stripe the size you want for the border. Now stencil a large motif (say, a fern) at random so that it fills the space. Wherever the stencil extends over the edge of the tape, it will be truncated. In fact, the truncation really defines the edge of the finished border, so make sure that most of the prints cross over the taped edges.

To make the border even bolder, paint a background color first.

COMBINE BORDERS

A fairly simple border can often be made more ornate by adding a second, narrower border on either side of it. Separate them by only a thin margin so that they look as though they belong together.

Chapter 6

ALL-OVER PATTERNS

Trying to keep the repeat prints lined up for an all-over pattern is a little harder than stretching a horizontal line across the wall as a guideline for a border stencil. Basically, what you have is multiple rows of motifs that must be kept parallel to each other, stacked from floor to ceiling. However, the individual motifs within those rows must also be spaced correctly with respect to the motifs above and below. For example, the motifs might be arranged on a rectangular grid pattern or staggered in a diamond formation.

For the purposes of stenciling, most all-over patterns fall into one of two groups. So-called powdered ornament is a pattern in which the motifs are either scattered randomly over a surface or spread in an unconnected but organized fashion. A diaper pattern, on the other hand, is an interlaced form of repeated ornament, where the elements are tightly connected. Its pattern is based on some kind of geometric or undulating framework, such as a lattice, grid or weave.

All-over patterns can be stenciled on furniture, decorative objects and fabric, as well as walls and floors. Most of this chapter will focus on the wall connection, but as with the previous chapter, the information is equally relevant to other surfaces.

Powdered Ornament

This is the easiest type of pattern to stencil, because the elements are not tightly connected and you can get away with some inaccuracies and fudging on the registration. There are many ways to organize the layout of the motifs, but we'll just look at some of the simpler ones here. (If you wish to know more, refer to a good design book; see suggestions in Further Reading.)

Although the idea of an irregular, or random, scattering of motifs like these Japanese butterflies may sound like the easiest way to cover a wall, I usually find it the hardest. "Random" sounds great until you actually have to place the stencil in that random spot. Then it becomes: Should it be up half an inch or a little more to the right? I think young children are the only ones truly able to achieve random. The rest of us agonize too much.

A regularly spaced pattern of motifs is easy to execute. First, set up a grid that shows exactly where each stencil should be placed. The simplest patterns are based on a rectangular (above left) or diamond layout (above right), where the motifs are placed at the intersections of an imaginary grid. Either of these can easily be made more complex by adding a secondary motif placed on a second, overlapping grid.

With a rectangular grid, an evenly spaced row of motifs is first stenciled across the wall. Then the second and subsequent rows are added so that they fall directly under the first, separated by a predetermined distance. With a diamond grid, the rows are staggered —the motifs of the second row are placed midway between the motifs of the first row, and so on.

Diaper Pattern

A diaper pattern is based on an interlaced framework that forms part of the design itself. The framework can be derived from any number of geometric forms, both linear and curvilinear. In a stenciled version, it may have bridges or not, but even if it does, the overall design is very tightly connected. There is little latitude for registration error when positioning repeats.

Guidelines

LAYOUT

Stenciling an all-over pattern requires some advance planning and a good deal of measuring. Because a diaper pattern comes with its own registration, there are fewer decisions to make. You just need to determine how to handle the corners of the room.

With powdered ornament, you must decide what kind of layout you want and how far apart the motifs will be. This is partly determined by the size and shape of the motifs, because they should be laid out in such a way that you can fit complete repeats onto the wall and avoid corners entirely.

First, create a paper plan. Outline the wall on grid paper, then mark the layout of the design. With a colored marker, add intersecting grid lines that show the position of each stencil placement.

PUTTY ADHESIVE AND STRING ARE EASY TO REMOVE, AND WALLS STAY CLEAN

MEASURING

1 Now transfer the grid lines to the wall. If the stencils have registration points, these lines are used as a backup check on your position to ensure that you haven't drifted off course. In this case, you don't need to mark the position of every single repeat—just enough to verify that things are okay.

2 There are many ways to transfer grid lines to a wall. The example shown at left leaves no marks on the wall itself. In this case, the stencil motifs will be widely separated in a diamond layout. I wanted the grid points to mark the center of each stencil print—yours could mark the corner or one of the registration points.

3 I laid out vertical grid lines with lengths of string, fastened at top and bottom with pieces of putty adhesive (sold as Fun-Tak or Easy-Tak). To get the spacing right, cut a piece of cardboard the same length as the distance between the grid lines. Use this to measure the top and bottom positions of each string along the floor and ceiling. Mark the positions with a chalk pencil, then fasten the lengths of string in place.

4 Instead of using the same kind of horizontal guidelines (string tends to sag when it's stretched out horizontally), I simply marked the points

where the horizontal line would intersect the vertical lines. First, I used a cardboard spacer, as before, to mark the line spacing along the left and right edges of the wall. Then I had two helpers stretch a string between two pairs of those points, while I marked the spots where this horizontal string crossed the vertical strings. To avoid marking the wall itself, I stuck small pieces of tape on the wall, behind the strings, and put the marks on the tape.

5 As you can see from the photos, the layout used here is a diamond, so I just marked every other intersection on the grid.

NOTE: You may wish to use a spirit level or plumb line to compare the guidelines to true vertical and horizontal. Depending on the outcome, some of the lines may need to be adjusted, but remember to keep the ones closest to the edges of the wall parallel to the side corners and to the floor and ceiling.

■ The easiest way to lay out a grid on a wall is to use snapped chalk lines. However, this leaves you with a very marked-up wall that must be cleaned off later. If your chalk is close to the wall color and you've tested for removability, then it's a good method.

CENTERED REGISTRATION

1 The grid that you have laid out on the wall will allow you to position each stencil repeat without any unhappy surprises. There's just one thing left to do: Mark corresponding lines on the stencil so that you can easily line it up. In this case, the marks on the wall indicate the center of the stencil and the strings show the vertical alignment, so I've drawn vertical and horizontal lines through the middle of the stencil itself. Their intersection is the center point.

2 For your first stencil print, slip the stencil under one of the string lines and position it so that the vertical center line marked on the stencil matches up exactly with the string line and the center point matches up with the tape mark on the wall. This ensures that the center of the motif is in the right place and that the image is aligned straight and level.

3 Secure the stencil to the wall with low-tack painters' tape or stencil adhesive. Unstick the bottom of the string line, and move it aside temporarily. If necessary, reach under the stencil (without moving it) and remove the marker tape.

4 Paint the stencil using your preferred method (see Chapters 2 and 4). Remove the stencil, and retack the bottom of the vertical string line. Move over to the next position in the row, and repeat. Once you have stenciled the first overlay at every position, remove the grid lines. Any subsequent overlays are positioned with respect to the print of the first overlay, not to the guidelines.

AVOID CORNERS BY PLANNING STENCIL PLACEMENT IN ADVANCE

CENTER LINES MARKED ON STENCIL ARE MATCHED TO GUIDELINES

PULL STRING AWAY WHILE STENCILING PATTERN

Guidelines

USE STRINGS AS VERTICAL GUIDELINES

BEGIN BY STENCILING COMPLETE REPEATS

USE REGISTRATION POINTS TO LINE UP REPEATS

POINT REGISTRATION

Many all-over stencils that come with point registration have repeats which are close together and tend to cover most of the wall. The nature of the particular design determines the shape of the stencil itself—it might be rectangular, diamond or some amorphous shape.

1 Lay out an abbreviated grid on the wall. Most of the stencils will be positioned according to their registration points, but an occasional grid line will allow you to correct for small misalignments.

■ It is generally easier to plan an approach that allows you to avoid working right into the corners; otherwise, you'll have to fold a bulky stencil into the corner. For example, leave a plain margin of an inch or two around the edges by placing painters' tape along the corners, then stenciling right to the edge of the tape.

Alternatively, stencil a straight, narrow border along the edges of the wall first. Then mask the borders with painters' tape, and fill in the remaining space with the all-over pattern.

2 Begin your all-over pattern by stenciling the complete, unbroken repeats. Use the grid to line up the first stencil. You need only a partial grid, because most of the time, you rely on point registration.

3 Work in a systematic way to stencil the repeats. Start at the center and work out; start at the top and work down; or start at one side and work across.

4 Each time you reposition the stencil, use the registration points to line it up in relation to the repeats already painted. Most of the time, you'll be aligning the stencil with two adjacent finished prints (for example, above and on one side). Make any adjustments (they should be minor) whenever you encounter grid lines.

5 Fill in the gaps at the edges when all the unbroken repeats are finished. Use the registration points to position the stencil, and paint the print right up to the taped edge. You will have to bend the stencil slightly for this, but because of the margin at the edge, it won't have to be folded sharply.

TIME SAVER

A large part of your time is spent first measuring and marking the position of each stencil repeat, then moving and realigning the stencil. So if the stencil can be made large enough to contain several repeats, the amount of work will be cut down considerably. For example, suppose you need to stencil 20 fleurs-de-lis in each of 10 rows to cover a wall. If you work a single motif at a time, that's 200 repeats—200 grid points and 200 stencil moves. But if you take a little extra time at the outset to cut five properly spaced fleurs-de-lis into your stencil instead of one, then the grid points and moves are reduced to a mere 40.

Corners

PATTERN IS TRUNCATED AT CORNER BORDER

The subject of dealing with corners has already been addressed, so we'll just do a little recap here. First, with most powdered designs, it is possible to plan the layout to avoid having to fit motifs into a corner.

With diaper patterns or very dense powdered layouts, place a narrow border, either plain or stenciled, along all four edges of the wall, and truncate the filled-in pattern where it meets the border. This gets you close to the corner but not so close that you have to fold the stencil or worry about matching up the other side.

Occasionally, there may be no other option but to fold the stencil into the corner. In this case, work it exactly as you would a continuously wrapped border. Mask one side of the corner. Place the stencil on the unmasked side, letting it go free on the masked side. Print it, using a brush and a stippling motion to get paint right into the corner. Remove the stencil and the painters' tape. When it is dry, mask the side just painted, place the stencil on the unpainted side of the corner, and stipple as you did on the first side.

If your all-over pattern is done in a damask style or with faint, transparent colors, you can modulate your application so that parts of the prints fade in and out randomly. At the edges of the wall, you can then fade out any parts that are tricky to fold into the corners. That way, you don't have to be very precise when folding the stencil or matching one wall to the next.

STENCIL UNMASKED SIDE

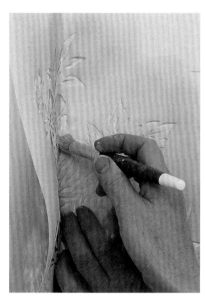

REVERSE PROCEDURE

Stripes

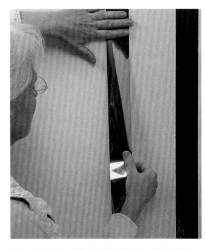

FOR THICK/THIN STRIPES, ALTERNATE WIDE HAND-CUT MYLAR STRIPS WITH THIN MYLAR PARTY STREAMERS

PULL OFF WIDE STRIPS, EXPOSING STRIPES TO BE PAINTED

ROLLER STENCIL EXPOSED STRIPES

REMOVE THIN STRIPS, EXPOSING STRIPES OF ORIGINAL WALL COLOR

Border stencils are frequently used vertically to create patterned stripes over a wall, but plain stripes can also be fashioned using a stenciling method. The hardest part is cutting long, straight, even strips of Mylar. (I use a 3-mil thickness because it's easy to cut.) Cover a table or clean floor area with pieces of cardboard. Put a Mylar roll at one end of the area, pull the Mylar out the length of the cardboard, and cut full-length strips. Use a knife and a metal ruler to keep the lines straight. Then, unroll another length and continue cutting the same strips until they are long enough. A convenient substitute is a roll of Mylar party streamer. Just pull off the length you need and snip. The only drawback is that it's available only in a few widths.

1 Start with straight strips of Mylar cut the width of the desired stripes and the height of the wall. You don't need many because the strips can be reused.

2 Lightly spray the back of each Mylar strip with stencil adhesive, and let dry.

3 Place the first strip in position on the wall, making sure that it is properly vertical. Place the next one adjacent to it, carefully butting the edges together. Position several more the same way.

4 Now remove every other strip. Use a stencil roller to stencil the exposed stripes.

5 Leave the leading piece of Mylar in place, and remove all the others. Use them to mask off the next set of stripes.

6 Check the vertical alignment of the stripes from time to time to make sure tiny errors are not accumulating.

NOTE: Of course, this technique requires a little planning before you begin so that you don't start with a six-inch stripe on the left side of the wall and finish with a half-inch stripe on the right. Sometimes it's best to start in the middle of the wall.

APPLYING CLEAR GLOSS STRIPES OVER FLAT BASECOAT

This method works particularly well for damask stripes, which require a transparent medium with a different sheen from that of the basecoat.

Chapter 7

FREEFORM STENCILING

So-called freeform stenciling is a way of creating images with templates without producing the stereotypical look of stenciling. This method lacks the traditional stenciling characteristic of the same motif repeated over and over at regular intervals. Instead, stencil prints are grouped and overlapped at the stenciler's discretion to create a unique composition. It might be a rambling vine with tangled foliage or a lush and abundant bouquet. Although most freeform stenciling tends to focus on botanical themes, it could also be something completely abstract. The finished results look more like freehand painting than stenciling. Indeed, freeform stenciling is often combined with freehand work in such a way that the role of the templates may not be immediately apparent. This approach can be applied on any scale, from greeting cards to furniture to entire walls.

NOTE: The key to freeform stenciling is the overlapping of stencil prints, layered to give the impression of depth or dimension. Overlapping prints can be tricky, because it is easy to end up with one large, blended mass (or mess!) of what should be individual elements. To ensure good results, pay careful attention to shading and color choices. Generally, use colors that recede (cool, dull colors) for background layers and colors that advance (warm, bright colors) for foreground layers. If a piece is looking too sedate, liven it up by slipping a really warm zippy color in between foreground and background. (If you are not familiar with these color properties, read the section on color in Chapter 1.)

■ When painting (as opposed to stenciling) with acrylic paint, it is customary to start with the background, then work forward, adding layers of paint over the background. It doesn't matter whether clear, bright colors are painted on top of dark, somber tones or whether complementary hues are layered one over the other, because the paint can be applied as thickly as necessary to obscure whatever color lies directly underneath. Adding bright yellow accents over a navy-blue background, for example, simply means piling on the yellow until it jumps out over the blue.

When using stencils, however, this is not possible. The paint layers must be very thin to avoid bleeding, and a single layer will never totally obscure the color beneath it. If the work is fairly monochromatic and subdued in color, that won't necessarily be a big problem. It may be possible to work one layer overlapping another quite successfully.

But if the work encompasses large contrasts in temperature and intensity, a different approach is required. Start with the brightest, clearest colors—these are usually in the foreground—then mask them and work backwards so that the background ends up being stenciled last. While the final result looks as though the images are layered, each one is, in fact, stenciled over the same clear basecoat.

■ There are several ways of overlapping stenciled images or of making them look layered. Which one you use depends on the effect you want and on the shape of the stencils.

Layering Images Without Masks

FOR A TRANSPARENT OVERLAP, SHIFT STENCIL AND ROLL A SECOND PRINT OVER THE FIRST; POST-IT NOTES MASK AREAS TO REMAIN UNPAINTED

TRANSPARENT LAYERS

Because each coat is so thin, stenciled images often tend to be somewhat translucent, unless they have been built up with several coats of paint. This can sometimes be used to advantage.

1 For example, to stencil a branch of overlapping leaves so that they have that sun-dappled transparent look, make the first print of leaves with the stencil.

2 Shift the stencil to an overlapping position, and roller stencil the second layer of leaves. The paint layers should be just translucent enough that the overlapping areas show up clearly.

NOTE: Using a roller instead of a brush keeps the edges of the first layer crisp. (The rubbing action of a stencil brush tends to blur overlapped edges unless the paint is thoroughly dry.) The overlap lines will show up even if the same color is used for each layer.

Stenciling layers that look opaque must be done a little differently. Below and on the following pages are two approaches that work well for me.

OPAQUE LAYERS: OPAQUE MEDIUM

1 I make a first stencil print of a leafy branch, for example, using a color that is cooler and more pastel than the foreground colors. I might add a few overlapping leaves, letting the lap lines show (they are eventually covered up). The idea at this stage is to sketch in the overall shape of the entire image, knowing that this first layer will be mostly hidden, except for what peeks out between and beyond the foreground leaves.

2 The foreground layers must end up looking opaque, and this takes a little more work. If the background layers are sufficiently subdued, a more vivid opaque layer of leaves can be stenciled on top, either by roller or brush. It might take two coats to

SUBDUED BACKGROUND LAYER   OVERLAY WITH OPAQUE FOREGROUND LAYER   ADD ADDITIONAL MID-RANGE LEAVES

build up enough opacity, but they can be done one after the other without moving the stencil. Adding a little white to the first coat gives it more hiding power. Any lap lines that remain slightly visible while the stencil is still in place tend to disappear (or at least recede to the point of unimportance) once the stencil has been removed. One or two layers can be added this way, as long as there is enough color difference between them.

3 Because the top layer is the most visible, the most in focus, it should be perfect. Any hand-painted details, such as veins or contoured shading, should be added at this point.

4 A layer of perfect opaque leaves now overlaps another layer (or two) of more faded leaves. To give the composition more depth, bulk things up by making it appear as though there are many different layers, from near to far. It is difficult, however, to keep adding one opaque layer on top of another indefinitely. So

start adding individual, partially overlapped leaves, tucking them in behind the foreground leaves so that they seem to lie somewhere between the background and the foreground.

This is not as difficult as it sounds. Place the stencil in an overlapping (or "underlapping") position with respect to a foreground leaf.

5 Using a paint color that is slightly different from the one in the foreground layer, start stenciling the leaf along the edge farthest from the foreground leaf. Let the stenciled color gradually fade away by the time it hits the foreground leaf. Don't worry if some of the color gets onto the foreground leaf—it will be quite faint.

6 If it's a bit too visible, simply touch up the foreground leaf later. Bunches of these "tucked-in" leaves can be added very quickly with a little practice. Simply hold the stencil in place with one hand, and add color with the other.

Layering Images Without Masks

WITH LEAF STENCIL IN PLACE, REMOVE
COLOR USING SOFT CLOTH

OPAQUE LAYERS: TRANSLUCENT MEDIUM

Another way to produce opaque layers is to use slower-drying mediums, such as solid oil paints or a paint to which a retarder has been added. Although these mediums tend to be translucent, the stenciled layers will seem opaque if the top layers look as though they completely hide the layers underneath.

1 Stencil the background, or farthermost, layer first. In this case, it's a pear. Now let's add a green leaf that looks as though it's in front of the pear. Normally, this might be problematic, because the red on the pear is quite strong and would show up under the green of a stenciled leaf. Not only would the edge of the pear be visible through the leaf, but the red would muddy the green.

2 After being stenciled, the pear should feel somewhat dry to the touch but not dry enough for any kind of permanence. Place the leaf stencil over the pear. If using a water-based medium, slightly dampen a stencil brush with a little clear glaze or a touch to a damp sponge. Work this around through the leaf stencil by stippling or swirling gently, then carefully wipe the opening with a clean, dry cloth. This should completely remove the color of the pear.

   If using a solid oil paint, be very careful when placing the leaf stencil, as the pear colors will smudge easily. Wrap a piece of clean, soft cotton around your finger, and gently wipe off the paint from the area that shows through the leaf stencil.

3 Remove the leaf stencil. There may be a very fine line of color outlining the leaf shape, color that got pushed into the edge of the stencil. Don't worry about this—it will give extra definition to the edge of the leaf.

4 Let the pear dry completely, then replace the leaf stencil and add green.

NOTE: This method works only on hard surfaces.

Layering Images With Masks

Sometimes, the most straightforward and effective way to stencil overlapping images is to use a mask, as described in Chapter 2. Masking is particularly useful when you want to overlap two very different colors or keep all the colors strong and opaque or avoid any fading away of background colors.

For example, suppose you want to place a leafy vine behind a pink tulip. If the vine is stenciled first and the flower on top of it, the green will show through the pink. Although the green could be whited out first, it would take several coats of stenciled white to cover up enough of the green, and the result might not be completely successful. On the other hand, if the tulip is stenciled first and not protected with a mask, the vine must then be faded away sufficiently that absolutely no green gets onto the pink. If it does, it will be very noticeable.

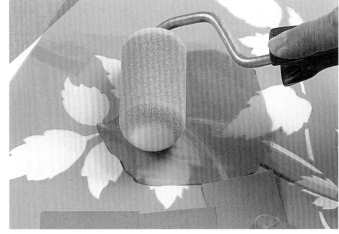

PLACE MASK OVER STENCILED TULIP

ADD VINE STENCIL AND PAINT LEAVES, USING POST-IT NOTES TO MASK ANY LEAVES THAT ARE TO REMAIN UNPAINTED

REUSABLE MASKS

A mask is sometimes included with a commercial freeform stencil. If it isn't, it is very easy to make one. First, stencil the image onto a piece of paper. Then stick a piece of Mylar over the paper, and carefully cut out the shape with a craft or utility knife, following the edge of the print. Try to be as exact as possible. When finished, write an identifying word on the mask with a permanent marking pen. This will help you see the mask (clear Mylar pieces are *very* easy to lose) and will indicate which is right side up. Store the mask taped to its stencil.

1 For this example, start with a stenciled tulip and align the mask over the flower and stem. Secure it with stencil adhesive or painters' tape, and position the vine stencil on top of everything.

2 Then stencil the vine normally, going right over the mask, since the mask will protect the bloom from any green paint.

3 Remove the mask, replace the vine stencil, and paint the one branch that appears in front of the tulip stem. Because it's green, it's easy to paint it over the stem.

Layering Images With Masks

APPLY LIQUID FRISKET TO PETALS THAT NEED MASKING

DRIED FRISKET FILM PROTECTS RED PETALS FROM GREEN OVERLAY

LIQUID-FRISKET MASKS

If the flower to be masked is a freeform creation (i.e., a mass of individual blossoms, such as this geranium), there is no point going to the trouble of cutting a Mylar mask. The mask could be used only once, since the geranium clusters will be different every time.

1 In a case like this, where a high degree of accuracy is required for a onetime mask, the solution is to paint on liquid frisket, which is rather like whitish rubber cement. Apply it carefully with either a small brush or a special frisket tool, as shown in the photograph (above left). I find the tool easier to use (and clean) than a brush. Different brands of liquid frisket are available from art-supply stores. Do a test run first to make sure the frisket doesn't alter the colors and can be removed without damaging the surface.

NOTE: Covering the geranium with frisket is not unlike painting an image in a coloring book very obsessively—you *must* stay within the lines. Any frisket that goes over the edge of a petal translates into a white gap between petal and leaf; any that stops shy of the edge of a petal results in green overlaying the petal.

2 As soon as the frisket has dried completely, lay a leaf or stem stencil over the geranium and apply the green paint. Work gently, though, so that no frisket is rubbed off.

3 Let the paint dry thoroughly, then gently rub off the frisket using a frisket eraser, an art eraser or clean fingers.

ONCE PAINT HAS DRIED, FRISKET CAN BE REMOVED

AD HOC MASKS

Most stores that cater to airbrush artists sell Mylar or plastic masks in a variety of shapes. While these will not conform exactly to a particular stencil, their edges and shaped curves can be very useful as quick ad hoc masks. Pick out a segment that fits the required shape, and hold it over the work as you stencil. For a disposable mask, it's hard to beat Post-it Notes. Shape them with a pair of scissors, if necessary. The low-tack adhesive strip holds them in place.

Composition

"Freeform" does not mean the same thing as "free-for-all." It takes planning to get a freeform design right—planning and a number of draft exercises, either sketched or stenciled. While everything doesn't have to be planned down to the last tendril, you do want to know beforehand where you're going to start, where you're heading and where you want to end up. Sometimes, a spontaneous and natural-looking composition just happens serendipitously, but sometimes, it takes a lot of work. Plan in advance how you're going to paint around doors, windows, paintings, mirrors and furniture. If the room is empty, find out what furniture will be there eventually and where it will be situated. You don't want your best work to end up behind a china cabinet.

With a plan or sketch in hand, rough in the layout right on the wall with an easily erasable piece of chalk, chalk pencil or watercolor pencil (pick a color similar to that of the wall, just in case). If your planning stage stops short of a full dress rehearsal, then a lot of ad hoc decisions must be made as you work. Move this branch up or down, left or right, half an inch here, two inches there. A very helpful aid in this situation is a set of preprinted individual stencil elements. Stencil separate leaves, blossoms, fruits or whatever onto clear Mylar or other transparent film. Or stencil them onto poster board and cut them out. Make flip copies of everything, and use all these pieces as layout guides, holding or taping them in place temporarily so that different variations in the composition can be evaluated. When you are happy with the layout, simply replace each individual element with its corresponding stencil, and paint.

SIMPLE FREEFORM

These few examples illustrate various aspects of freeform stenciling. If you want to start with something simple, consider modifying a traditional border, such as this vine. Add individual and clustered blossoms to some of the repeats so that every repeat is slightly different.

The honeysuckle border is shown first as the original purchased stencil. I then fattened it up by adding extra blossoms and vine segments and layering the clusters of leaves. All the extras were stenciled using parts of the original stencil, with unwanted bits masked by Post-it Notes.

Composition

The topiary was built up from two small branch stencils and a trunk.

1 The first step was to rough in the overall shape with the palest of the leaves and just a hint of the trunk.

2 The branches were then filled in with several layers of overlapping leaves.

3 Finally, some extra mid-range leaves were tucked into the top layer. The trunk was restenciled to bring out the parts not covered up by leaves.

The example at left was done with transparent colors, which often look best over some kind of subtle faux finish, as they let the finish show through. For this composition, I masked the fruit when stenciling the leaves and used the technique described for translucent mediums when building up the leaf clusters. The fine outlines created by the erasures show up to good effect here on the leaves. The glaze used for the ribbon was wiped off through the stencil as well, because I wanted to produce the same outline effect. To see a larger version, please turn to the chapter opening on page 138.

STENCIL INDIVIDUAL FLOWERS ONTO
POSTER BOARD, THEN CUT AND ARRANGE

In creating the bouquet, I relied heavily on poster-board proofs for the composition and precut masks for the execution.

1 After creating a composition with poster-board proofs, I stenciled the foreground flowers.

2 Then I masked these and added the next layer of partially hidden blooms, using slightly more subdued colors.

3 This layer was, in turn, masked, and the back layers were stenciled in the palest tones.

4 The foliage and stems were added last, after the foreground flowers were masked.

STENCIL FOREGROUND FLOWERS FIRST

MASK FOREGROUND FLOWERS, AND
ADD MID-RANGE FLOWERS; STENCIL
BACKGROUND FLOWERS LAST, AFTER
MASKING MID-RANGE BLOOMS

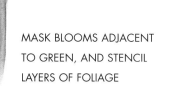

MASK BLOOMS ADJACENT
TO GREEN, AND STENCIL
LAYERS OF FOLIAGE

Chapter 8

PROJECTION STENCILING

Projection stenciling is harder to describe than it is to do. It's like a big paint-by-numbers method of creating images as large as you wish, using a disposable paper stencil that prevents you from painting over the lines.

Now, don't skip this chapter just because you don't have a projector! It is used only to enlarge the pattern. I used this same technique for a long time, relying on photocopiers and the old grid system to blow up my designs, until my sister finally convinced me that it was a lot easier (and faster) to beg, borrow or buy a projector.

Projection stenciling is not much different in principle from methods used by airbrush artists, except that it can be extrapolated cheaply to very large surfaces by substituting freezer paper for frisket film and stencil rollers for the airbrush.

Here's how it works. For small projects, the pattern is transferred onto freezer paper or adhesive shelf liner, which is then stuck to the surface to be decorated. For large projects, such as a wall mural, it is usually easier to cover the wall with freezer paper first and then transfer the pattern by projecting it using either an opaque or an overhead projector. This allows the degree of magnification to be adjusted on location. You trace the projected image onto the freezer paper with a permanent felt-tip pen.

Next, you create stencil openings by cutting out sections of the freezer paper along the pattern lines. Cut right on the wall, using a very sharp blade. Peel away one cut-out section of freezer paper. Stencil that section in an appropriate color, usually with a stencil roller. As soon as it is dry, cover it up with the freezer-paper piece previously removed so that the section is completely masked. The next section is done in the same way. You keep exposing, painting and masking sections until the whole thing is finished. The result has no bridges and does not look stenciled.

Projection stenciling can be done on any scale—from pencil box to wall mural—although the projection part isn't necessary for small projects. It works best with images that are highly graphic in nature but can also be adapted to other styles, as we'll see in later chapters.

The Stencil

MATERIALS

For large-scale projects, there are a couple of choices for the stencil material. By far the cheapest is plain freezer paper, available at supermarkets in 18-inch-wide rolls. This is basically a utility paper coated on one side with a very thin plastic film. Some brands are white; others are brown. Make sure the freezer paper is rolled with the plastic side out to ensure good contact with the surface. If it is rolled the other way, reroll it to change the curvature. To use freezer paper for stencils, spray the paper side with stencil adhesive, and after letting it dry, place this side on the surface to be stenciled. The paint is applied to the plastic side. Another material suitable for large projects is called TransferRite™, which is a type of adhesive paper used in the sign-writing industry. It works well but is expensive and harder to find.

For smaller projects, where cost is not such a factor (because very little is used), the choice is much wider. In addition to freezer paper and TransferRite™, there are also low-tack frisket film, MacTac™ and low-tack shelf paper—anything that prevents paint from passing through, has a bit of stick on one side and is easy to cut.

Avoid films that tend to stretch with handling. There is no need at all for the material to be transparent, because the stencil is never moved. Do a few tests before starting a project, however, to make sure the stencil material will hold well but not so well that the paint will peel off when the stencil is finally removed. Also, check to see whether it leaves any adhesive residue on the surface. This can be easily removed by wiping the finished wall with paint thinner or mineral spirits, but if this step can be avoided, all the better.

CREATING A PATTERN

Projection stenciling works best with relatively simple graphic images that translate into straightforward line patterns. It is possible to use it for highly complex pictures, but unless you *really* like stencil cutting, I wouldn't advise it. A combination of projection stenciling and traditional stenciling can be used to create images that look very detailed. For example, refer to the faux-drapery projects in Chapter 9. These elaborate constructions of faux textile begin with a simple line drawing that does no more than outline each fold of the fabric. This is the projection pattern. Then within each "fold" outlined on the pattern, a normal, repeatable Mylar stencil is used to decorate the fabric.

1 Patterns are easy to create. When looking for ideas, however, keep reminding yourself to simplify. For inspiration, start with a greeting card, a poster, clip art or even a photograph. Create an outline, then modify it to suit your needs, making sure the proportions match those of the surface to be stenciled. When you have what you want, make a clean copy.

The final pattern must be a size that works with your chosen method of enlargement. If it's the low-tech grid method, then any size will do, but it's probably more accurate to work with something a little larger than letter size. A convenient size might be 11 by 17 inches, which is the largest sheet regular photocopiers can handle.

2 When using an overhead or opaque projector, choose a pattern size to fit the projector. Remember, too, that any little flaws in the pattern will be magnified when projected. These flaws may not even be visible to the eye on the original pattern. Also, what may seem to be a lot of detail on a small pattern might end up looking like a gross simplification when enlarged to fill a wall. So to create the best possible pattern, enlarge the clean copy a few times on a photocopier—say, to an 11-by-17-inch size. Add any details that seem to be missing, and correct any flaws that appear in the enlargement. Make another clean copy, working as precisely as possible. Then, using a photocopier, reduce the pattern to the size that will fit the projector.

NOTE: If you are adept at computer graphics and have a scanner, then all this enlarging, reducing and correcting can be done with the appropriate software and a copy printed out. This method is not necessarily faster (indeed, it can be very time-consuming), but some people may find it easier.

3 Enclose the pattern in an outline that replicates the shape of the surface to be stenciled (e.g., wall, tabletop, toy box). For a wall, I also like to superimpose a rectangular grid—just a few lines, unless I'm using a grid system to enlarge the pattern; in that case, I'll use as many lines as necessary to make an accurate enlargement. To distinguish the outline and grid from the pattern, use a different color.

■ The outline, combined with the grid lines, provides a frame of reference that helps you position the pattern correctly. Horizontal and vertical pattern lines, for example, can be superimposed on guidelines previously marked on the wall.

Preparing the Surface

1 Start with a clean, dry wall surface painted with flat or eggshell latex. If the wall has been freshly painted, allow enough time for the paint to have cured.

2 Cut pieces of freezer paper large enough to cover the surface, and lay them flat on the floor, paper side up. Apply stencil adhesive in a well-ventilated area. Even better is to do this outside (weather permitting), laying the paper on any dry, flat surface. Place sheets of newspaper under the freezer paper, extending well beyond the edges of the freezer paper to catch any overspray of adhesive. Cover the paper completely with an even spray of stencil adhesive. Do not miss any spots.

3 Let the adhesive dry, then position the pieces of freezer paper on the wall, smoothing out the wrinkles with your hands. This works better with two people when there is a large area to cover. If more than one length of freezer paper is needed, use clear packing tape to cover the seams where the sheets meet. Do this after the sheets are on the wall. It's also a good idea to secure all the outside edges of the freezer paper to the wall with painters' tape.

Transferring the Pattern

TRACE PROJECTED PATTERN LINES ONTO FREEZER PAPER ON WALL

Now that the wall is covered with sheets of freezer paper, the next step is to enlarge the pattern and trace it onto the freezer paper.

For large projects, the easiest way to transfer the pattern to the wall is with an overhead or opaque projector. If you don't have one and can't borrow one from a library or school, rent one. Get the strongest-lit system available. This will allow you to work in a dim light rather than in total darkness. For an overhead projector, the pattern should be copied onto a transparency; for an opaque projector, it should be copied onto paper.

1 Find a stand for the projector that will put it at a halfway height for the image. Center the projector left to right as well. This will minimize the distortion in the projected image. Now turn on the projector, and darken the room until the projection is visible. Focus the projector and move the pattern so that the design is more or less centered. This is when it comes in handy if some guidelines (i.e., horizontal, vertical and center) have been drawn on both freezer paper and pattern to help you position the image so that it is straight up and down and sized correctly.

NOTE: For a very large project, the image may have to be projected in stages to reduce distortion, especially if it is highly geometric, with well-defined verticals and horizontals. When working in a small room, it may not be possible to move the projector back far enough to get the proper enlargement. In that case, project and trace the image in a larger room, then transfer the freezer paper to the small room.

2 Once everything is positioned, tape the pattern down on the projector, and brace the table on which the projector is sitting to minimize the chance of something shifting.

3 Now, using a fine permanent felt-tip pen, trace the projected pattern lines onto the freezer paper on the wall. Use a ruler to keep straight lines straight. When you have finished, turn on the lights, and check each part of the image very carefully to be sure nothing has been omitted. Only then should the projector be moved.

■ Small details within part of a large mural may have to be projected separately. This will allow you to use a different, more accurate scale for those parts of the pattern.

Stenciling the Images

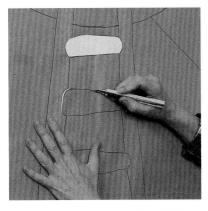

CUT SECTIONS WITH A SHARP KNIFE

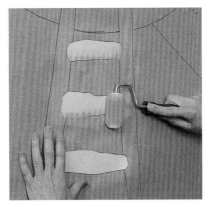

STENCIL AND SHADE EXPOSED SECTIONS

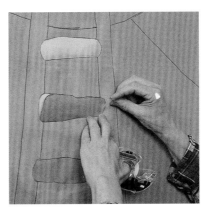

COVER PAINTED SECTIONS

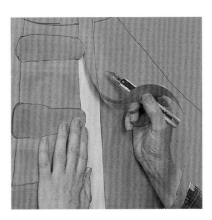

EXPOSE NEXT SECTION

CONTINUE CUTTING, EXPOSING, STENCILING AND MASKING SECTIONS
UNTIL ALL SECTIONS ARE DONE

1 With a very sharp knife, cut out one section of the pattern at a time, and stencil the section. For large areas, use a stencil roller. (For cutting straight lines, use a straight edge to guide the blade.) Add whatever shading is appropriate. Use only water-based paints. Do not use solid oil paints, because they can dissolve the lines made with the felt-tip pen and dry too slowly to be masked.

2 Give the section a blow from a hair dryer to get it slightly more than dry to the touch, then cover it up with the same piece of freezer paper that was cut away. There is still some moisture in the freshly painted section, which makes the stencil adhesive less grippy, so secure the cut-out piece to its neighboring pieces (not to the wall!) with Scotch tape.

3 Now cut out and remove another section of freezer paper, stencil the revealed wall with its appropriate color, let dry, and cover it up again.

Continue stenciling, section by section, until the entire piece is done.

4 By the time you have finished cutting, painting and replacing sections, the freezer paper will be looking rather disheveled. Check that no spots have been missed before removing all the freezer paper.

5 Carefully inspect the finished project for tiny gaps in the painted sections. Sometimes the freezer paper will have shifted by a hair, leaving the thinnest of bridges unpainted. These are easy to touch up freehand with a fine artist's brush. At this time, handpainted embellishments can also be added, if desired. For example, elements can be outlined with a paint pen to reinforce a cartoonlike style.

6 If the work will be subject to a lot of wear and tear, protect it with a clear sealer. Otherwise, a top coat shouldn't be necessary.

Stenciling the Images

The one thing about this whole process which amazes people is the fact that the stencil is cut right on the wall. They can't believe this doesn't damage the surface. Of course, it will cause damage if you hack away with a dull blade and use a lot of pressure. But if the knife is sharp enough, a light touch is all that's needed, and the wall will barely be scratched. Such faint scratches should not be noticeable and are usually filled in with the paint.

More examples of this technique can be found in *Projection Stenciling* and *Projection Art for Kids* (see Further Reading).

Chapter 9

IMITATION TEXTILES

Ihave always been fascinated by the way textiles were rendered in the sumptuous portraits left by the grand painters of centuries past. How can it be possible, with merely a brush and some paint, to conjure an image of cloth with such astonishing realism that just by looking, you can "feel" the texture? Be it wispy transparent voiles, crisply starched laces, thickly napped velvets or shimmering crushed silks, the painted image somehow travels through your eyes and comes out through your fingertips.

Of course, the talent for such alchemy is not usually within the grasp of most decorative painters, even the professionals. For the do-it-yourself enthusiast, it's the impossible dream. Still, I used to wish I could capture the effect of swagged textiles on my wall—a much more modest effect, to be sure, than that of Rembrandt but one which didn't require a lifetime of study. Imagine the possibilities: swags, curtains and glorious excesses of draped cloth, all for the price of a little paint.

Then, on a trip to Paris in 1986, I visited the newly opened Orsay Museum and discovered two painters whose work I had never seen: Pierre Bonnard and Édouard Vuillard. They both had a very graphic way of depicting cloth in flat patterned sections, with no depth at all. Their style was similar in a way to that of Gustav Klimt, only more orderly. It looked very Japanese. These paintings were completely different from those of the old masters, but for some reason, they stopped me dead in my tracks. I bought the museum guidebook and all the Bonnard and Vuillard postcards I could find in the gift shop to make sure I wouldn't forget the details. Those paintings had given me an idea that just might work for a mere stenciler.

Back home, I put that idea to work, trying to reproduce the blue gingham curtains in my son's room. I outlined each section with flexible painters' tape, then stenciled it with a flat gingham pattern, just as Bonnard had painted in *Femme à la robe quadrillée*. For adjacent sections, however, I made sure there was a break in the pattern. Not a gap but, rather, a shift up or down and a slight rotation of the gingham grid. This was really easy to do with a

Woven Texture

stencil, but the effect was magical. It didn't matter that there was no contouring or perspective within each fold of the curtain; the discontinuity between folds tricked the brain into seeing gathers and folds. In photographs of the stenciled curtains painted right next to the real ones, it was difficult to tell which was which.

The first improvement I made to this method was to adopt the airbrush technique of cutting frisket film in situ, but instead of using proper frisket film, I substituted much cheaper freezer paper and stencil adhesive. I stuck the freezer paper onto the wall, traced the outline of the drapery on the paper, then cut out the sections to reveal and mask them for painting. The basic approach is exactly the same as for projection stenciling, described in the previous chapter, except I was not using a projector at the time. An overhead projector makes this method much easier.

Eventually, I tried various ways of contouring each fold of "cloth" with shading and highlighting, giving a slight curve to the patterns stenciled on the folds. None of this is difficult. This chapter shows you how, starting with flat "textiles" and finishing with draped ones. More examples can be found in *Stencilling on a Grand Scale* (Firefly Books).

The projection method discussed in Chapter 8 is ideally suited for this subject. To create life-sized draperies with traditional Mylar stencils would require several overlays, and the logistics of creating, using and storing stencils at this scale are daunting. Moreover, such a tool will only produce identical copies of the same drapery. Not only is projection stenciling cheaper and faster, but a few quick changes to an overhead transparency will produce a brand-new creation every time.

It's not really necessary to give faux textiles a woven look, unless you plan to make them plain (without a pattern) or unless the work is for a small piece that will be seen up close. For the example shown below, a linen finish was applied with thick gesso. To do this, drag a wallpaper brush horizontally across a layer of fresh, thick gesso. Let dry. Apply another layer, and drag the brush vertically. When the gingham and doily are stenciled over it (see pages 163 and 164), the woven texture shows through. Other textile effects can be produced with a combing tool (coarse weave) or a wood grainer (taffeta).

Flat Textiles

A "flat" project is a good way to get started when stenciling faux textiles—a tablecloth painted onto a tabletop, a rug painted onto a floor, an "upholstered" door or furniture panels.

Just as with real textiles, an infinite variety of patterns can be used for faux textiles. Calicoes, damasks, toile de Jouy and other prints are simply all-over patterns with designs of varying size and complexity. Pick a relatively simple design with an appropriate scale and easily positioned repeats.

Lace, gingham and tartans are also very effective as faux textiles. Here are some relatively simple ways to stencil them.

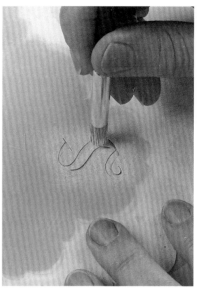

DRAG BRUSH ACROSS WHITE GLAZE · ADD EMBROIDERY WITH OPAQUE PAINT

SHEERS AND WOVEN LACE

1 This effect shows up best over a deep-colored background. Stencil the textile shape with a transparent basecoat that contrasts well with the background. Here, I roller stenciled the scalloped square with a very transparent white glaze.

2 Immediately drag a wallpaper brush across it, with the stencil still in place. Let it dry, then apply another coat, and drag the wallpaper brush at right angles to the first coat.

3 Wipe off any bleeds right away with a Q-tip, or cover them by stenciling a solid white scalloped border.

4 Then stencil any lace pattern or embroidered details over this, using opaque white paint.

5 Simulate folds or creases by blending a hint of white along a fold line.

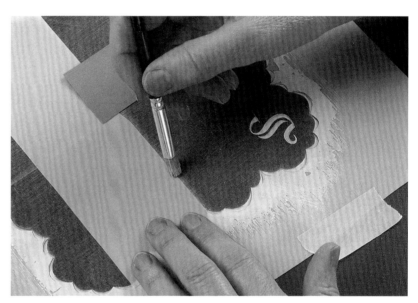

USING A LIGHT TOUCH, SIMULATE FOLD LINES (NOTE THAT FOLDS ARE STRAIGHT EXCEPT WHERE THEY COME TOGETHER AT CENTER)

Flat Textiles

CROCHET LACE

To stencil this crocheted border, you can use a cut stencil, as I did here, or a piece of curtain lace (stiffened with shellac) to add the holes.

1 If the original surface is white (as it is here), cut a long scalloped mask. Stick it across the surface to mask that shape while painting the entire surface. (If the original surface is colored, stencil a solid-white scalloped strip across it, then stencil crochet holes over it with the same color that surrounds the border.)

2 Remove the mask.

3 Cut a single repeat of the stencil pattern with all the holes. Use this overlay to stencil the holes over each scallop. This approach minimizes the amount of stencil cutting. The black lines on the stencil are for registration.

4 Add freehand shadows.

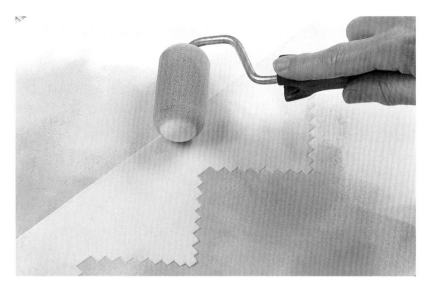

USE A LONG MASK TO CREATE A SOLID WHITE SCALLOPED STRIP

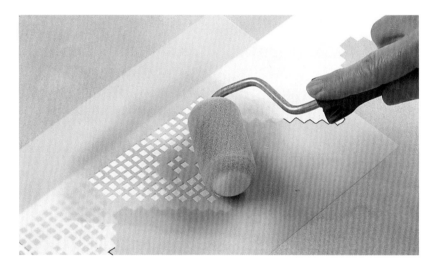

STENCIL CROCHET HOLES OVER STRIP WITH A "ONE SCALLOP" OVERLAY

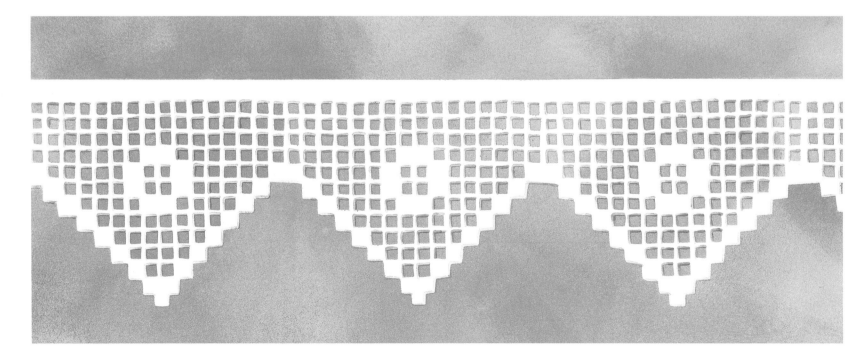

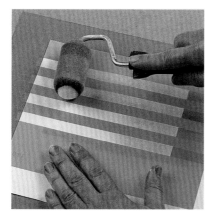

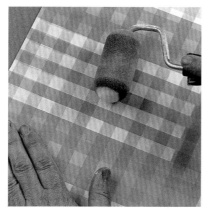

ROLLER STENCIL PARALLEL STRIPES

ROTATE STENCIL 90 DEGREES

GINGHAM

1 Start by roller stenciling a set of parallel stripes. You can make stripes longer by tapering the ends and blending them into an adjoining set of stripes. Let dry completely.

2 Rotate the stencil 90 degrees, and roller stencil another set of stripes over the first set.

3 Use a translucent medium and a light touch so that wherever the two sets of stripes overlap, the overlap is clearly visible as a darker rectangle. If a glaze is used for this, it must be fast-drying, because the second set of stripes can't be done until the first set is completely dry; otherwise, the edges of the overlapping parts will be blurred. I find a tinted acrylic varnish works well.

NOTE: It's important to use a stencil roller instead of a brush to help keep the overlapping edges crisp. Vary the size and spacing of the stripes to create a variety of plaid patterns, as shown here.

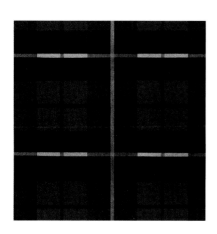

To create the tartan, I started with a red background, then stenciled the black stripes. The narrow yellow stripes were added with an extra overlay.

TRADITIONAL GINGHAM WITH STRIPES AND GAPS THE SAME WIDTH

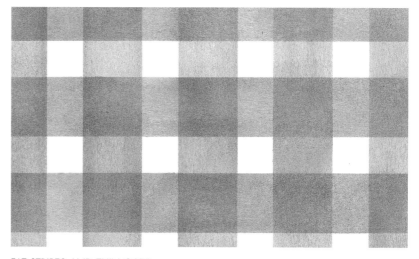

FAT STRIPES AND THIN GAPS

ALTERNATING FAT AND THIN STRIPES AND GAPS, ARRANGED ASYMMETRICALLY

Flat Textiles

DOILIES

Paper doilies can be used to add a very realistic touch to flat imitation textiles. Start with a white surface, then set the doily in place as a mask with stencil adhesive. Stencil the textile basecoat color and pattern over the entire surface. Create a gingham effect by roller stenciling fat stripes first crosswise and then lengthwise (see page 163).

Another version of this project appears on page 160. Because that surface was given a gessoed linen effect before any stenciling was done, it has the look and feel of a woven texture. Using a stencil roller instead of a stencil brush left more color in the grooves than in the gessoed ridges.

Remove the paper doily, and you are left with its image in white, the textile pattern showing through its cutwork. Use a fine artist's brush to add shadows freehand.

BASECOAT OVER SURFACE MASKED WITH DOILY

ADD GINGHAM STRIPES RIGHT OVER DOILY

REMOVE DOILY TO SHOW LACE AND GINGHAM

ADD SHADOWS FOR THREE-DIMENSIONAL EFFECT

Draped Textiles

Of all the techniques presented in this book, this has to be my favorite. It is so simple, yet the results are spectacular, especially when applied on a grand scale. Featured here is the projection process I described in the introduction to Chapter 8.

To start, decide on a stenciled textile pattern or faux-textile effect and an all-over layout for the way the simulated cloth is going to hang. Then combine stenciling with the faux-textile method of your choice.

DRAPED EFFECT

When a geometric pattern such as gingham is applied to a stenciled drapery, the gingham stencil can be modified so that the pattern enhances the illusion of three-dimensional folds. The example here was done with a curved set of stripes for the horizontal stencil and a straight set for the vertical direction. Detailed nongeometric patterns don't really need any modification, as long as the appropriate shading is added.

Draped Textiles

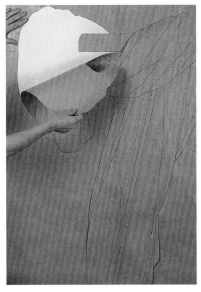
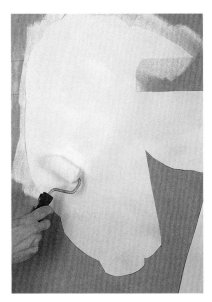
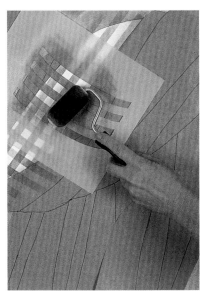

CUT OUTSIDE EDGE OF FABRIC PATTERN · PEEL OFF CUT PIECE OF FREEZER PAPER · ROLLER STENCIL DRAPERY BASECOAT · STENCIL GINGHAM ON EXPOSED FOLD

DESIGN LAYOUT

Choosing the draped pattern is the most important part of this type of project. Start with sketches and rough layouts, combining ideas from a variety of sources: magazines, paintings, photographs and real-life studies. To work out the mechanics of the fold structure, I find it helpful to use plain sheets as models, arranging them in different poses—hanging, tied back, swagged, draped over furniture. It is essential to come up with a line drawing which portrays the folds of the cloth in a manner that is both realistic and artistic. The realism part has to capture the weight and substance (or lack of substance) of the cloth, while the artistry part must give the composition a certain flair, an unpredictability that imparts an air of realism.

If the fabric is to be stiff and heavy, like a rich velvet or brocade, then the folds will tend to be large, with angular breaks wherever the fabric is pulled back. A lightweight silk or muslin will form small folds when gathered and smooth curves when draped. Starched cotton might fall somewhere in between, with smallish gathers and angular curves.

If you're lucky enough to find a photo that's almost exactly what you want, trace the fold lines, enlarge the tracing on a photocopier to a workable size and play with different modifications to perfect the design. Then trace out a clean copy to use as a pattern that can be projected onto the wall. If you need to work from a real model but feel your sketching skills are not up to the task, take some photographs (snapshot quality is good enough). Try to exaggerate the lighting so that the folds will show up well. Now, make photocopy enlargements of the 4-by-6 photos, trace them onto tracing paper, and work from there. There's no need to let a lack of drawing talent stop you.

BASIC TECHNIQUE

1 Once you have a clean line drawing to use as a template for the draped composition, transfer it, enlarged, to the freezer paper that will serve as the main stencil. To do this, cover the wall surface with sheets of freezer paper (using stencil adhesive, as described in Chapter 8), project the line drawing onto the paper and trace the lines with a fine permanent felt-tip pen. If the room is too small for projection, project and transfer the line drawing to the freezer paper in a larger room, then move the freezer paper into the smaller room. If you cannot obtain a projector, enlarge the drawing manually, using the grid system.

2 When the freezer-paper pattern has been fixed in place (tape the outside edges as well, even though you've also used stencil adhesive), cut along the outside edge of the entire drapery. Remove the piece and save it. Using a roller-stenciling method, fill in the exposed area with the base color of the cloth. Be generous with the paint, except near the edges of the cutout, where you must take care (by offloading excess paint)

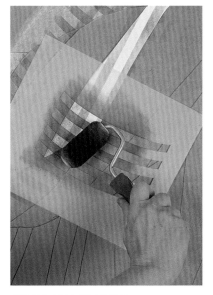

STENCIL ADJACENT FOLD

DO NOT MATCH UP BETWEEN FOLDS

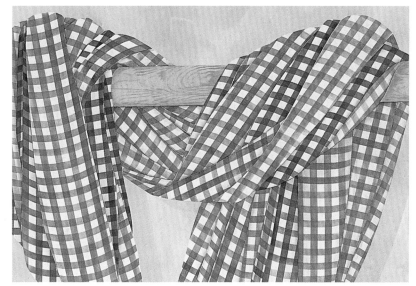

to avoid bleeding under the stencil. Let this section dry thoroughly, overnight if possible.

3 Now cover up the newly painted section with the freezer paper that was cut out in step 2. Position the piece exactly, and press it into place. Tape it to the rest of the freezer paper in several places with Scotch tape. Don't use painters' tape for this —you want a strong hold and a tape that's easy to cut.

4 Cut away one of the main fold sections of the drapery. Shade any receding edges, making them slightly darker and less intense. Decide how the overlaid pattern (in this case, a gingham) should be oriented, and roller stencil it over the section. Give the section a quick blow from a hair dryer, then cover it up with its piece of freezer paper, Scotch-taping some of the edges for security.

5 Cut away a second section adjacent to the first. Shade any receding edges as before. When positioning the gingham stencil, lift up an edge of the freezer paper on the first section to make sure the stencil does *not* line up with the gingham already stenciled. The angle of the gingham should change slightly, and the horizontal stripes should be higher or lower. A good rule of thumb for alignment is to make the pattern of each fold section more or less parallel to the leading edge of the fold.

Sometimes, clear vapor-barrier plastic makes a better stencil material than freezer paper. The transparency allows you to see the pattern orientation on adjacent sections, making it easy to "misalign" the pattern between sections. This plastic stretches, however, so it must be handled with care.

6 Continue to cut away, stencil and cover up sections of the drapery until the whole thing is finished. By this point, the freezer paper will be looking rather forlorn—cut up, taped together and covered with random splotches of gingham colors.

7 If the trompe l'oeil drapery is to cast a shadow, now's the time to add it. Since the drapery usually hangs parallel to a wall surface, a drop shadow works well. Leave in place the taped-together piece of freezer paper that is covering the finished drapery. Untape the section of freezer paper that surrounds the drapery, and shift it slightly down and to one side. This opens a gap below and beside the drapery. When the gap is exactly where you want it, tape the freezer paper in place. Roller stencil the gap with a transparent glaze tinted with the shadow color. I usually use a touch of raw umber, but check Chapter 3 for other suggestions. If you prefer, the shadow can be added freehand.

8 Remove all freezer paper. Check the drapery for small slivers of unstenciled space between fold sections, which can occur when the masking is not completely precise. Fill these in using a small artist's brush.

NOTE: For this example, I used a faux wood treatment on the sections making up the crossbar.

Textile Characteristics

Once you have learned this basic method, there are all sorts of variations you can employ (and invent) to expand your repertoire. Most of these involve ways of trying to imitate different types of textiles.

HEAVY TEXTILES

When it comes to type of material, texture and sheen, heavy textiles can differ from each other as much as night and day, but the one characteristic they share is the way they drape. Heavy cloth forms wider, thicker folds that fall heavily. Highlights and shadows are therefore broader, spread out over larger areas. They will be sharper and more brilliant on a shiny surface like satin but soft and diffused on dull surfaces like velvet and wool.

■ Satin and brocade need sharp highlights and strong shadows to bring out their shine; their broad folds should break in fairly sharp angles.

■ The sheen of damask, on the other hand, can be quite flat, especially if the fabric is woven out of cotton or wool. In this case, the highlights and shadows should be more subtle and blended gradually with the base color. To emphasize the fact that the woven pattern may disappear in certain angles of lighting, go over sections of the folds freehand afterward with a translucent coat of the base color, thus making the pattern almost disappear in places.

■ For taffeta, use a wood-graining tool to produce watermarks rather than applying a stenciled pattern. Be careful to avoid messy bleeds. With a fold section exposed, roller stencil a layer of tinted glaze over the whole area. Immediately pull and rock the wood-graining tool over the surface in parallel sweeps along the direction of the warp. As soon as the section is finished, brush it lightly with a blending brush, again along the warp direction—just enough to soften the grain marks without obscuring them. There may be some bleeding at the end of the section where the sweeps end, because the tool pulls the glaze in this direction. Carefully lift this edge of the freezer paper,

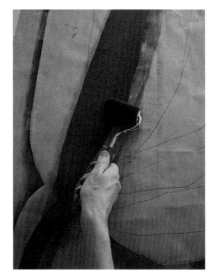

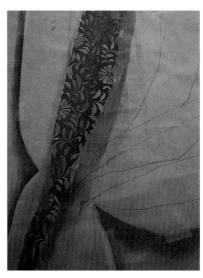

SHADE EDGE OF FOLD   ADD NONGEOMETRIC PATTERN

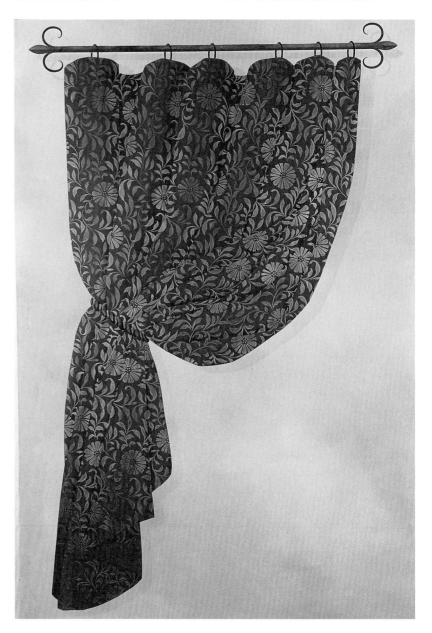

and use a Q-tip to remove any glaze that has crept under the edge. Use a hair dryer to dry the glaze—otherwise, it takes too long before the section can be covered up. When working on adjacent sections, alter the angle of the grain.

■ For plain velvet, try stippling a dark glaze over a slightly lighter basecoat. Stipple dark shadows along each fold. Any highlights should be soft, diffuse and low in contrast.

■ For a crushed velvet, apply a glaze slightly deeper than the basecoat, using a bunched-up rag as the applicator. When that coat is dry, stipple a final translucent layer on top. As with all plain fabrics, there is no pattern to shift between folds, so make the shading and highlighting strong enough to show the structure of the folds in the drapery.

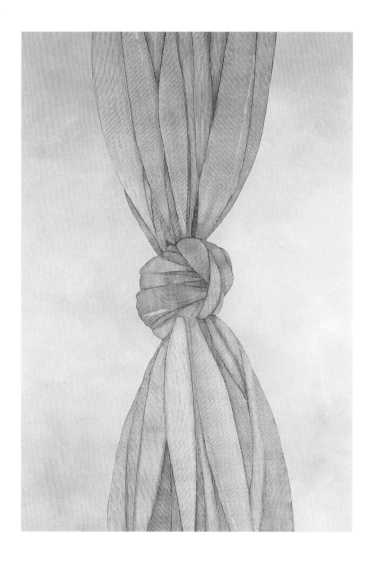

"STARCHED" SWAG HANGS IN ANGULAR FOLDS OVER STENCILED HEADBOARD

LIGHT TEXTILES

The finer the fabric, the narrower its folds, the more it can be bunched up and the less weight it has to make the folds hang straight down. If it is crisp, like starched and ironed cotton, then the folds will be sharp and linear, as will the highlights and shadows. If the fabric is soft, the folds will be smooth and curved, with soft, blended highlights. The example at left was striped with a graining comb.

Textile Characteristics

TRANSPARENT TEXTILES

For sheer fabric, a couple of things must be done a little differently. First, the pattern should have some lines that show overlapping folds, since you would normally be able to see through two or more layers. The overlapping parts are painted twice—once with each section they belong to. This will make those parts look a little more opaque than areas with just one layer of fabric.

■ The second difference is that you should work with a very transparent medium instead of straight paint. Mix a little paint and water with a clear medium that's not too slow-drying, or use any similar medium with which you are comfortable. For example, I find that a mix of paint, Floetrol and water works well. It doesn't take forever to dry, and it can make the paint as transparent as you wish. Do a few small trials to get the right amount of translucency.

■ Choose colors with enough contrast that the cloth will show up well over the background, even though it is painted with a very transparent medium. White sheers over a dark background, for example, always work well. If you want white over a lighter background, the edges and fold shadows must be somewhat more opaque to show up.

■ Finally, I get better results if I do not apply an overall basecoat. Instead, I start working right away on individual fold sections.

1 When a fold section is opened up, roller stencil the medium over the whole area, moving the roller back and forth parallel to the long side of the fold. This way, any lap lines will simply resemble small undulations in the fold. Try to build up slightly more opaque color near the long edges and anywhere else that the fabric is bunching up.

2 If the fold is too opaque all over, wipe down the middle of the fold with a dry rag (or one that's barely damp) to thin out the glaze layer there to almost nothing.

■ To make a plain sheer textile look embroidered or lace-like, add a stenciled pattern to each section. Use an opaque acrylic in the same color as the transparent sheer.

3 Once the entire piece has been finished and the freezer paper removed, brush in some opaque highlights where the fabric is bunched up and wherever it receives a glance of full light. At the same time, freehand some transparent shadows wherever it seems appropriate.

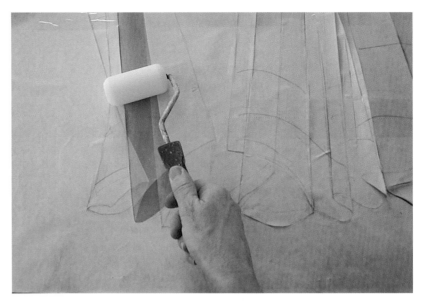

FOR ULTRASHEER FOLDS, STENCIL OVERLAPPING PARTS MORE THAN ONCE

SEMISHEER HAS "EMBROIDERED" PATTERN STENCILED IN SOLID WHITE

Borders/Accessories

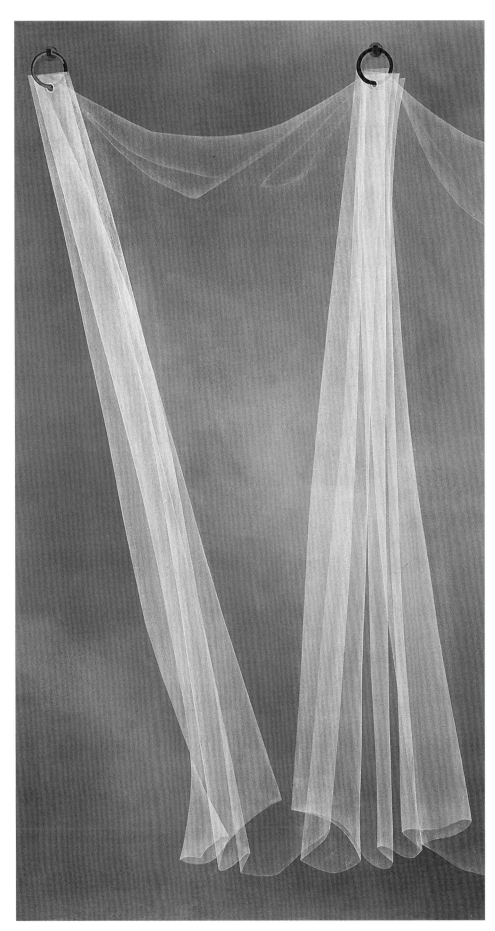

A border can be added to a curtain hem, especially if the composition features a fair amount of exposed edge. However, a draped hem is almost always curved to some degree, so a straight border stencil cannot be applied as is. The stencil could be redesigned so that it follows a curve, but then not all the folds would have the same curvature. It's easier to pick a border design with a small broken repeat, which can be easily manipulated to follow a change in direction.

■ All sorts of accessories can be added to a drapery composition, each of which will enhance the sense of realism. Curtain rods, exotic finials, tiebacks and fringes can be stenciled in the standard way, with special attention to shading, highlights and shadows. Finishing touches can be hand-painted or penned, depending on the level of detail desired.

RODS, RINGS AND FINIALS ARE EASY TO STENCIL

Chapter 10

ARCHITECTURAL ELEMENTS

If they were the real thing, the features discussed in this chapter would require a hammer and nails and some measure of carpentry skills to install. But if your budget is inadequate or if you need temporary effects because the landlord wants the apartment left in its original condition when you leave, then the painted fakes described here might be the answer. Of course, it doesn't have to be a question of resources or constraints—you may simply want to make an elaborate trompe l'oeil statement.

You might think that fake architectural elements require an extraordinary level of painting skill, but that is often not the case, especially when you rely on a good set of stencils to do the heavy lifting. It is surprising how much realism can be portrayed with a few simple stenciled shapes. My first attempt at architectural embellishment was a very basic painted crown molding, roller stenciled in gray (no shading!) on a white basecoat. I wasn't completely satisfied with the result and debated whether to paint it out.

Then a couple of neighbors happened to remark on the interior renovations they'd spied as they walked past the front window. Oh, that new wall color and that wide crown molding look so good, they said. When I looked at it through their eyes, it did, indeed, appear real.

In this chapter, you'll see a wide range of stenciled effects, some quick and easy and some that require a serious investment of effort. None of the steps involved is difficult in itself, but the sum of the steps may take time. The central requirement, in addition to patience, is that you have learned and practiced the shading methods described in Chapter 3.

For almost all the shading work shown here, I have used transparent acrylic glazes or solid oil paints (and the instructions refer to them accordingly). I prefer these mediums because one or two colors (for example, raw umber) work well over just about any basecoat color and because they let the patterns of any faux finishes show through. However, you don't have to use glazes for form shadows if the basecoat is plain. Opaque acrylics work fine as long as you pick a subtle range of colors to stencil or taper over the basecoat.

Faux Moldings

Once you can stencil a solid shadow and a tapered linear shadow (Chapter 3), these effects can be combined in different ways to create faux moldings of varying complexity. It's useful to have reference materials at hand in the form of short pieces of actual moldings and molding catalogs from companies that manufacture architectural millwork. Build up a collection of foot-long pieces of molding from a local lumber store, or scavenge scrap pieces from a carpenter.

1 The first step for faux molding is to stencil or paint the basecoat. This doesn't have to be plain. It can be fake marble or wood or some other kind of faux finish. Let it dry thoroughly.

2 The next step is to give the basecoat the illusion of shape by stenciling form shadows and cast shadows over it. A transparent medium such as an acrylic glaze or a solid oil paint works best. The more transparent, the better, because the effect must be subtle, allowing any marble veining or wood graining to show through. Stick to a fairly monochromatic scheme for all shading. I used raw umber for most of these examples.

3 Use a very transparent medium for cast shadows. Roller stencil large cast shadows to obtain even coloration. Small shadows can be done with a stencil brush.

NOTE: When working on the linear shading for straight strips of molding, use small brushes for small curvatures and sharp shading. Use big brushes for large curvatures and soft, even shading. Use a pencil line for sharp contrast to demarcate the deepest part of a crevice.

CHAIR-RAIL MOLDING

1 For a long, straight piece of molding, lay down strips of painters' tape to mark the top and bottom edges of the entire strip.

2 Then basecoat the strip with low-sheen latex paint, using a roller-stenciling technique to avoid bleeds under the tape. Leave the tape in place until the top edge of the strip has been highlighted and the bottom edge shaded.

3 To create wide contours, lay a Mylar straight edge along the line of deepest shadow. Mark the line with a pencil, then brush linear shading along the Mylar, over the pencil line. For narrow ridges, use a thin strip stencil. Color it evenly. Overlap and blend the ends of adjacent strip sections to extend the shape along the chair rail.

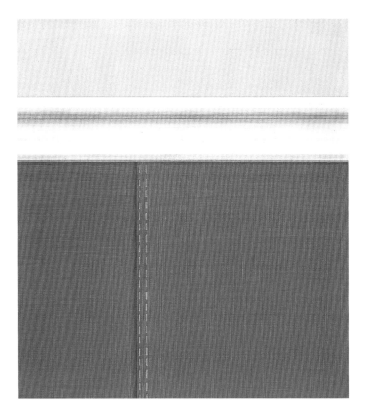

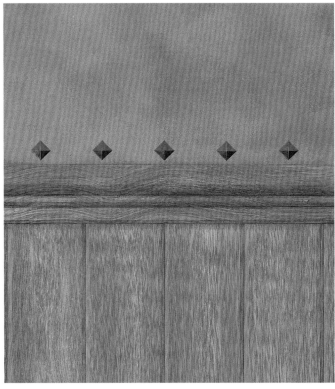

A FEW EXTRA STENCILED FEATURES ARE SHOWN IN THESE TWO EXAMPLES. TOP: LINEAR SHADING AND STENCILED STITCHING EMPHASIZE SEAM ON DENIM WAINSCOTING. ABOVE: STENCILED TACKS ACCENT EDGES OF LEATHER PANEL. BEVELED EDGES OF FAUX-WOOD BEAD BOARD IN BOTH TREATMENTS WERE ALSO STENCILED.

DOUBLE DENTIL MOLDING

One of the easiest fake moldings to stencil, this is also one of the most impressive, especially when seen from a distance. It is made up of solid, stenciled form shadows. Most of it can be done quickly with a stencil roller. Add some linear brush shading in between the "teeth" for an extra touch of realism. Here, the molding has been stenciled onto a fake marble basecoat.

EGG AND DART

This very classic molding is also the most time-consuming of all the examples shown here, because it requires individually brush-stenciled form shadows for each section.

Carved Decoration

Tapered stenciling with transparent color works especially well with reverse stencils. Using a very small stencil brush, blend the color over just the edges of the cutouts. This creates a combined form-and-cast shadow that makes the cutout parts look carved or recessed. This can be done over any type of basecoat, plain or faux. For the "stone" border shown here, an overlay added a little more carved detail to the scroll. This basecoat is a textured compound, but it was troweled flat.

I stenciled the carved faux-wood border a little differently, using a stencil roller for the initial reverse stencil. Then, with a damp cloth wrapped around my finger, I wiped off the glaze from the middle of the cutouts. This left just a hint of color over those areas and a thin line of dark color along the carved edges. I used an overlay to add relief to the motifs.

This same technique can be used to create larger "carved" shapes on a wall: any kind of alcove or niche, for example, or chunks of "missing" plaster.

Faux Panels

One of the main drawbacks of using water-based products for faux finishes is that they have less open time than equivalent oil-based products, which means there is a limited timespan in which to apply the glaze and manipulate it to the required effect. If the section being worked on starts to dry before you move on to the adjacent section, the lap line between the two sections may show up as a darker line wandering through the finished wall. It is possible to avoid this, but it usually means being very organized and having a partner to help. Even then, you must work quickly.

A second solution, and one that imparts a very elegant effect to the room, is to divide the work into well-defined panels by masking off an area only as big as you can handle in one pass. Of course, some effort must be expended beforehand in planning the size and placement of the panels for optimum effect. If the panels are to abut each other exactly, work on every other one, let them dry overnight, then do the in-between panels so that the painters' tape does not disturb the finish.

A SIMPLE STENCILED MOLDING SEPARATES "FABRIC" PANEL FROM REST OF WALL; A MORE ELABORATE CARVED MOLDING IS SHOWN ON PAGE 172

An alternative that allows you to do all the panels on the same day and to avoid the corners of the room as well is to "frame" the panels and space them slightly apart. The framing, which is done with stencils, can be plain or fancy. Plain could be a simple stenciled stripe or a fake molding, while the fancier styles might imitate the kind of gilt-framed panels of brocade found decorating the baroque walls of European palaces.

In Europe, it is not uncommon to "wallpaper" with textiles, an expensive and labor-intensive process. A very similar effect (visually, if not acoustically) can be created with a little paint and some stencils. Tricks for making panels look like cloth include using a dragged linen effect under or over a stenciled pattern or using a graining tool to make taffeta watermarks.

On a slightly smaller scale, a plain flush door, or hollow-core door, makes an ideal surface for stenciled panels. It's also a great project with which to start: At less than two square yards, it's not very intimidating. For ideas, check out styles shown in door catalogs. The same patterns can be used on furniture and kitchen-cabinet doors or on a chest of drawers, like the one shown at left. First, I primed the unpainted chest. Then I applied a thin ivory crackle finish over an uneven taupe basecoat before stenciling the panels.

Stonework

BLEND DARKER COLOR ON EDGES

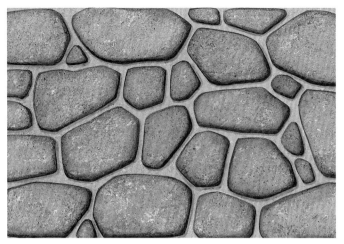

SHADING MAKES STONES POP UP FROM GROUTING

For stone blocks with little or no mortar between them, the bridges on a one-piece stencil would have to be vanishingly thin. Instead, cut a stronger stencil of non-adjacent blocks and use an overlay to fill in the others. Since there is little mortar or shadow to create boundaries between the stones, make subtle changes from one stone to the next by roller stenciling slightly different transparent colors for each stone over the faux-grout basecoat. Add definition to the edges of each block by blending a line of watercolor crayon and wiping it back to the stencil edges.

PAINT

Whether you want the look of a cobblestone pathway, fairy-tale-castle ramparts or a garden wall, paint and a stencil create an inexpensive substitute for the real thing.

1 I like to start with a painted stone finish over the entire surface that I want to cover with fake pavers or blocks. Use whatever kind of stone effect you want, but choose the color carefully, because this finish will end up as the grouting between the stones. If the same type of medium (water-based or oil-based) is used for the entire job, then let the basecoat dry completely (at least overnight) before continuing.

2 Lay the stencil over the dried basecoat. To alter the color of the stones from that of the grout or basecoat, apply a thin coat of color over the stencil with a stencil roller. The medium must be transparent enough that the color texture and variation of the basecoat show through.

3 To give the stones three-dimensional relief, brush darker color along the edges of each stone. The way the color is tapered—fast or slow, in a broad or narrow band—will affect whether the stone looks flattish, gently rounded or sharply cut. The sunny side of each stone should have only a little added color at the very edge, just enough to make it look like an intersection between stone and grout. I used watercolor crayons for the shading (solid oils also work well). These have a lot of pigment, and I find them useful for making very sharp color gradients. To do this, trace the crayon around the inside edge of the stencil. Blend it by rubbing a brush dampened with glaze along the stencil edge. If it gets too dark, wipe it back with a slightly damp cloth.

4 Add cast shadows freehand. Apply a protective finish. If it has the same solvent as your shading material (oil varnish and solid oil paint or water-based varnish and watercolor crayons), then apply a clear spray first to seal the shading and prevent smudging before adding the protective finish.

STENCIL DESIGNED WITH NONADJACENT STONES

DARKEN NARROW GROUT LINES WITH FINE BRUSH

TROWEL GROUNDSTONE OVER BASECOAT AND VINYL STENCIL

WHEN DRY, PEEL STENCIL AWAY TO EXPOSE GROUT LINES

FINISHED IMPASTO SAMPLE

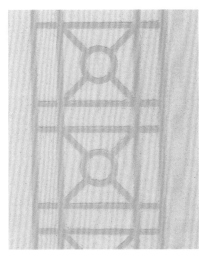

SAME METHOD, DIFFERENT STENCIL

IMPASTO MEDIUM

This method creates a surface that not only looks like stone but feels like it as well. For the example here, I've used "Groundstone" products (from Briste Group). You may find textured products from other manufacturers that can be used in a similar way.

1 First, trowel a thin layer of textured basecoat onto a primed surface. This coat will end up being visible as the grout between the stones.

2 Then lay a single-use, high-adhesive vinyl stencil sheet, precut with the desired stone pattern, on the dried basecoat.

3 Next, apply a Groundstone topcoat (or other textured medium) with a trowel, and smooth it.

4 After this topcoat has dried, pull the stencil off to reveal the grout. Create different patterns of stone blocks by using a variety of stencil shapes.

TIGHT STONE WALKWAY: USE OVERLAYS TO CREATE A CLOSE-PACKED LAYOUT

Plaster Decoration

Like elaborate moldings, plaster ceiling rosettes can get expensive. A cheap and easy alternative is to stencil them with either paint or an impasto medium, using the method and materials described in Chapter 4. For some ideas, refer to one of the Victorian stencil collections by Dover Publications. These collections have a number of ceiling-rosette designs (meant for paint, but just fine for plaster too), along with matching corner and border stencils. The rosettes can be quite elaborate, but it's not necessary to cut a stencil for the entire thing. Most have some kind of rotational repeat, so it's possible to get away with cutting, say, a quarter (90 degrees) of a rosette. Print it, then rotate 90 degrees, and print again. Do it twice more, and you have a complete rosette.

Breaking a rosette stencil into wedges makes it easier to work around a light fixture. It means the fixture does not have to be removed to fit the stencil in place.

■ Working on ceilings is physically demanding and particularly hard on the neck. If you can get scaffolding that lets you lie on your back, it's easier, but wear safety glasses, because anything that falls or drips will land in your face. If you are farsighted and normally wear bifocals, buy a cheap pair of full-lens reading glasses at

CEILING ROSETTE MADE WITH PLASTER MEDIUM

the drugstore. This way, you'll be able to focus up close no matter which direction you look.

■ Another problem is the pull of gravity. It's best to use stencil adhesive on the back of the stencil to maintain good contact. Using tape alone on the edges will allow the center parts of the stencil to sag away from the ceiling. If using an impasto technique, make sure the medium is thick enough that it won't sag or drip off once applied.

■ The most common ceiling color is white, but that doesn't mean the rosette can't be

SHADOW STENCIL ROSETTE DONE WITH PAINT

done in white too, as long as you use a plaster-type product that gives a real three-dimensional relief. White on white is stunning and classic, as long as there are real shadows to pick out the shape. White plaster also looks great over a nonwhite ceiling.

■ If you want to use only paint, rather than plaster, then you need some color to make the shapes visible. Or if you must stick with all white, then design the rosette as a shadow stencil. In this case, the directional quality of the shadows makes the design nonsymmetric, so you must cut out the entire rosette as a stencil.

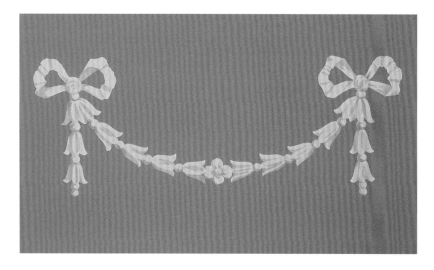

Ceiling rosettes are not the only types of plaster decoration that can be imitated by using stencils. Look through some of Dover's historical design books for all kinds of ideas for plaster swags, borders and cartouches that can be adapted to stenciling. This swag was stenciled first with ornamental gesso (a plasterlike acrylic product), then an overlay was used to add painted form shadows.

Columns

Fake columns can add a note of elegance to a long, boring wall, either on their own or topped by a stenciled crown molding. You don't have to be much of an expert to accomplish this if you use a commercial stencil. If you prefer to design your own, look at historical design books in the library or at some of the Dover Publications books on architectural features. Or take a photo of your local courthouse, and work from that.

1 Once you have a stencil, make a paper print of the capital (the top part) and the pediment (the base part). Use the prints to decide where to position the column.

2 Then measure and mark the edges of the column shaft so that it falls directly below the capital and extends to the top of the pediment.

3 Frame the boundaries of the shaft with painters' tape. Basecoat the shaft, then remove the tape at the top and bottom only.

4 Replace the paper prints with the corresponding stencils. Stencil the basecoat for the capital and the pediment. Leave the tape along the sides of the shaft for the time being.

NOTE: For best results, roller stencil the basecoat of each part of the column. This is the fastest way to get good coverage over such a large area. Several coats are required to build up an even basecoat.

5 Before stenciling the details, a simple marble or stone finish can be added over the basecoat, if you wish, provided you use a fairly dry method that won't bleed under the edges of the column shape. Let any such finish dry at least overnight before continuing.

Now you have what looks like a silhouette of the entire column shape, without any details. The next step is to stencil those details as form shadows, using a transparent medium and the methods described in Chapter 3 and in the molding section on page 174.

6 Creating the crown and pediment is straightforward stencil work, using a couple of overlays. Leave the shaft plain or make it fluted, depending on the amount of work you're prepared to do. It takes time to get the fluting right—stencil with a small brush and use a transparent, blendable medium such as a glaze or solid oil paint.

CAPITAL, SHAFT OF PLAIN COLUMN

STENCILED ROPE, MOLDING ADD FORM

FLAT MARBLE SILHOUETTE

STENCILED FLUTES AND MOLDING

Latticework

Fake latticework is a common design feature for murals, furniture and wallpaper. It is usually done as part of a garden theme, and the most common form it takes is that of a regular grid, square or diamond-shaped. If this is the type of trellis you want, the first thing to consider is the scale of the work and whether it would be easier to use a stencil or long strips of painters' tape. For covering an entire wall, the tape approach is generally better. Otherwise, many, many repeats of precisely registered stencil prints must be made, and many of those prints will have to be worked into wall and ceiling corners.

For something less ambitious, however, where the lattice is used for a border, a door or a piece of furniture, a stencil can be the most practical approach. The easiest and fastest way to stencil a trellis pattern is to use a reverse stencil as a mask for the lattice pieces. Start with a surface painted the color of the eventual latticework, and stencil background color over it. Suitable colors must be used for this to work, because the background color has to look true when stenciled over the lattice color. White or near-white latticework is ideal, because any background color can be used.

By using tape or large cardboard templates as masks combined with a lattice grid stencil, you can create arches, panels or columns of latticework.

REVERSE STENCIL

A reverse stencil for latticework requires only a single overlay (except for shadows). It is essentially a large-scale diaper pattern (see Chapter 6), which means that registration and positioning must be precise. In this example, we start with a white basecoat and roller stencil a light blue, which results in a white lattice over a blue "sky." For an even more skylike background, play with the color before removing the stencil, adding clouds, for example, or sunset colors.

Using a stencil makes more decorative forms of latticework just as easy as straight diamonds and squares. Below is an example taken from a book of Chinese designs.

BLUE "SKY" AND "CLOUDS" ROLLER STENCILED OVER WHITE BASECOAT WITH DIAMOND GRID STENCIL

SAME PROCESS WITH CHINESE-STYLE LATTICE; SHADOWS WERE STENCILED WITH OVERLAY

CAST SHADOWS

To make the trelliswork more lifelike, add shadows. There are several ways to do this, depending on how much work you want to put into it. The easiest way is the one that offers no perspective to the strips of lath. Wherever one lath crosses over another, there is a simple cast shadow on the shaded side and a barely discernible diffuse shadow on the other. The latter is created by running a stencil brush along a straight edge. This is a good method to use when covering an entire wall, because it avoids awkward decisions about how the shadows need to change with perspective.

To mimic a trellis mounted against a solid wall (instead of freestanding, with sky behind it), consider stenciling shadows cast onto the wall as well as onto other lattice strips. For seamless shadows, use a stencil roller and a very transparent glaze. The shape of the cast shadows should reflect the structure of the trellis (i.e., one set of lattice strips closer to the wall than the other) as well as the direction of the light source.

Latticework

FORM SHADOWS

For latticework that appears to be above eye level, add form shadows to define the bottom edge of each lattice strip. The sample at right shows a form shadow stenciled onto the foreground strips only, while the sample at lower right has it stenciled on both sets of strips. For latticework that is below eye level (for example, a fence), your eye sees the top highlighted edges rather than the bottom shadowed edges, so stencil strips of highlight along the upper edges of the lattice pieces instead of shadows along the lower edges. Keep only the small cast shadows on the lower edges where one lattice piece crosses another.

FORM SHADOWS STENCILED ONLY ON FOREGROUND STRIPS; NOTE THAT LATTICE APPEARS TO BE ABOVE EYE LEVEL

CHANGE STRUCTURE OF LATTICE BY CHANGING FORM SHADOWS

FORM SHADOWS ADDED TO ALL LATTICE STRIPS; AGAIN, LATTICE IS ABOVE EYE LEVEL

ANOTHER CHANGE IN FORM SHADOW MAKES A FLAT LATTICE

Changing the shape of the form shadows completely alters the look of the lattice. The trelliswork shown in the two samples at left was done with the same basic stencil used for all the other diamond lattice examples on pages 182-184. Only the shadow overlays are different. Yet another choice of shadow overlays could make the lattice look woven, although in this case, one would also expect to see a slight curve to the lattice strips.

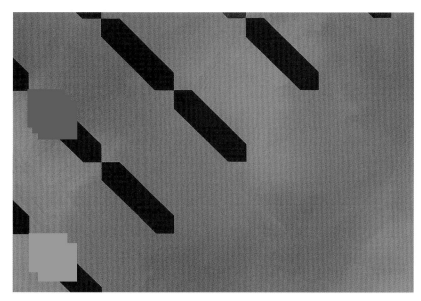

WITH BACKGROUND PAINTED, STENCIL FIRST OF TWO OVERLAYS BLACK

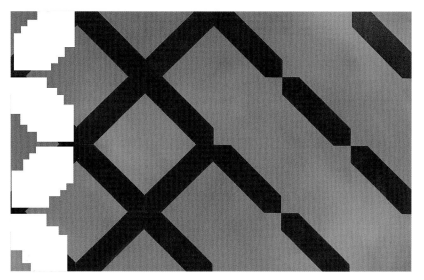

ADD SECOND OVERLAY TO CREATE BASIC LATTICE GRID

ADD GOLD HIGHLIGHTS TO GIVE SHAPE TO LATTICE

DIRECT STENCIL

S ome color combinations just won't work with a reverse stencil. If you want a black lattice, for example, the best method is to paint the background color first, then use a two-part stencil to create the lattice, as was done here. Instead of form shadows, gold highlights have been stenciled on this one.

Latticework

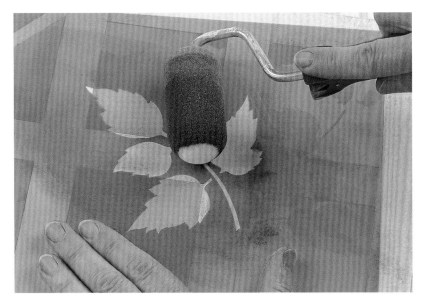

ADD BACKGROUND FOLIAGE WHILE LATTICE MASK IS DOWN

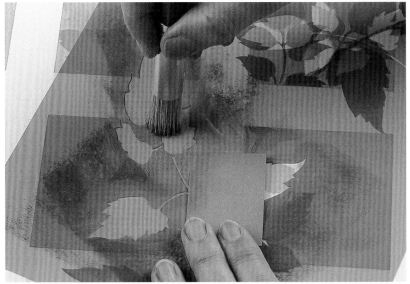

REMOVE LATTICE MASK, AND ADD FOREGROUND LEAVES

ENTWINING FOLIAGE

A lattice on its own is sometimes enough. But if you plan on creating a painted garden, you'll want to add some botanical interest. After all, real garden latticework is generally used as a support for plants.

1 Using a reverse stencil for the lattice makes it easy to do this, since the stencil itself is a mask for the trellis. Because the stencil shields the "woodwork," vines can be stenciled on willy-nilly, and they will seem to be growing on the other side of the trellis, visible only through the holes when the lattice stencil is removed.

2 Remove the lattice stencil/mask, and add vegetation that appears to be poking through the lattice into the foreground.

3 Don't forget to add any shadows cast by leaves onto the lattice or a wall behind it. Make sure the shadows stop short of any "sky" appearing behind the lattice.

ADD TRANSPARENT SHADOWS CAST BY LEAVES ONTO LATTICE

Gingerbread Borders

1 Bridgeless Victorian gingerbread is easy to stencil in one step when using a reverse stencil and even easier if the entire wall is being repainted. Ideally, start with the wall painted the color that will end up as the border color, and use the stencil to mask the border design while you repaint the wall. Obviously, a short stencil is not going to work here.

2 Fold a long strip of freezer paper zigzag style, with each section exactly the length of the pattern repeat. The piece should be long enough to make four or five folded sections—the number of layers that can be cut through at the same time with a sharp knife.

3 Transfer the pattern to the top fold, then cut it out, cutting through all the layers. Unfold the freezer-paper strip. Cut enough strips to make up the length of the wall,

then piece them together into one very long stencil.

4 Spray the back of the stencil with low-tack adhesive, and place it on the wall along a horizontal guideline.

5 Now, paint the wall in normal fashion, but switch to a foam roller and roller-stenciling technique whenever going over the freezer-paper stencil. Several thin coats will be required over the stencil to equal the coverage of a normal nap roller on the rest of the wall.

6 When the entire wall is done, peel off the stencil (reuse it on the other walls). I have added hand-painted form shadows to the example below to make the whole piece look hand-painted rather than stenciled. If your colors do not have much contrast, shadows also help the image stand out.

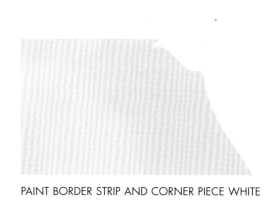

PAINT BORDER STRIP AND CORNER PIECE WHITE

STENCIL WALL COLOR OVER WHITE AREAS

1 If the border design has straight outside edges, it's not necessary to repaint the wall. Simply paint a white strip the width of the design across the wall, using painters' tape to ensure straight edges. In the example above, I also stenciled a white patch for a corner piece.

2 Next, place the stencil over the white strip (a short stencil is okay here, because repeats work fine), then roller stencil over it using the same paint that's covering the rest of the wall. Do the same thing with the corner piece.

NOTE: To avoid having to stencil right into the corner, paint a straight white strip along the edge of the wall from floor to top of border.

Windows

Stenciling a closed window is no different in principle from stenciling a trellis. The grid openings are generally larger, and you might add fake moldings around the perimeter or a curtain off to the side, but otherwise, it's very similar.

1 Start with a white or off-white rectangle the size of the overall window, and use a reverse stencil in which the cutouts are the individual window lights and the Mylar shields the muntins that separate the lights.

2 Then stencil a sky or a garden through the window-light cutouts.

3 The final step is to stencil form shadows on the muntins and moldings.

NOTE: For very large multi-paned windows, it's less work to mask the muntins with tape than to cut and work with an unwieldy stencil. In this case, avoid excessive measuring by cutting a stencil with, say, four window lights, then using it as a movable template to pencil in guidelines for the tape.

MASK FINISHED CURTAIN

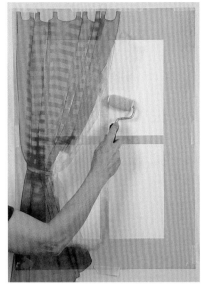

PAINT SKY WITH STENCIL IN PLACE

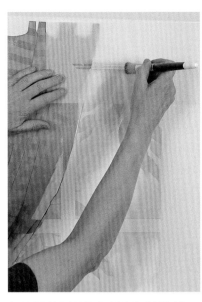

ADD FORM SHADOWS TO CASING

It is not difficult to combine a painted curtain with the window. Begin by painting a white rectangle the size of the eventual window. Using the method described in Chapter 9, draw up a curtain pattern and stencil it in the appropriate position. Cover up the finished curtain, as shown, with the freezer-paper pieces used to stencil it. This will protect it while the window is being stenciled.

1 Position the window stencil over the masked curtain, carefully lining it up with the white rectangle.

NOTE: Stenciling French doors or casement windows that are *open* is a little more complicated, because now we're dealing with perspective. All those window lights, muntins and even the form shadows must be tapered and shaped correctly, or the illusion won't work. If this seems daunting but you *really* want an open window, then look for a precut stencil from a commercial stencil company.

2 Following the reverse-stencil method for a lattice (page 186), stencil a sky and some trailing tree branches or other pieces of scenery.

3 Remove the window stencil (but leave the curtain shield in place), and stencil form shadows on the muntins.

4 Use stencil-shading techniques to add casing around the window or to create an inset window ledge. Finally, remove the curtain shield.

For highly colored or dark window frames, a different approach is needed, just as it was for latticework.

1 Start with a white background to get clear colors for the stenciled "view." Do steps 1 and 2 at left.

2 Mask the view before applying the dark color to the frames. The easiest way to do this is to cut Mylar or freezer-paper masks in the exact shape of each window light and stick them in place with stencil adhesive.

3 Then tape the outside edges of the entire window area, and use a roller-stencil method to color the casing and muntins all in one step. Following this, stencil any form shadows.

Fences and Balustrades

A good fence is a useful part of a muralist's repertoire. Whether simple or elaborate, it can tie together a variety of other design elements along a stretch of wall. Stenciled fences tend to fall into one of three categories: wrought-iron barricades, picket fences and stone balustrades.

IRONWORK

I find ironwork the easiest, and it's one that looks great just on its own. For the example shown below, I started with a simple background done as a well-blended color wash of ivory and raw sienna. The ironwork was then roller stenciled in acrylic paint, using a simple two-part commercial stencil. Gold highlights were done with linear shading.

PICKET FENCES

The main problem with picket fences is that almost everyone wants them white, with pale skies and big gardens stenciled behind them. Now a single stenciled layer of white paint does not show up well against a pale background, nor does it make a very opaque cover over stenciled tulips and poppies. It takes many repeat coatings to do a good job of either, and this is what makes the work tedious. A couple of approaches can make the project easier.

1 Rather than painting a garden first and overlaying a white fence, stencil the fence first. Trace picket shapes with a pencil before roller stenciling to make them stand out.

2 Shield the fence, several pickets at a time, with a mask (cut several pickets out of thin Mylar or freezer paper), and stencil the garden that appears behind the fence. Remove masks, and add foreground plants. Add shadows.

Another approach is to use an impasto medium, either a plaster or an extremely thick paint, for the fence, applying it with a spatula. This totally opaque layer will cover any garden scene that's already been stenciled. It's what I did to paint the example shown above.

Refer to Chapter 4 for a refresher on this method. Experiment first with a *vertical* sample board to brush up on your technique and to make sure the medium is thick enough that it won't run or sag. Remember to alternate the repeats so that one part of the stencil never overlaps wet plaster. Once the fence is finished and completely dry, stencil shadows and any flowers protruding in front of the pickets.

One other technique is to treat the fence as a form of lattice created with a multiple-picket reverse stencil. Paint a white basecoat on the area where the fence will go. Position the stencil, then use a stencil roller to build up the background color to match and blend in with the color on the rest of the wall. If you can't achieve a perfect blend, hide or break up the seam with clouds or tall plants. Leave the stencil in place as a shield, and fill in the garden behind the fence with freeform plants. Remove the stencil, and add foreground plants and shadows.

STONE BALUSTRADES

I like to design balustrades without perspective. This way, they look pretty good from any angle, as opposed to looking perfect from one particular spot and somehow a little wrong from everywhere else. This approach also makes them very easy—all you need is a single overlay and some linear shading.

NOTE: For plain balustrades (a single color plus shading), you can stencil one baluster at a time, but if you want to do them in a fake-stone technique, it's much faster to cut a large stencil that includes half a dozen or more balusters. With freezer paper, this is easier than it sounds. Fold the paper as you would for cutting paper dolls, and cut three to five at a time, then piece several sections together on the wall.

■ By using multiple cutouts, you can let one step of the fake stone dry on the first balusters while you proceed with the same step on subsequent balusters. After the initial pass, go back to the first balusters and do the next step. Not having to move the stencils saves time and means that the basecoat can seal the edges, allowing you to work a fairly messy fake stone without risk of bleeding under the stencil.

1 For this example, I started with a roller-stenciled basecoat of pale yellow ocher.

2 When this was dry, I sponged on irregular patches of sharper ocher, warm brown and ivory, with a very small amount of black.

3 Then, when the sponging was almost dry, I rolled a rubber brayer over the surface, lightly at first, then heavily. This gave a rough blending of any patches of paint that were still a little wet and lifted irregular patches from parts that were drier.

4 Let everything dry overnight, if possible. (If one giant stencil was used, leave it in place.) For shading with water-based products, let it dry for a couple of days so that the shading process doesn't reactivate the stone paint and overblend it. If using solid oil paints, such as Oil Bar™, Paintstiks™ or stencil creams, overnight drying is sufficient.

5 With the original stencil still in place (or back in place), add some overall shading to each baluster using a large stencil brush and either a transparent water-based glaze or transparent solid oil paints. You want to achieve a fairly large range in value without obscuring any of the variation that creates the illusion of a stone texture.

LONG FREEZER-PAPER STENCIL

LINEAR SHADING ACROSS BALUSTER

RAILING AND FOOTING ADDED TO FINISHED BALUSTERS

6 Now it's time for a lot of linear shading (see Chapter 3). Use a straight strip of Mylar for tapered linear shading or various widths of rectangular cutouts for solid linear shadows. Place the Mylar across the baluster stencil so that it lines up with one of the various shadow or groove positions. Run a small stencil brush or blending brush along the straight edge, building up the shadow gradation. For the deep grooves, draw a sharp pencil line along the innermost edge before doing the shading.

7 Once the balusters are finished, tape off a strip for the footing and another for the top railing, and paint these areas with the same fake stone that was used for the balusters. Again, use linear shading to "carve" their shapes.

Chapter 11

FAUX MARQUETRY

Marquetry is a centuries-old technique used in the decoration of furniture and accessories. It entails fitting thin, shaped pieces of wood or stone together very precisely to form a decorative veneer that's usually used as the surface of a piece of furniture. The concept is like that of an elaborate jigsaw puzzle, with the pieces taking on the shapes of leaves, petals, birds, musical instruments—a whole array of fantastic elements.

The image created might be a simple geometric pattern or an elaborate trompe l'oeil composition made with pieces of wood, marble and metal or with such exotic substances as mother-of-pearl, ivory and tortoiseshell.

The real process, however, is a dying art—and a very expensive one. The imitation marquetry described here is a very affordable (if not quite as sumptuous) substitute. And, with the help of some stenciling tricks, it's not difficult. This technique is ideal for decorating small boxes, tabletops or other objects with flat surfaces. We'll look at two different methods: one with traditional stencils; and the other with the cut-as-you-go disposable stencils used in projection stenciling (see Chapter 8).

We'll also consider two types of surface—real and fake, or faux. On real wood, all the examples shown here were done using transparent colors (water-based gel stains or Oil Bars®) and either traditional or disposable stencils.

The faux surface can be any material, as long as it is flat and has a suitable basecoat of paint. Every part of the surface is given some sort of faux treatment to imitate wood or stone. In this case, the process does not work with traditional stencils, so the composition is all done with disposable ones.

I use only a few of the easier faux-wood and faux-stone methods here, but for more exotic alternatives, check Further Reading for instructional material. The methods described in this chapter would normally be used on fairly small-scale projects, so the choice of mediums does not require a long open time, as it would if you were working on large-scale faux finishing.

Real Wood

When working with a real-wood surface, whether it's plywood veneer or solid, choose a wood with a smooth, tight grain and no knots. It must be unfinished and sanded very smooth. Raise and sand back the grain before applying any water-based product (see Chapter 1). Treating the wood with a wood conditioner before staining, especially when using softwood like pine, will make staining more even and more predictable.

1 The medium should be transparent for both the basecoat and the stenciling. Craft stores usually sell a range of tinted wood stains in the small quantities needed for a novice project. For a basecoat, pick any stain that is suitable for the particular type of wood you have chosen.

2 For the stenciling itself, gel stains work best (oil- or water-based)—they are less prone to seeping under the edge of the stencil. To get the best results, think of gel stains as a type of temperamental transparent paint. Do *not* overwork the stain; this just moves the pigment particles around at the same time the binder is drying, resulting in a blotchy coloration. Instead, when applying the stain through the stencil, work quickly to ensure even and thorough coverage, then stop.

3 For a darker stain, wait until the first coat has thoroughly dried (speed up the process with a hair dryer, if necessary) before adding a second coat—as would be done with paint. Adding more stain before the first coat is completely dry will lift out some of the first coat; then you will truly have a mess.

NOTE: Artist-quality solid oil paints (see Chapter 1) also work well for wood stenciling. They can be worked around as much as you want without blotching problems. To make the colors more transparent and help them settle into the topography of the surface, dampen the brush by wiping it lightly across a paper towel moistened with turpentine. (To avoid an excess of fumes, keep the paper towel in a zip-lock bag between swipes.) Then pick up color on the brush from the surface of the palette, and work it into the bristles.

4 For the finish coat, use a compatible topcoat. I prefer an oil-based varnish, because it brings out the natural golden cast of wood. Make sure the stains have thoroughly dried (i.e., cured) before applying the finish coat, especially if the topcoat has the same solvent as the stain. Otherwise, the finish coat may smudge the stenciling. Check the manufacturer's label to determine how long it should take to dry. If you are concerned about brush marks or smudging, use a spray for the finish coat.

BEFORE WORKING ON A LARGE PIECE, EXPERIMENT WITH PATTERNS AND COLORS ON WOOD-VENEER SAMPLES; THESE WERE DONE WITH TINY DISPOSABLE STENCILS (SEE PAGE 196)

REPEATABLE STENCILS

Using conventional commercial stencils with gel stains or solid oil paints on wood is not much different from stenciling on other hard surfaces, except that mistakes can't always be wiped away unless the wood has been sealed before the stain is applied.

Also, because the colors are completely transparent, you must work from light to dark in terms of overlays and basecoats. In other words, the first step is to stain the entire surface with the lightest color (the equivalent of a basecoat), then use darker stains to stencil the pattern. If the pattern has overlays that put color on top of previously stenciled color, they must be done in successively darker stains.

This kind of stenciling looks most effective when you pick a pattern similar to one that might actually be used in marquetry—for instance, fret borders and geometric diaper patterns.

Try to cut the stencil so that it enhances the effect of "joins" in the inlaid pattern. For example, in the fret border shown below, two overlays were used (one for horizontal bars, one for verticals) to imitate the mitered cuts. The cuts were emphasized by allowing a hair-width overlap along those lines.

Allow the stain to cure, then apply several clear finish coats.

THESE FAUX-MARQUETRY BORDERS ON CLEAR MAPLE WERE DONE USING COMMERCIAL STENCILS

Real Wood

SCORE WOOD AS YOU CUT STENCIL

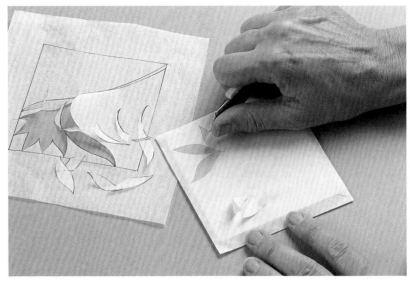

PEEL OFF PATTERN, THEN LIFT STENCIL PIECES FOR FIRST STAIN COLOR

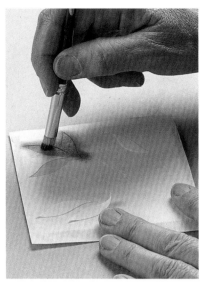

STENCIL EXPOSED WOOD PARTS

SINGLE-USE DISPOSABLE STENCILS

A small-scale version of projection stenciling, this technique does not require a projector, and it produces truly magical results. The scored lines add a tactile dimension and give a really crisp definition to the stain colors. Even woodworkers find it difficult to distinguish this stained version from the real thing.

1 Apply an overall basecoat stain in the lightest color. Let it dry overnight.

2 Trace the pattern onto thin tracing paper, or transfer it directly to the shiny side of a piece of freezer paper large enough to cover the project surface. I prefer to use tracing paper, as it is more accurate.

3 Spray the back of the freezer paper with stencil adhesive, and let dry. Smooth the freezer paper over the project surface. If using a tracing-paper pattern, position it over the freezer paper (here, I'm using TransferRite™ instead), and stick it in place with stencil adhesive.

4 Cut all pattern lines before starting to stencil, drawing the knife through pattern and freezer paper. Use a very sharp blade, and press hard enough so that the knife scores the surface of the wood. This will help prevent stain from bleeding into adjoining sections. Stain also tends to accumulate in the score lines, darkening them and enhancing the impression of real inlaid work.

5 Proceed very carefully— wrong cuts cannot be corrected and will be visible in the finished work. When the cutting is completed, remove all pieces of paper pattern, leaving only the freezer paper.

6 Starting with the lightest stains, lift sections of stencil paper to reveal the parts of the surface to be stained the same color. These pieces have to be replaced later, so number them or stick them to a copy of the pattern.

7 Press down the edges of surrounding exposed openings, using your finger or a burnishing tool. Apply stain or solid oil colors to the openings, more than one coat, if necessary. Work the color into the edges of each cut line for sharp definition.

8 Dry thoroughly; use a hair dryer to save time. Drying is very important, because each area will be masked after it is stenciled. If it is not dry, the mask may not stick properly or may lift some of the stain.

9 When each section is dry, cover it up with the corresponding piece of freezer paper, and lift away the sections to be stained the next color.

10 When all sections are complete, remove all stencil paper, let dry and finish with several coats of varnish. If your stain and varnish have the same solvent, spray the first coat of varnish to prevent smudging.

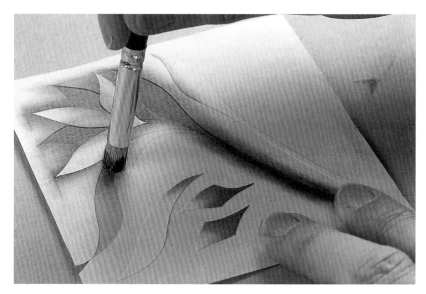

MASK FIRST AREAS STENCILED, THEN REVEAL AND STENCIL NEXT AREAS

For a two-tone variation of this process, try removing color from an already stained surface using the disposable stencil. This works particularly well if you start with a piece that's stained very dark. Wear protective gloves and goggles while doing this.

1 Use a stencil film that will adhere well. Cut the pattern lines, scoring deeply as you go. Remove the cutout pieces of the stencil film. Burnish the cut edges against the wood surface to make sure they are uniformly stuck. Using a worn-out stencil brush (just in case of damage), stipple some gel paint stripper (I used Citristrip) over the stencil. Within a few seconds, the finish and the stain should begin to loosen; swirl the brush around to remove it. Wipe the surface a few times with a clean cloth. Repeat the process until the exposed area is as clear as possible. Wipe the whole area clean of stripper, and wipe down with a neutralizer, if applicable.

2 Remove the remaining stencil pieces. Wash or wipe the surface according to whatever directions apply to the stripper you have used. Allow to dry, then apply a topcoat. This process may not work on all previously stained surfaces, so it's best to do a little testing beforehand.

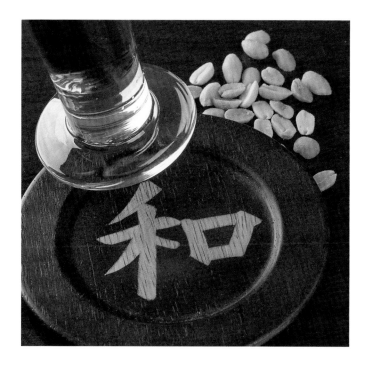

Faux Wood

You need a very smooth painted surface as a base for this treatment. Painted wood, medium-density fiberboard (MDF) and metal are all good candidates.

1 First, prime the surface with a suitable primer. Basecoat the surface with several coats—either white or a paint color appropriate to the wood you want to imitate. Using white allows you to apply different basecoat colors to each faux-wood section as you come to it.

2 Create a pattern that outlines the shapes to be filled by each type of faux wood.

3 Follow the same steps as for disposable stencils (see page 196), with two excep-tions. First, instead of staining each section, you will be applying a faux-wood tech-nique. Second, when cutting through the freezer paper, do *not* score the underlying surface. It's all right to scratch the paint layer, but don't cut right through the base-coat and primer. It may cause the paint to chip, and in the case of MDF, it will cause localized swelling. For this reason, you need a very sharp blade and a stencil material that is very easy to cut. I used freezer paper, but you may find low-tack frisket film easier.

4 Wood-grain effects are produced by manipulating glazes over a colored basecoat. If the project is small, however, you do not need or want a slow-drying glaze, so pick something with a short open time. Even so, use a hair dryer to speed up the drying process.

5 Now follow the basic projection-stencil-ing method. After each section has been given a faux-wood finish, let it dry, then re-place the stencil piece to cover it up. Expose the next sections, give them a different fin-ish, and continue until the surface has been completed. Remove all stencil pieces.

6 Let the faux-wood treatments dry thor-oughly. Finish the surface with several coats of varnish in a satin or glossy sheen. Since most wood tones have some degree of yellow in them, oil-based varnish can be used, if you wish, without affecting the colors adversely.

LIFT FREEZER PAPER TO EXPOSE LARGE DIAMONDS, AND APPLY MAPLE FINISH

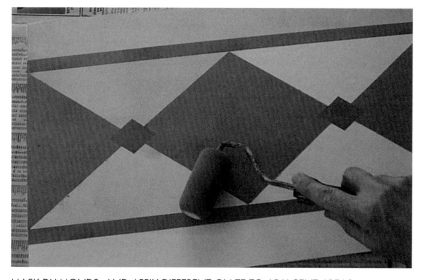

MASK DIAMONDS, AND APPLY DIFFERENT GLAZE TO ADJACENT AREAS

MANIPULATE GLAZE TO CREATE DIFFERENT WOOD GRAINS

SIMPLE FAUX WOOD

1 To do a simple faux wood, start with an eggshell or semigloss basecoat in the lightest color you want showing. It could be yellow, raw sienna or terra-cotta, for example, depending on the particular wood you want to imitate.

2 When the basecoat is fully dry, apply a colored glaze—usually some kind of brown—then manipulate it to produce graining marks. When working with a disposable stencil, use a thick glaze or even a gel stain to minimize the chance of bleeding. Apply the glaze thinly with a roller-stenciling method.

NOTE: Another way to avoid bleeding is to roller stencil a fresh basecoat over each new section. As it dries, it will seal the edges of the freezer paper, allowing you to faux to your heart's content.

3 For the look of inlaid wood, you must simulate several kinds of wood by using different glaze colors and different graining methods. Each type of tool that is dragged through the glaze (graining comb, folded burlap, graining rocker) will produce a different grain pattern. These basic patterns can then be modified by adding or removing glaze with an eraser or an artist's brush.

4 After using a graining tool, soften the impressions made in the glaze by stippling or blending with a very soft brush. More complex wood imitations can be achieved by combining methods and creating multistep processes. There are several references to instructional books in Further Reading.

Faux Stone (Pietre Dure)

The process here is exactly the same as for the faux wood, except that paint and glaze are used to imitate marble and other stones instead of exotic woods (see page 81). Further Reading contains references to many possible "stone" recipes. Those illustrated here are very simple.

Stone inlay can have a fine grouting between the sections. To imitate this, outline the pieces in acrylic ink after the whole surface has been finished. The pattern used here was adapted from a centuries-old Italian tabletop of pietre dure.

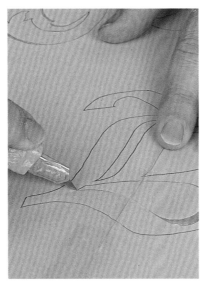

CUT WITHOUT SCORING SURFACE

LIFT BACKGROUND PIECE OF FREEZER PAPER

WITH SCROLLS AND MONOGRAM MASKED, SPONGE TWO COLORS FOR FIRST STEP OF MARBLE FINISH

REPLACE BACKGROUND MASK; EXPOSE CORNER SCROLLS AND MONOGRAM   CREATE LIGHT MARBLE INLAY

Chapter 12

FAUX TILES

Simulated tiles can be a very useful decorative element, especially on surfaces where it might be difficult to install real tiles or where you want to match specific colors and motifs. Faux tiles and faux mosaic can be applied almost anywhere—on furniture, floors and decorative objects, as well as wall borders. Remember, though, that faux items are just a painted illusion. No matter how well they are sealed, they do not have the durability or water-repellent quality of real tiles. They are therefore not appropriate for any surface exposed to water, steam or vigorous cleaning.

Use stencils and paint for a traditional approach to faux tiles, or replace the paint with a plaster medium for an impasto effect (see Chapter 4). There are a few pointers to keep in mind when designing tiles. Using a less-than-perfect placement grid and a slight variation in individual shapes gives the tiles more of a hand-made look. To impart an aged appearance, include some chipped and broken pieces and some worn corners. If you need inspiration, check out some tile catalogs or books on tiles and mosaics. Ancient Romans were particularly fond of mosaic floors and left behind a wealth of exquisite designs, so it's worthwhile to check your library for books on Roman architecture.

Terra-Cotta Tiles

1 Paint the entire surface in the color you want for the grout between the tiles. For the effect of plain concrete grouting, roll or brush out about 90 percent coverage in taupe. Before it dries, use a sea sponge to apply white and a small amount of black randomly. Blend the colors roughly with the sponge. The color variation should appear random.

2 When the surface has dried, spatter it with fine dots of watered-down brown paint, followed by a spattering of black paint. (If the spattering paint is too thick, it will leave small raised bumps on the surface.) The dots of color should be flat and look like grains of sand. My favorite spattering tool is an inexpensive rotating brush by Loew-Cornell. It provides

pretty good control, unlike the old standby toothbrush.

3 Let the grout basecoat dry overnight before stenciling the tiles. Several stenciled coats of paint are needed to cover the grout. Pick an opaque color for the first coat; it should be similar to the final color, but at this point, opaque coverage is more important than exact color. Use

a stencil roller for speed and uniform application. As soon as this first coat is dry enough, roller stencil a second coat. If the first coat provides opaque coverage, the second coat can be terra-cotta in color; otherwise, do one more basecoat. Let the terra-cotta color dry completely before proceeding.

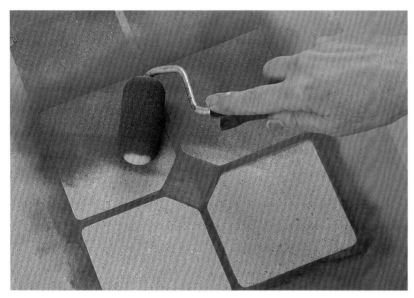

STENCIL SEVERAL LAYERS OF PAINT TO COVER FAUX-GROUT BACKGROUND

ADD COLORED STREAKS WITH FLAT ARTIST'S BRUSH OR BLENDING BRUSH

RUN SHARP PENCIL FIRMLY AROUND EDGE OF ALL STENCIL OPENINGS

FOR SHADING, RUB MIX OF GLAZE AND RAW UMBER OVER PENCIL LINES

4 Reposition the tile stencil. Select two colors to add some variation to individual tiles—for example, a very warm yellow and a terra-cotta that's different from the original, maybe darker or more orange. Use a flat artist's brush to apply these colors in streaks and patches, working on one tile at a time (to prevent bleeding, avoid brushing right into the edge of the stencil). As soon as the paint has been applied, stipple it or blend the streaks to eliminate brush marks. Make each tile slightly different.

5 Stencil the small accent tiles in a different color. Here, I've used white. Let the tiles dry overnight.

6 The next step is to make everything look less flat by shading the edges. Place the stencil back over the tiles. Trace the edge of each tile with a sharp lead pencil, keeping the point of the pencil right next to the stencil edge. With a small stencil brush (¼-½ inch), rub a mix of glaze and raw umber along the tile edges. It will cover and blend with the pencil lines, leaving a fine dark line at the very edge of the tiles and tapered shading that indicates the curve of the tile surface. If the shading expands too widely, wipe it back with a damp cloth wrapped around your index finger.

7 For projects that call for a large area of stenciled tiles, the shading does not have to be quite so detailed, especially if the work will not be viewed up close. In this case, skip the pencil outline, and do brush shading as you go.

8 Let the work dry for a few days, then apply several clear finish coats in a semigloss or gloss sheen. Use a product formulated to go over a painted surface. When this is dry, you may wish to apply a flat finish coat over the grout lines only, working freehand with an artist's brush. However, if this is a floor treatment, you might be better off leaving the entire surface glossy, since flat finishes underfoot tend to grab onto dirt.

Glazed Tiles

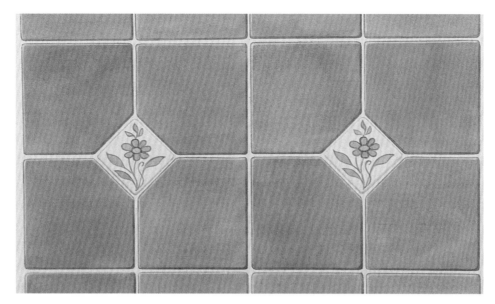

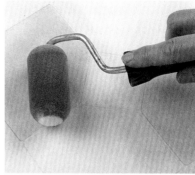

ROLLER STENCIL BASE COLOR OF TILE

ADD PATTERNS AS DESIRED

RUB SHADOW COLOR ALONG EDGE
OF TILE STENCIL WITH SMALL BRUSH

The method for faking regular glazed tiles is almost the same as that for terracotta tiles, except the grout is usually quite plain and the tiles are generally placed closer together. This means starting with a plain basecoat. You can even use white and add any grout color by hand at the end. If the stencil material is thin, cut only a single tile into the stencil or cut every other tile to avoid having fragile bridges.

1 Begin by making a thin pencil outline through the stencil. This gives greater definition to the boundary between tile and grout, especially with pastel tiles. Then roller stencil the base color of the tiles, using more than one coat, if necessary. The paint seals and mutes the pencil lines.

2 Stencil any overlays that add pattern, and let these overlays dry overnight before continuing so that the process of shading the tile edges does not smudge the pattern.

3 Now add form shadows on all shaded edges of the tiles. The easiest way to do this is a version of the drop shadow. Leave the stencil in place (rather than shifting it),

and use a shifted mask over the tile to cover all but a narrow strip on the shaded sides of the tile. (For the mask, simply use the cutout left from cutting the stencil.) Stencil this strip with transparent shadow color.

4 If you prefer tapered shading, use a very small stencil brush to rub shadow color along the edge of the tile stencil.

5 Highlights can be added to the other edges of the tiles with the same methods used for shading or by doing them freehand with a fine artist's brush or a fine paint pen.

6 Let the work dry for several days, then seal it with a few coats of a glossy sealer (one formulated to go over paint).

7 If you want a contrasting sheen on the thin grout lines, go over them freehand with a flat sealer, using a fine artist's brush and an elevated straight edge (i.e., a ruler with spacers underneath that raise the edge up enough to prevent bleeding and to let the ferrule rest against it). Or seal the entire surface first with a flat finish, then roller stencil a glossy finish onto the tile shapes only.

Glazed Tiles Antiqued With Crackle Finish

1 A transparent craquelure finish will instantly age faux glazed tiles. First, stencil the tiles as outlined in the previous section. Let the paint dry thoroughly. Review the craquelure method described on page 112.

2 For a large surface, you may find it easier simply to purchase a craquelure kit rather than do the traditional gum arabic method. Follow the manufacturer's instructions to apply the clear craquelure finish to the entire surface. This is easier than trying to apply it to individual tiles through a stencil. Let this dry overnight.

3 Apply a raw umber glaze to the surface, or depending on the product instructions, rub a little raw umber artist's oil paint over the surface. Wipe off the excess, leaving color only in the cracks. Apply whatever clear finish coat is recommended in the craquelure kit.

4 Finally, use a fine artist's brush and an elevated straight edge to repaint the grout lines (covering up the cracks in the grout), and add highlights.

Faux Tiles in 3-D

This is a variation on the impasto stenciling methods described in Chapter 4. There are a couple of different ways to start this process, depending on how you want the grout to look. In this example, I have opted for the simplest approach—one where all parts of the surface end up the same color. If you want the grout to be a different color, basecoat the surface with the grout color before adding the tiles.

1 Stencil the basic tile shapes with a plaster medium. Let this dry slowly and fully. For colored tiles, either pretint the medium or apply color after the surface has dried.

2 To add a raised motif to the tiles, apply a second layer of plaster with an overlay stencil. Two overlay applications were used on the tiles that are shown here: one for a broad "X" shape and the other for the decorative motif. Let each overlay dry completely before adding the next one on top.

3 Apply a sealer to the tiles, if necessary (i.e., for nonacrylic mediums). If you haven't used a tinted medium, now is the time to add color—either to the whole surface or, with the help of the first square stencil, to the tiles only.

4 To accentuate the relief of the tiles, finish by rubbing them with a tinted glaze or tinted sealer so that extra color accumulates in the crevices.

COVER BASIC TILE SHAPE WITH BROAD "X" OVERLAY AND PLASTER MEDIUM

FOR DEPTH AND DETAIL, ADD OVERLAY STENCIL WITH RAISED MOTIF

Mosaic Tiles

Mosaic tile has a timeless appeal and is currently enjoying a resurgence in popularity at both hobby-craft and professional levels. Faux mosaic offers the do-it-yourself enthusiast many creative possibilities on different scales of endeavor. It can be stenciled over entire floors, used as borders or applied to furniture and myriad small decorative objects.

The pieces used in a real mosaic are called tesserae and can be stone, terra-cotta, marble or glass. There are two main categories of historical design, both given names by the ancient Romans, who were masters of mosaic design and installation. Opus tesselatum refers to a mosaic composed of almost identical rectangular pieces (about ¾-inch square) arranged to form either a geometric or a pictorial design. Opus vermiculatum is a mosaic made up of pieces that are not uniform and are often not rectangular. The pieces are set in curving paths that follow the contours of the design. You can design your mosaic stencil in one style or the other.

NOTE: If you plan to stencil with paint only, separate the pattern into overlays according to color. If you are using an impasto medium such as plaster, however, the entire piece should be cut as one stencil. In any case, the stencils must be cut with great care, as the bridges (i.e., the spaces between the tesserae) should be narrow and are therefore easy to cut through accidentally.

Mosaic Tiles

STENCIL BLACK TILES OVER SPECKLED
GROUT BASECOAT

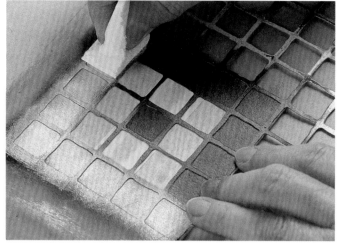

REPAINT SELECTED TILES IN WHITE, USING A DIRTY STENCIL AND
TAPPING LIGHTLY WITH A MAKEUP SPONGE

NOTE: If you want to get
the feel of the mosaic pattern
without even pretending it's the
real thing, try making a "ghost"
print. Stencil the design over
the grout basecoat using very
subdued colors. Then load a
clean stencil brush with a slow-
drying colorless glaze. Offload
any excess onto a paper towel,
and work the brush around over
all the stencil openings, using a
circular motion. This should re-
open the paint and push some
of it into the edge of the openings. Wipe with a clean, soft
cloth, picking up the paint in
the middle of the openings.
When you lift the stencil, all
the tesserae should be almost
grout-colored, with only a thin
outline defining the shapes.

MOSAIC WITH PAINT

1 The technique for sten-
ciling faux mosaic with
paint is pretty much the
same as for the faux-tile
methods already described.
Paint a basecoat that will be
the grout, then stencil the
mosaic pattern over top,
using as many overlays as
there are colors. Stencil
a couple of coats to get
opaque coverage. For a
long border or a floorcloth
that won't be seen up close,
that's all you need to do.

2 A very small project,
such as a set of coasters
or a little box, might require
more detailed shading. The
usual methods don't work
well, because the tesserae
are small and close to-
gether, making it difficult
to shade individual cutouts.
What you can do, instead

—especially for the light-
colored pieces that need
sharp contrast to pop out
visually from the grout—
is stencil them first with a
very dark color, even black.
Use a clean stencil, and
work the paint right into the
edge of the stencil cutouts.
I use a roller for quick basic
coverage, then use a brush
to get into the edges.

3 For the next step, you
need a dirty stencil—
one with enough paint
buildup that the cutouts
are a hair smaller than on
a clean stencil. Place the
stencil precisely over the
dark print you just did. Use
the flat end of a makeup
sponge to make a new print
in light-colored paint. Tap
the sponge gently so that the
color does not go right into
the very edges of the cutouts. You want good coverage, but you also want that

"halo" effect, with the white
print ever so slightly smaller
than the black one. In the end
result in this example, the
white pieces have a very fine
black outline. It should look
a bit like dirt caught in the
grout at the edge of the tile.

OPUS VERMICULATUM BORDER WAS DONE WITH STRAIGHTFORWARD APPLICATION OF PAINT AND THREE-OVERLAY STENCIL

IN THIS VERSION OF SAME STENCIL, PAINT (SUBDUED COLORS) WAS SOFTENED AND IMMEDIATELY WIPED OFF WITH STENCIL STILL IN PLACE

Mosaic Tiles

MOSAIC WITH IMPASTO

The impasto stenciling method works wonderfully with mosaic stencils. The plaster not only gives completely opaque coverage of whatever grout colors you choose but also gives a tactile sense that the mosaic pieces are slightly raised above the grout. The only drawback is that you must use a single-overlay stencil, creating an entire repeat in one pass. This means that the whole piece is initially stenciled with the same color of plaster, since the medium is scraped over the stencil with a large spatula. Color is added later. If you wish to try this approach, review the section on impasto stenciling in Chapter 4.

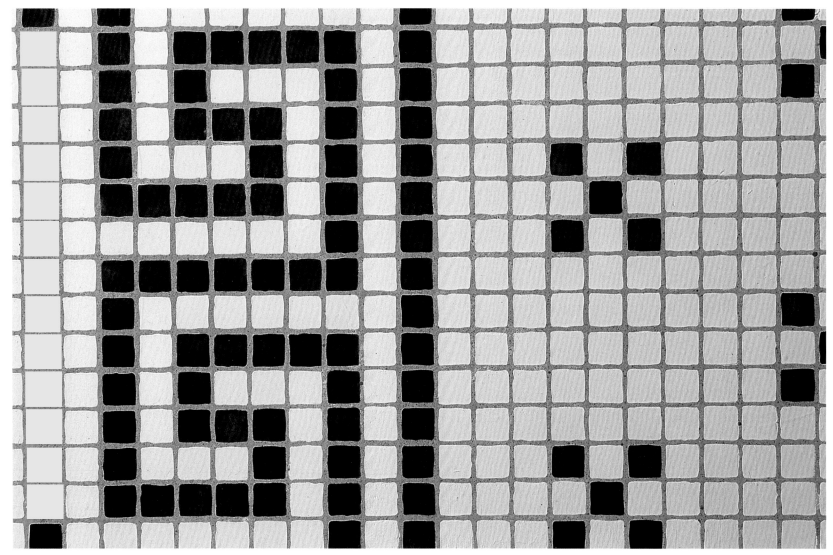

OPUS TESSELATUM DESIGN

USE LARGE SPATULA TO PULL LAYER OF PLASTER OVER TILE STENCIL

INITIALLY, ALL TILES ARE SAME COLOR

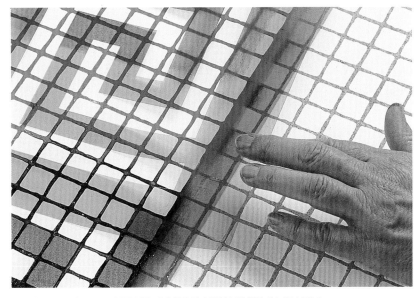

REPLACE CLEAN TILE STENCIL; POSITION FRET OVERLAY ON TOP

TILE STENCIL MASKS GROUT WHILE FRET PATTERN IS STENCILED

1 Start with a surface basecoated to look like grout. Here, the basecoat was sponged and spattered with "concrete" colors.

2 Use a single-overlay stencil to cover the surface with plaster mosaic. (When it is dry, the plaster will shrink a little in thickness, so if you wish to increase the relief, reposition the stencil and make a second plaster application.)

3 Once the plaster has dried and been sealed, apply stenciled paint color to selected parts of the dried plaster by careful use of stencil and masks, as shown above.

4 Paint selected tiles to make either borders or scattered motifs. To do this without getting paint on the grout or without cutting detailed overlays, mask the grout with the original tile stencil and cover the tile stencil with an overlay that reveals only the broad areas to be stenciled.

5 This means placing a clean tile stencil over the dried white tiles, as shown here, then laying a fret stencil on top so that the tiles which make up the fret pattern can be stenciled black.

6 The fret motif can be moved along for repeats as long as the tile stencil is still under it to mask the grout. When you reach the end of the masked area, lift both stencil pieces and move them to the next section.

Chapter 13

GLASS, CERAMIC TILE

The creative possibilities for stenciling on difficult surfaces such as glass and ceramic tile have expanded enormously in recent years, because chemists in the hobby-paint industry have developed new products specially designed for these surfaces. It's important to pick the right product for the job, however. For example, some paints work better than others with stencils (most are meant primarily for freehand work), and some are more permanent than others. Several types of glass and ceramic paint must be cured in the oven to harden, so that obviously won't work for windows. Also, because the surfaces are so slippery, the usual methods for making a basic stencil print aren't very effective.

Etching Glass

This treatment is the real thing, and it's permanent. It etches the actual surface of the glass, leaving a very fine, evenly frosted finish. The process is easy and inexpensive, and it works well with stencils. The only drawback is that the chemical product can be tricky to use on a vertical surface, because unless it's extremely viscous, it may slide off the stencil. The etching creams that I've tried have varied a lot in consistency, from yogurt softness to cold-peanut-butter stiffness. Unless you get the latter, you generally have to count on working on a horizontal surface, which is easy for tabletops, mirrors or even doors but can be problematic for windows, especially those old ones painted into the frame of the house.

Etching requires contravening the most basic diehard rule of stenciling, which is "offload, offload, offload." Instead, the etching cream is literally spooned on top of the stencil. If you haven't done this before, you just *know* it's going to bleed under the edge of the stencil. But, amazingly, it doesn't, not if the stencil is firmly adhered to the surface. The reason is that the etching cream or gel is thixotropic—its normal state is at least as viscous as thick yogurt, too thick for capillary action. However, if stirred, it liquefies. This is the same property possessed by river delta soils; if shaken by a severe earthquake, land that normally supports tall buildings and freeways becomes liquid enough to swallow them up.

Etching works best with stencils made of self-adhesive vinyl (e.g., shelf liner) cut out directly on the glass itself and with commercial stencils cut from various kinds of adhesive plastic, because these stencils have a solid film of adhesive (instead of a spray of droplets) that resists bleeding. But it also works surprisingly well with ordinary commercial stencils, as long as stencil adhesive is used to keep the template in close contact with the surface.

PATTERN UNDER GLASS, STENCIL ON TOP

SPOON CREAM OVER EXPOSED AREA

USE SPATULA TO REMOVE CREAM

THE PROCESS

1 Clean the glass or mirror surface with alcohol, vinegar or soapy water, and rinse thoroughly. Dry with a paper towel or lint-free cloth.

2 A precut stencil should be either self-adhesive or sprayed on the back with stencil adhesive. Position the stencil, and rub firmly in place with a lint-free cloth or paper towel. Proceed to Step 3.

2a If the design is relatively simple and you're working with a hand-cut stencil, consider cutting a single-use stencil right on the glass. Cover the surface with a sheet of self-adhesive vinyl, such as MacTac™ or Rubbermaid Con-Tact Ultra™ (in clear or translucent white).

2b Stick the pattern to the other side of the glass so that it is visible through the vinyl.

PRECUT SELF-ADHESIVE STENCIL

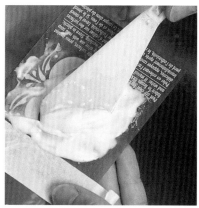

PILE ON CREAM, THEN SCRAPE OFF

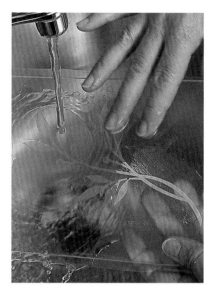

RINSE THOROUGHLY WITH WATER

PEEL AWAY STENCIL

2c Use a sharp utility knife to cut the vinyl along the pattern lines, and remove the cut-out pieces. To avoid distortion caused by the thickness of the glass that separates the pattern and the vinyl, look straight down on the pattern while cutting. For maximum adhesion, rub down all cut edges with a credit card.

3 Here's the part that is hard for fastidious stencilers. With a small spoon or spatula, scoop etching cream out of its container, and spread it over all parts exposed by the stencil. For stencils with large cutouts, spoon the cream onto the stencil margin and pull it smoothly over the area with a spatula to ensure even etching. Let the cream sit for the time recommended on the label. Do *not* use a brush. Do *not* work the cream around —this will only liquefy it.

4 Use a spatula to remove most of the cream, and re-turn it to the jar for reuse.

5 With the stencil still in place, flood the glass surface thoroughly with water to remove all remaining cream.

6 Remove the stencil, and rinse again, or simply remove the stencil under water. Make sure that no etching cream gets on a spot that's not supposed to be etched.

SURGICAL BRUSH HELPS RINSING

REVERSE ETCHING

1 To etch most of the surface and have the motif clear, leave the motif "sticker" part of the cut stencil in place, and remove all the rest of the vinyl. Rub the sticker down firmly for good adhesion.

2 Apply a large amount of etching medium to one end of the glass, then spread it quickly over the whole surface with a wide spatula or squeegee.

3 Let it sit for the time recommended on the label before removing the excess and rinsing under running water. Then remove the sticker.

NOTE: Etching is easy and yields beautiful results. The only precaution is that the etching chemical is toxic, so this is not a product for kids' crafts. Read the label carefully, and follow the safety instructions.

Painting Glass and Glazed Ceramics

There are two types of paint for glass and glazed ceramics: those which air-dry to final hardness and those which need baking in the oven to cure. The application is the same for both.

In general, the heat-cured paints are more resistant to scratching—they pass the fingernail test. But if you need to get rid of them, they do come off with a razor blade and a little elbow grease. These paints are not acrylic (so don't confuse them with ordinary craft paints), but they are water-based, and soap-and-water cleanup will work for your tools.

■ The air-dried paints may take a week or so to become fully resistant, depending on both the brand and the thickness of application. From my own experience, they can take anywhere from a few hours to 10 days. So it's important to read the label carefully, lest you be too cavalier with your objet d'art before it's ready.

■ Whether air-dried or oven-cured, the paints should be dishwasher-, oven- and microwave-safe, but once again, check the instructions for each particular brand to make sure. Also check to see whether the paint is officially approved as food-safe. If not, then the painted decoration of any kitchen utensil or dinnerware must be confined to parts that won't end up with dinner served on them or have teeth chewing them. This is not really a big problem; the underside of a clear-glass plate or the part of a glass that does not come into contact with food or lips can be stenciled. Inadvertent contact with food is not usually a health hazard. However, if you cut up a steak over some stenciled ivy, you're going to create scratches—hazardous to your artwork, if not your health. To be absolutely sure that something is safe, call the manufacturer and ask. All companies have toll-free help lines as well as e-mail addresses for just this sort of question.

■ I must stress the importance of making sure you have the right product for the job. A single brand name may offer more than one line of so-called glass paints, but look closely, because one may be specifically designed for glass only, whereas another may be the better choice for ceramic tiles or porcelain teacups.

DELIBERATELY TEMPORARY

When we were kids, our mother used to let us paint the windows at Christmas. There was a catch, though: We had to use her homemade paint. The formula was simple and pretty clever. She mixed up the same runny white paste she used for cleaning the windows—Bon Ami® (a powdered cleanser) and a little water. We could tint it with poster paints if we wanted, but mostly, we used it plain white to paint snowflakes on every window within reach. It was a great way to keep three little kids happy, and Mom got clean windows when it was time for us to wash it all off.

This "paint" works with stencils too, and it's perfect when you don't want the decoration to last forever. Apply it by pouncing with a fine sponge. Ordinary latex paint can also be used for temporary decoration. It's not meant to bond to glass and can be cleaned off without too much effort.

SNOWFLAKE MODELED AFTER A MICROSCOPIC PHOTO POSTED ON THE INTERNET

FAUX ETCHING

One of the problems with etching glass for real is that it's definitely permanent. Also, most etching products generally must be applied to a horizontal surface. If your surface just has to stay vertical or if you might want to change the design in a year or so, then it's time for faux etching. This is very easy, involving no more than stenciling with translucent white glass paint. Several companies make their own brands of paint for this very purpose. If there is a choice of finishes, choose frosted or flat sheen to imitate real etched glass. The effect of this faux treatment is very realistic, although when placed beside the real thing, the latter has a noticeably finer texture.

FAUX ETCHED BORDER GIVES DAMAGED GLASS NEW LIFE

1 The first step in the process is to clean the glass or mirror. Wash, rinse thoroughly, and dry completely. Then clean it with alcohol to make sure there is absolutely no grease left. Some brands of paint require their own special conditioner to prepare the surface and a glaze to seal the paint afterward. Do not skip these steps if called for.

APPLY PAINT WITH MAKEUP SPONGE

2 As with real etching, use a standard reusable stencil or a single-use stencil cut directly on the glass surface (see Etching Glass on page 216).

3 Stencil large areas with a roller-stenciling method, using a high-density foam stencil roller and offloading well beforehand. Apply several thin layers.

■ For small projects, use a makeup sponge, applying the paint with a light pouncing action. Again, it is very important to offload the sponge and to use a light touch to avoid bleeding. Glass has no absorbency whatsoever.

4 Remove the stencil. Any mistakes can be scraped off with a knife blade, although it's much easier to get it right the first time.

■ For air-dried paint, allow the object to cure undisturbed for whatever time is indicated on the paint label. It is very vulnerable to scratching during this time. If a sealer is required, apply it according to the label instructions.

■ For heat-cured paints, follow the label instructions. This usually means air-drying for 24 hours, then putting the glass piece into the oven, turning it on to a specified temperature and baking for a set time. When it is done, turn off the oven, open the door and let the piece cool down with the oven. Don't be dismayed if the colors appear burned when you first look in the oven. They revert to normal as they cool.

■ To add fine frosted lines as a frame or decorative accent, use the neutral frosted felt-tip pen sold by Pebeo. This pen makes lines that are virtually indistinguishable from real etching.

Painting Glass and Glazed Ceramics

CERAMIC TILES, DISHES, GLASSWARE

This process is exactly the same as for faux etching of glass (see page 219), except there's a huge choice of colors and sheens, including satin, glossy and frosted. Again, if the label recommends a particular preconditioner and topcoat, be sure to use them.

1 When using Mylar stencils, stick to flat surfaces. Otherwise, use thin adhesive vinyl or freezer paper, which can be molded, to a certain degree, to fit the shape required. Try to burnish the edges down as much as possible.

2 While thin stenciled layers pounced or rolled on with dense foam produce the perfect translucent, slightly textured coat needed to imitate etching, they won't give you intense color. Glass and ceramic paints show up to best advantage when applied generously, an approach that usually spells disaster for stenciling.

3 For strong color, stencil a first coat, then use this as a pattern for going over the whole thing freehand with an artist's brush, carefully following the stenciled design. Use a generous coat with your freehand painting.

4 Another way to make thinly stenciled color stand out is by outlining the shapes, as described in Chapter 4. Apply the same paint with a fine squeeze bottle for a strongly colored outline. Or purchase an outline pen made expressly for glass and tile surfaces.

POUNCE PAINT ON TILE WITH MAKEUP SPONGE

FOR A BOLDER LOOK, OUTLINE PATTERN FREEHAND

Gold Leaf

STENCILED TO UNDERSIDE OF GLASS COASTER, GOLD LEAF WON'T BE SCRATCHED FROM USE

Gold leaf looks stunning on glass. However, it's a very fragile medium, and at first glance, it might seem more appropriate for decorating objects that are only looked at rather than used.

The solution is to apply the leaf to the underside of the glass so that it doesn't get scratched. (Painted glass can be protected the same way. Just remember that the first paint layer applied will appear to be on top of the other layers when viewed from the reverse side. Therefore, the background color must be the last layer painted.)

1 Stenciling gold leaf on glass is the same process as the method described in Chapter 4, except that it is stenciled on the back of the object. After cleaning the surface, tape the stencil in place. Use a fine makeup sponge to stipple gold size through the stencil.

2 Remove the stencil, and let the size dry to the prescribed tackiness.

3 Lay down a leaf of real or composition gold over the size. Tap it in place with a very soft brush. As the brush is worked around, it will fix the gold in place where there is adhesive and dust away the excess where there is not. Apply sealer to finish.

Impasto Stenciling

USE UNIFORM BEAD OF GEL

HOLD SPATULA AT LOW ANGLE, AND DRAW GEL ACROSS STENCIL

At the time of printing, there was just one product available for tough relief stenciling on glass: a thixotropic water-based medium called Gel Crystal, by Pebeo. It adheres well to a variety of surfaces, but the results are most stunning on glass. The process is quite simple and works best with a thick (7-10 mil) stencil. With anything thinner, the colors are rather pale. Such a thick stencil, however, can really only be used on a flat surface.

1 After the usual cleaning and degreasing of the glass surface, place the stencil flat on the glass, with stencil adhesive holding it firmly in place.

2 Squeeze a small amount of gel along the edge of a clean paint spatula or palette knife slightly wider than the stencil motif.

3 Holding the spatula at a low angle, pull it slowly over the stencil opening in one fell swoop, pressing very slightly. The stencil opening should be filled uniformly, level with the thickness of the stencil material.

4 Hold the stencil on opposite edges, and very carefully lift it straight up, to prevent smudging. (Stencils with floppy parts can be difficult to lift cleanly, so start with well-bridged, stable stencils.)

NOTE: Because the medium is available in crystalline, opaline and iridescent colors, there's lots of opportunity for creativity. For the look of fossilized amber, for example, try embedding a mosquito in an ocher or amber-brown sample.

Faux Stained Glass and Cloisonné

These effects can't be called stenciling by any stretch of the imagination, but they do allow stenciled motifs that may appear elsewhere in your decor to be replicated. For example, suppose you have a flight of stenciled butterflies rambling across a wall that has a glass-fronted cabinet. That line of butterflies could be continued on the glass in the cabinet as "stained glass" or "cloisonné." Or the motif could extend across a window by placing the butterflies on glass suncatchers.

The two methods are the same, except for the color of the material used to outline the stencil. Make sure you pick paints and liners within the same product line so that they will be compatible and have the same curing requirements.

1 Work on a horizontal surface. If it's a cabinet door, unscrew the hinge and place the door flat on a worktable.

2 Tape the stencil to the underside of the glass to act as a pattern.

3 Before doing the outline on glass, squeeze some liner onto a paper towel to get rid of air bubbles that sometimes form in the tip.

4 Hold the tube of liner product like a pencil, and squeeze it gently while drawing the tip along the edges of the stencil cutouts, seen through the glass. The line—black for stained glass, gold for cloisonné—will appear slightly three-dimensional. Let it dry.

5 Now fill the sections with transparent glass paint, following the label directions. The liner keeps each color confined to one area. Allow to dry and cure according to the instructions.

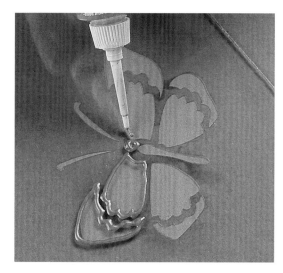

OUTLINE TRAPS GLASS PAINT

Chapter 14

UNDER FOOT

O f all the restorative and decorative options available for sprucing up a floor in dire need of rescue, paint has to be the least expensive choice and the one that offers the most creative possibilities. Whether it's hardwood, vinyl, concrete or simply the plywood subfloor of a cottage that will see another decade of seasonal occupation before completion, as long as you can get a primer or a floor paint that will stick to the surface (and nowadays, there are specialty paints for just about any surface), then you can bring out your stencils and unleash your imagination on a pretty big scale.

Floor treatments don't have to be reserved only for old and worn surfaces. Some of the decorative options, such as stenciled borders and stenciled parquet patterns, are just as appropriate for new floors.

The stenciling methods used on floors are much like those already described in previous chapters, except that you have to work on your hands and knees, which can be physically tiring. Another difference with floors is the amount of abuse they must endure. Your artistic efforts may have to shrug off the wear and tear of boots, runners and high heels, spilled milk and broken dishes, dragged furniture and muddy dogs.

This means choosing your materials with care and with an eye to endurance. Use paints and stains that are meant for use underfoot, and finish with several coats of sealer for protection. Ordinary acrylics are fine for the stencil work, as long as they are topped with a protective sealer.

Stenciled Floors

Preparation is a huge part of a successful floor project, no matter how simple or elaborate. Start by making a scaled-down diagram on grid paper, laying out the dimensions of the floor and the stencil elements. Borders and all-over patterns underfoot are no different from those on a wall, so a review of Chapters 5 and 6 will help you figure out the logistics of arranging the motifs.

FLOOR PREPARATION

It is essential to prepare the floor to provide a good working surface. This doesn't necessarily mean stripping and sanding back to bare wood, unless you want the look of new wood. If you plan to paint the floor, just sink any protruding nails, fill nail holes and sand the surface sufficiently to give it tooth for the primer to hold. For vinyl, strip any wax, clean thoroughly with TSP or ammonia, rinse well, and sand to a dull finish. Concrete should have cured for at least a month. Etch the surface of the concrete by applying one part muriatic acid to three parts water, then rinse well with water.

■ Choose a primer suitable for the floor material. If in doubt, ask your paint dealer to recommend a product. Make sure the floor is completely clean, dry and free of any sanding dust. The easiest way to apply the primer is with a long-handled roller, after cutting in the perimeter with a brush. Let the primer dry according to the manufacturer's instructions, then apply the basecoat. Be-

cause you will have to walk and crawl around on the floor while stenciling, the basecoat should be allowed to dry for several days before you continue. Even then, work only in stocking feet (with clean socks!).

■ Before stenciling on bare wood, you may wish to stain the surface first. It's not always easy to obtain an even stain over such a large surface, so ask for advice on the best product for the type of wood you have. Consider treating the floor with a wood conditioner beforehand. This partially seals the surface, ensuring a more even stain application. Choose a finish coat or varnish at the same time you select the stain so that you'll end up with compatible products.

■ If you stencil on bare wood, there's not much that can be done to correct a mistake. However, if you apply a thin coat of clear sealer to the surface before you begin, the stenciled paint doesn't soak into the wood and can be more easily wiped off if caught in time. Don't use a chalk line on the bare wood—it won't come off without sanding.

PARQUET TILES CAN BE USED AS A GRID FOR BORDER PLACEMENT

REGISTRATION

For an all-over pattern, a registration grid must be marked on the floor to keep the pattern properly spaced. The easiest way to do this is with a chalk line (but *not* on bare wood).

1 To measure a grid on the floor, start by measuring and marking the center points of two opposite walls. Snap a chalk line between them. Do the same for the other pair of opposite walls.

2 Starting at the center of each side of the floor, measure off the intervals of the grid on both sides of center. Match up grid marks on opposite sides of the floor, and snap a chalk line between them. This will produce a complete grid. The lines may have to be fudged a little when you get close to the walls, because the room may not be perfectly square.

3 Wherever you can't use a chalk line (on bare wood, for example), use lengths of string instead, held in place with pieces of putty adhesive. You'll have to move carefully within the room to avoid tripping over or dislodging the strings. And, of course, each string must be moved temporarily when you are stenciling under it.

NOTE: Sometimes it's possible to get away without any of this detailed measuring. Regularly spaced floorboards, parquet squares or embossed vinyl flooring can act as a guideline for a perimeter border or as a grid to align all-over motifs.

STENCILING

Once the floor has been prepped to the point of a painted or stained basecoat and a grid of guidelines has been set in place, the stenciling and finishing are pretty much the same, no matter what the surface. The job will go easier and faster, however, if you pay some attention to its ergonomics.

■ Buy well-cushioned knee pads or a thick kneeling pad. Set the palette, paints, brushes and rollers on a large rimmed tray. At regular intervals, stand up and stretch your legs. (For extra protection, place the tray on a piece of drop cloth large enough for the stencils as well. As you move, drag the cloth and tray with you.)

■ Consider using a stencil roller instead of a stencil brush, as it is much faster. Or make a compromise, and do the basic stenciling with a roller, and the details or shading with a brush. Although you don't want to be careless in your work, you don't have to be obsessively fastidious for a floor. It generally won't be seen any closer than from about four feet, so if there's a tiny misalignment, it won't be noticed.

FINISHING

After the basecoat and stenciling have been given enough time to cure, apply several clear finish coats to protect the thin layers of stenciling and to give the entire surface a uniform sheen. There are many oil- and water-based clear finishes available that are tough enough to do floor duty. Just remember that all oil-based products impart an amber cast to whatever they cover. Only water-based finishes give a colorless coating.

■ One more *really important* point is that not all varnishes and clear finish products, particularly polyurethane, are meant to be applied over paint.

ALL-OVER PATTERN WITH NO MEASURING: STENCILED STARS AND STAINED BLOCKS ALIGN WITH PARQUET SQUARES

Some are strictly for wood. Before buying a product, read the label. If there is any doubt as to its suitability, ask your paint dealer or phone the manufacturer's help line. Most of the companies that make paints and glazes for decorative work also manufacture clear topcoats to go over them, so that's a good place to start.

■ When the finish coats have been applied, the room must be barricaded from foot traffic, including pets, for several days. After that, stocking feet only until the finish has cured. Painted floors need a maintenance regime that's in keeping with the amount of traffic they receive. When adding a new coat of varnish, prepare the surface carefully, so as not to damage the stencil work.

A TRAY HOLDING YOUR SUPPLIES CAN BE EASILY MOVED ALONG FLOOR; DON'T FORGET KNEE PADS

Faux Rugs

Fake rugs are a bit of a hybrid: From a design point of view, they are like floorcloths; from an application point of view, they are like a painted floor.

1 After you've done a scaled-down sketch on grid paper, tape off the shape of the rug directly on the (clean) floor surface. Pay some attention to placement, because this is one piece of carpet that can't be moved.

2 Sand the area enclosed by the tape just enough to give it some tooth. If the sandpaper damages the tape, replace the tape after the sanding is finished. Carefully wipe away any sanding dust.

3 Paint the enclosed area with a good primer. Use a roller-stenciling technique along the edge of the tape to avoid bleeding under it. This means using several coats of an offloaded stencil roller around the edge and as much paint as you like elsewhere.

4 When the primer has dried, do a basecoat. The basecoat can be plain or can include colored border strips. It can be a faux finish or any kind of uneven coloration that suggests the texture of a woven or knotted rug. Add stenciling over basecoat.

5 Remove all tape. Add shadows and a fringe, either freehand (with brush, paint pen or liner) or stenciled. Give it all time to cure, then apply several coats of clear finish with a product meant to cover paint.

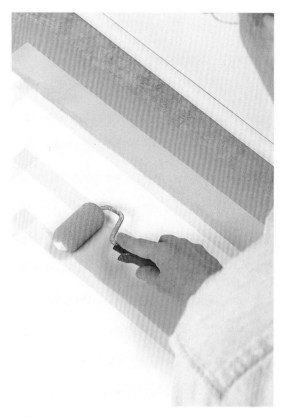

AFTER TAPED RUG AREA IS PRIMED, BORDER AREAS ARE TAPED AND BASECOATED

BEFORE STENCILING, EACH AREA OF RUG WAS DRAGGED WITH SECOND COLOR FOR TEXTURE

FINISHING TOUCHES: FRINGE AND SHADOWS

Floorcloths

Floorcloths originally became popular as floor coverings in the 18th century. Since then, their fortunes have waxed and waned as other flooring products were developed and marketed. Today, they have reclaimed a place in home decor as a piece of furnishing that combines practicality and artistic expression.

A floorcloth is simply a piece of canvas that has been primed, painted, embellished with painted decoration and varnished many times for protection. It functions as a long-lasting, flexible, cleanable floor covering. It is meant to be used only over smooth, hard flooring. With a soft substrate, there is a risk of cracking the paint film on the canvas.

Some artists make floorcloths from pieces of linoleum or vinyl flooring, but this section deals with the traditional floorcloth made from canvas. If you wish to work with a flooring material, refer to the previous section on stenciled floors.

There is no single *correct* way to make a floorcloth. Floorcloths have been made over the centuries by merchants, artists and homemakers alike, and each artisan develops his or her own particular method. And as long as it works, what does it matter? Experiment with some of the alternatives by making small samples. If you make them about 12 by 18 inches, the finished pieces can be used as one-of-a-kind place mats.

MATERIALS

The most widely used material for traditional floorcloths is probably #10 duck canvas. This is a nice compromise between weight and ease of handling. It's tough but still flexible enough to hem. If you don't plan on a hem, then you could try a heavier weight (i.e., a smaller number, such as #8). However, the #10 is generally more readily available, in widths of up to 120 inches, and is less expensive. Other types of canvas with different weaves will also work, as long as they are the right weight. It's worth trying whatever product you can obtain easily and inexpensively before looking further afield. Canvas is sold at art-supply stores, mail-order or Internet sources, tent and awning manufacturers and marine suppliers. Some sources sell it already primed, but this is more expensive.

■ Try to transport the canvas rolled on a tube to avoid folding it. (A good source of indestructible tubes is PVC pipe, sold in the plumbing section of building-supply stores.) Folded creases are hard to remove if the canvas isn't stretched (see next section).

■ When calculating how much canvas to buy, add in any hem allowance if you plan a hem, as well as extra length for shrinkage if the canvas is not going to be stretched.

■ You need acrylic gesso for priming the canvas and paint for the basecoat and stenciling. I use exterior or porch and floor latex paint for the basecoat, as it is flexible and tolerant of temperature changes. I stencil with both acrylic paints and my basecoat latex. Some artists use solid oil paints for stenciling.

PLACE MATS ARE A GOOD PROJECT TO WORK OUT TECHNIQUE AND PATTERN

ROLL ACRYLIC GESSO LIBERALLY OVER CANVAS STAPLED TO BOARD

CLOSELY SPACED STAPLES PREVENT CANVAS FROM SHRINKING AS IT DRIES

PREPARATION

The first step in preparing the canvas for painting is to prime it with acrylic gesso. This seals the canvas, creating a smooth, paintable surface. When canvas is wet, whether from water or paint, it tends to stretch and buckle, then as it dries, it shrinks. With large pieces of canvas, some surface distortion may be produced by uneven shrinkage. This can be avoided by stretching the canvas prior to priming. (Here, we get into one of those areas of personal preference: Some people prefer not to stretch; others always do. Try it both ways to see which suits you better.)

1 I use a sheet of ½-inch plywood for stretching. This will accommodate a canvas up to four by eight feet. Anything larger requires a wall or a proper frame (or the south side of a barn, as North American women were instructed in the homemaking magazines of the 1830s and 1840s). I don't really "stretch" the canvas the way an artist would. I rip the canvas to size so that the edges are straight with the grain. Then I square it and staple the edges to the plywood. I pull the canvas snug as I do this, working from side to opposite side and putting in staples every couple of inches.

2 Apply a generous coat of acrylic gesso to the entire surface of the canvas. (Some people prefer to mask off a hem allowance with tape, keeping the hem free of paint. While this does make it easier to turn the hem, it leaves the raw canvas more susceptible to dirt, unless it is painted afterward.) Gesso can be applied with a brush, a foam roller or a nap roller. For a very large canvas, however, a medium-nap roller works best, because it holds a lot of gesso. Work the gesso into the canvas. Don't be surprised if this uses a lot of gesso—thick canvas is very thirsty. The canvas may appear a little loose on its frame once it gets wet from the gesso. As it dries, it will try to shrink, but the staples prevent that. Instead, the threads get pulled very taut, leaving a perfectly flat canvas surface. Let the canvas dry completely (preferably overnight), still stapled in place.

3 Basecoat the stretched canvas, applying one or more colors. Fewer basecoats are required if tinted gesso is used for priming. Let dry completely. Then remove the staples holding the canvas to its frame, and trim the edges using a straight edge and a utility knife.

NOTE: Here's another point of personal choice: Some people prefer to leave the canvas on its frame until all the stenciling has been completed. For an example of this, see photographs on page 232.

Floorcloths

HEMMING

To hem or not to hem, another question of preference. For small pieces which will serve as place mats, I prefer not to hem, because I don't like a hem ridge that can make a wineglass unstable. Sometimes, the shape of a floorcloth precludes hemming (for instance, anything not rectangular). In this case, trim the edges, and seal them by making sure the background paint is applied right through the edges.

For canvases that will lie on the floor, I prefer a hem, as it makes them lie flatter. It's best to hem before too many layers of paint have been applied to the canvas. The hemming can be done right after the basecoat, or the hem allowance can be masked off until all the painting and stenciling are finished.

1 Measure and mark the hemline on the reverse side of the canvas, using a T square to get the corners square. Allow ⅝ inch to ¾ inch for a sewn hem and about 1 inch for a glued hem. Cut the excess from the corners at an angle.

2 Fold the canvas on the hemline, and reinforce the folds by rolling them firmly with a rolling pin or a wine bottle.

3 To sew a hem, work on one side at a time on a table large enough to accommodate the width of the canvas. You may find it easier to work with the canvas rolled on a tube with just the side to be hemmed unrolled enough to slide through the machine. Use a new heavy-duty needle (the kind used for heavy denim) and strong thread, in a shade as close to the background color as possible.

■ Practice with a scrap of canvas folded double until the tension is properly adjusted to produce long, smooth stitches.

■ Don't try to stitch more than two layers. If your electric machine strains with the effort, help it along manually by turning the wheel. Or take the piece to an upholsterer to be stitched. If you have an old treadle machine, you should be able to manage just fine.

4 If you prefer to glue the hem, you need flexible, waterproof glue that sets reasonably quickly. Work on one side at a time. Run a bead of glue along the inside of the fold, another along the edge of the canvas and a third that waves back and forth between the two. Fold the hem down firmly. Press a rolling pin or wine bottle along the folded hem repeatedly, pushing hard. Wipe off the excess glue that squeezes out of the hem. Weigh the hem down until the glue dries.

PARALLEL STREAKS OF SIMILAR COLOR GIVE HANDWOVEN LOOK TO BASECOAT

NAVAJO BORDER IS STENCILED TO ALTERNATE WITH SETS OF PLAIN STRIPES

HEM CAN BE ADDED BEFORE OR
AFTER RUG IS COMPLETE

DECORATION

Once the hem is finished, the basecoat may have to be touched up along the fold line, where the original paint may have cracked during hemming.

Now, bring out the stencils, and start having some fun. A floorcloth is a medium for self-expression. Some artists interpret it very literally and try to re-create carpetlike designs, while others paint whatever comes into their heads: a starry night, a koi pond, the family dog, maybe something totally abstract. Unless you work best in a completely spontaneous fashion, you'll find it useful to make a small-scale sketch or diagram first. This will help you keep track of colors and design placement.

■ Working on these decorative elements is usually easier if the canvas is mounted in a vertical position, tacked to a wall or to a plywood stretching board. As I mentioned earlier, some people prefer to leave the canvas attached to the stretching board until all painting is finished, before removing the staples, trimming and hemming.

FINISHING

The final step is to apply three to five coats of clear sealer or varnish, in a satin or gloss finish. Make sure this product is designed for use over paint. Most artists prefer to use a water-based finish to avoid the yellowing caused by oil-based varnishes. Apply it according to the manufacturer's recommendations, using a clean, soft, synthetic brush that is reserved for finish coats. Do not overbrush, as this may cause cloudiness. Let the varnish cure completely before walking on the floorcloth. This may take a couple of weeks.

■ Don't forget to add your signature and the date on the back of the floorcloth.

■ Normal periodic cleaning can be done with a damp sponge. Some people add a coat of removable picture varnish (such as Liquitex Soluvar) over the final coat of water-based varnish. Although the manufacturers don't really recommend this (because picture varnish is not all that tough), it does allow occasional super cleanups of the floorcloth. Simply remove all the picture varnish with mineral spirits or whatever special remover is sold with it, then apply a fresh coat of the same picture varnish.

■ Some artists prime both sides of the canvas to protect the underside from spills.

■ If you are worried about the floorcloth slipping underfoot, apply patches of non-skid medium (sold in hardware stores) on the reverse side. Do a test first to make sure that it does not affect the painted side. Carpet tape also works to keep floorcloths in place.

Sisal

A stenciled border is a good way to dress up a plain sisal rug. At first glance, it would appear not to be an easy surface on which to work, because it can be highly textured. In fact, sisal comes in a great variety of forms and weaves, some quite finely woven and others very coarse. The coarser the weave, the less detail that can be captured in the pattern.

1 Use a good-quality porch-and-floor acrylic paint, and pick simple stencils, without a lot of detail.

2 Spray glue is not effective in holding a stencil in place on sisal, so use tape. This is one instance where you can bypass low-tack tape and go straight for something with a lot more hold.

3 Like canvas, sisal can soak up a lot of paint, so the brush doesn't have to be off-loaded as much. Work with a stiff stencil brush, and pounce the paint on instead of swirling it. Use a straight up-and-down motion. You may have to work quite hard to get paint into all the nooks and crannies of the surface.

NOTE: Some people prefer to use spray paint or an air-brush for this. Although spraying does give better coverage, the image isn't usually as clean around the edges.

Hooked Rugs

This is an unusual application of stenciling, but a practical one nonetheless. In recent years, the craft of rug hooking has been making a comeback. This is where strips of fabric (traditionally re-cycled from worn-out clothing) are hooked into a base of burlap or stiff cotton mesh, following a pattern transferred onto the base. There are various ways of copying the pattern onto the base, but one of the easiest is with stencils. I use latex paint and a stencil roller. The pattern dries quickly and needs no heat-setting.

Chapter 15

FABRIC STENCILING

There are two main categories of products for adding color to textiles: dyes and paints. Fabric dyes have an ancient history and have always been important articles of commerce. Most dyes, whether natural or synthetic, are organic compounds that are generally used in water solution. The fabric is immersed, and the dye molecules undergo a chemical and physical interaction with the molecules that make up the fibers of the fabric. Often, the cloth must be pretreated with a mordant, an inorganic salt that helps bind the dye to the fabric. The important thing to remember here is that dyeing is a chemical process; the dye becomes part of the fabric and does not affect its physical properties, such as texture, softness and drape. Dyes are rarely used with stencils (unless with a stenciled resist), mainly because they are too fluid for controlled application.

Paint is a completely different type of medium. It is made of organic or inorganic pigments dispersed in a binder. As paint dries, it forms a film or coating that sticks to the surface of the cloth. Products sold as fabric paints are designed to adhere well enough that the painted cloth is washable and to be pliable enough that the cloth remains soft. Some manufacturers also sell fabric-medium additives that can be mixed with acrylic paint to make it more suitable for cloth. Most acrylic paints can also be used as is; acrylic adheres well to many textiles and is usually washable, but it does render the cloth rather stiff to the touch. Solid oil paints usually work well on fabric too.

I find fabric paints easier to use than regular acrylics. They have a longer open time, they blend easily, and they are often somewhat reversible, in that if they start to dry on the brush, all it takes is a slight dampening to make them workable again. Cleanup is straightforward: Usually no more than a brief soak in soapy water and a light scrub is all that's needed for both brushes and stencils.

It is generally quite easy to distinguish between dye and paint after application. Even with the most flexible paint, it is obvious to the touch that the paint is a film on the fiber, rather than an integral part of the fiber itself.

Unless you are thoroughly familiar with the materials, always test paint and fabric together before embarking on a project. Paints and textiles manufactured by different companies can have very different characteristics, and methods of paint application vary with each artist.

Materials and Preparation

TYPES OF FABRIC

When it comes to painting and dyeing techniques, plain cotton is the most versatile fabric. It has body, a smooth surface and an absorbent quality that makes the paint easy to control. Cotton fabrics come in many different weights and in a variety of weaves. All are easy to stencil.

■ Canvas is basically a heavy cotton and is also easy to stencil. Being so heavy, it tends not to move around and can be worked without special anchoring. It is very absorbent and thus not prone to bleeds. Canvas as used for floorcloths is a different sort of surface, however, because it has been gessoed or primed. This coats the fibers with a rather thick layer of paint, leaving the canvas with properties more akin to those of primed drywall than of cloth. For this reason, floorcloths are discussed on their own in Chapter 14.

■ As far as stenciling is concerned, most cellulose fibers (rayon, linen, hemp) share the same characteristics as cotton. Synthetic fibers are another matter and must be evaluated on an individual basis. Many fabric paints and dyes are meant to be used with natural fibers. They may or may not work with synthetics, so check the label and test paint and fabric together first.

■ Silk falls into a category of its own. Because the fiber is a protein, rather than a cellulose, it has different characteristics. Dyes and paints formulated especially for use with silk tend to give best results.

■ Lightweight varieties of silk, which allow colors to wick through the weave, are usually painted with what is known as a resist technique. For example, a flower shape would be outlined with a medium (like wax or Gutta) that blocks, or resists, paint and dye. When color is then applied, the resist medium keeps it confined within the flower outline. Traditional stenciling works better on the heavier types of silk or with paint that has been mixed with a thickening agent, such as sodium alginate.

■ The difference between dye and fabric paint is immediately obvious when you handle a piece of lightweight silk. Because the fabric is so fine, you can tell right away that the painted sample, no matter how soft and pliable, is made up of a paint film adhering to the surface. A dyed sample, however, feels no different from the original silk.

■ Very rustic cloth, such as burlap, makes an interesting surface for stenciling. It works particularly well with the roller method. Since it already has a very rough hand, you don't need to bother with fabric paints (which tend to be more expensive) but can just use straight acrylics or even house paint. Why decorate burlap? Because it makes great shopping bags, Christmas stockings, gift bags for wine or curtains for a cottage or garden room. And don't overlook the old craft of rug hooking. A century ago, stencils were often printed straight onto the burlap used for the rug backing. This made it very easy to follow the pattern when different colors were being hooked (see page 235).

FABRIC PREPARATION

For best results, prewash all fabrics to remove any sizing or additives left from the weaving and dyeing processes. If you want a dyed background color, this is the time to do it, but the fabric may have to be scoured first (see page 253), according to the type of fiber and the dye instructions. Press the fabric flat before starting to stencil.

NOTE: There is one preparation step I cannot emphasize too strongly: Practice your technique and test your products on scraps of fabric first. When a wall is stenciled, mistakes can be washed off or painted over, but with fabric, there's only one chance to get it right. So work out any potential problems, including washability, beforehand.

EMBROIDERY CAN BE APPLIED OVER A STENCILED PRINT FOR A SPECIAL TOUCH

COLOR FIXING

Most fabric paints need some kind of heat treatment to fix the color and make it permanent, although sometimes a very long curing time will have the same effect. Anything beyond throwing the piece into the clothes dryer can be a lot of work, especially when stenciling large areas. You'll find yourself at the ironing board, trying to give each small motif or iron-sized area of cloth two minutes of quality time without scorching it or missing a section.

1 The first step is to read the paint manufacturer's instructions to see what the options are.

2 Then cut up some test pieces, stencil them, and process each piece differently, keeping track of exactly what you did.

3 Throw the test pieces in the wash, and check the results. The method you pick is the one that produces the best results with the least amount of effort.

NOTE: Many fabric dyes (as opposed to paints) need fixing by steaming or a chemical bath solution. Since dyes are rarely used with stencils, this process won't be discussed here. Acrylic paints and house paints do not usually need heat-setting, just sufficient curing time.

Basic Stenciling

SECURING THE FABRIC

There are a few big differences between stenciling a wall and stenciling a piece of cloth. The first is that cloth is supple, instead of rigid, and therefore wants to move around when you apply the paint. One solution is to spray a *little* low-tack adhesive onto the work surface. Let it dry well. Spread the cloth out on the prepared surface, smoothing it to remove any wrinkles. There should be just enough friction to keep the cloth from shifting under the action of a brush or roller. (The adhesive does not need to be rejuvenated for each new piece of cloth; one spray is enough for a long time.)

It's a good idea to test the adhesive first to make sure none of it transfers to the cloth. My favorite work surface is a piece of laminated countertop material, the leftover part that gets cut out to fit the sink. Contact any kitchen-renovation company, and you can probably pick up a piece free of charge. Or use a piece of firm, flat cardboard (noncorrugated) or a sheet of freezer paper. Freezer paper makes an ideal disposable work surface. There is no need to apply adhesive, because freezer paper can be ironed to the underside of the fabric (with the plastic side of the paper facing the wrong side of the fabric). It will adhere temporarily, until the two are pulled apart. It does not leave a residue.

NOTE: For stenciling T-shirts, an adhesive work surface is essential, because the knit fabric is very difficult to keep still. Choose a surface that can fit inside the shirt to prevent paint from seeping through to the other side. Ironed-on freezer paper is ideal for this.

SECURING THE STENCIL

This part is easy. If it's a robust stencil (i.e., not a lot of fragile or floppy parts), simply tape it in place. Otherwise, apply a very light coat of low-tack adhesive to the back of the stencil, and let it dry. Then prepare a "cloth sandwich": Smooth and secure the fabric over the work surface (see above), then position the stencil on top; the adhesive acts as the mayonnaise to hold it all together. This works like a charm, firmly anchoring the fabric in place.

The hold of the stencil should be lighter than the hold of the work surface; otherwise, the stencil will tend to pull the fabric up every time it is lifted and moved. And you do *not* want the cloth to shift in the middle of a job. You'll never get it realigned exactly as it was.

SPRAY ADHESIVE ON WORK SURFACE

WORK PAINT WELL INTO FIBERS

LET PAINT DRY, THEN HEAT-SET FOR PERMANENCE

APPLYING THE PAINT

Once you start applying the paint, you'll notice other differences between fabric and walls. Apart from very fine, fragile fabrics, most textiles are more absorbent than a sealed sheet of drywall, and the absorbency increases with the weight of the fabric. This means less offloading, because the paint soaks straight in rather than spreading out. The other thing is that cloth has texture —it's fibrous—and the paint must penetrate the fibers and microfibers, rather than just sit on the surface fuzz. Otherwise, it's only going to end up in the lint trap. So whether using a roller or a brush, make sure the paint gets worked in as well as possible.

In spite of the obvious differences between a textile and a solid surface, many of the stenciling basics described in Chapter 2 can also be applied to fabrics.

OVERLAYS

1 For multiple overlays, mark all registration on pieces of low-tack tape positioned strategically on the cloth. A removable fabric marker can also be used, as long as you've tested it first.

2 Secure the cloth well (see facing page). Unless the stencil is very fragile, don't use spray glue to hold it in place, as it may cause the cloth to lift or shift when you change overlays. Once the grain of the cloth shifts, it's almost impossible to get it (and the stenciled image) back the way it was, which means the next overlay will not fit properly. Instead of adhesive, use a couple of small pieces of low-tack tape. When you need to lift one overlay, first hold the stencil and cloth firmly in place while you remove the tape so that nothing shifts.

OVERLAY STENCIL PRINTS

STREAKED COLORS

SOFTLY BLENDED COLORS

SHADING

B asic approaches to shading, blending and streaking of colors all translate directly from solid surfaces to cloth. The two examples here show harsh streaking on the prehistoric horse and soft color blending on the peony.

NOTE: One difference when working on cloth is that glazes are not used with the paints. However, most lines of fabric paints include a product called a colorless extender, which can be used to render the paint more transparent and to increase its ability to blend and taper. Unless the label specifies acceptable dilution rates, do *not* water down fabric paints. This dilutes the paint binder, and you need full-strength binder for proper adhesion. Use a proprietary extender or a diluting agent instead of water.

Basic Stenciling

ADDING FREEHAND SHADING

HIGHLIGHTING EDGES

FREEHAND

Stenciling and freehand do not usually complement each other side by side on fabric; they just look completely different. However, the two can be combined by using basic stencil silhouettes as a kind of pattern to get started on the freehand, as shown above with the sweet pea. The stenciled outline acts as a basecoat that is well worked into the fibers, providing a uniform surface on which to do freehand without having to scrub it into the cloth. The outline also defines the overall shape; the details can then be created freehand. It's a bit like doodling in the margin of a telephone book.

Freehand line details can be added by using a fabric-paint pen. Several fabric-paint companies sell these marker-type pens as accessories to accompany their regular lines of fabric paint.

BACKGROUND TREATMENT

We've seen how the marriage of stenciled images and interesting background finishes can produce very creative effects. With fabric, the repertoire is more limited. It is possible to stencil over printed cloth, of course, but most stencilers prefer to work with a plain surface.

If you are prepared to dye your own fabric, there are some simple techniques to create various background effects. Dyeing is beyond the scope of this book, but your local library or bookstore should have plenty of reference books. For the example shown at right, I applied blue colors onto wet silk with a sea sponge. Then I sprinkled the surface with pickling salt and left it to dry undisturbed. After shaking off the salt, I stenciled the pattern with opaque blue fabric paint.

OUTLINES

Outlined accents can make cloth look very dramatic. This piece was roller stenciled with gold paint, then the flowers were outlined in the same gold squeezed from a narrow-tipped bottle (an Air Pen™ also works). The thicker application of the outline produces a very rich gold and leaves a slightly raised relief.

For this example, I used inexpensive sheeting and acrylic paint—not the best materials to wear next to the skin but perfect for a dramatic tablecloth or for yardage from which to cut costumes for a high school performance of *Romeo and Juliet*.

Stenciling Fragile Fabrics

Fragile fabrics, including lightweight silks and very fine cottons, take much more care, because they really don't want to stay put. It's difficult enough just to get the piece to lie flat with the grain straight and no wrinkles. Then all it takes is a breath of wind or a heavy sigh to lift a corner, set it fluttering and deposit it in a different position. You cannot use a traditional silk-painting frame as an anchor, because it elevates the cloth. But with a little care, the two methods described on page 240 should work just fine.

1 Cut a piece of freezer paper the size of your fabric sample. Lay the fabric on an ironproof surface (such as a table insulated with layers of sheeting), right side down, getting the grain as straight as possible. Place the freezer paper, plastic side down, over the back of the fabric. If you need to use more than one piece, place them side by side but do not tape them together. Iron the back side of the freezer paper carefully (low to medium setting, no steam) to fuse the paper and the fabric. Try not to shift the paper as you do this. Test a corner to check on the degree of fusion before lifting the piece. Then turn it over, and place it on a hard surface for stencilling.

Alternatively, for a rigid anchor, pick a solid but movable work surface, such as a piece of countertop laminate material or flat plastic, of similar size to the piece of fabric. Spray it lightly with stencil adhesive, and let it dry. (Test the adhesive beforehand to make sure it won't leave any residue on the fabric.) Getting a piece of flyaway cloth to lie down straight and true on this surface is not easy unless you have four hands. Have a helper hold two corners while you hold the other two. Hold the cloth taut while carefully lowering it onto the tacky work surface.

2 If at all possible, avoid using stencil adhesive on the stencil, as it may pull up the cloth when the stencil is removed. If this happens, the chances of realigning the fabric the way it was are less than that of winning a lottery.

3 If you need to turn the fabric as you work, turn the whole work surface.

NOTE: Do not use a cardboard work surface. The paint often goes right through fine silk, and if it does, it will stick to the cardboard and dry there. When the cloth is peeled off, shreds of cardboard will be stuck to the back.

■ For delicate fabrics, use the very best fabric paint you can find—the one with the softest hand. It is worthwhile to buy samples of several brands and try them out before making your final choice.

■ Very fine fabrics, such as lightweight silk, bleed easily—a characteristic that is put to use in other methods of painting and dyeing silk. For stenciling, of course, it's a liability. So pay attention to your offloading, and proceed carefully. It's easier to work with viscous paints, as fluid ones can wick along the woven threads, past the edge of the stencil. Solid oil paint is also a good choice, as it doesn't bleed at all. Be careful not to smudge it, however.

STENCILING VELVETEEN

Fabrics with a thick nap or pile seem like unsuitable surfaces for stenciling because of all the fuzz. However, you can get striking results with cotton velveteen, especially when using very dark cloth and metallic fabric paint. The cotton takes fabric paints well, and the nap is shorter than that of velvet. The process works best with a single-overlay stencil that does not have a lot of small detail.

1 Metallic paint generally shows up well over a dark background, so apply this first over the whole stencil. Use a brush instead of a stencil roller. You can stipple with a normal stencil brush. Or, as I prefer, use a blending brush, and apply the paint in short strokes, always in the same direction—with the nap. That's the direction where you feel the least resistance when you run your hand over the surface. For the example shown at right, metallic gold was used.

NOTE: Because there is so much cotton to take up the paint, you don't need to offload much. As you get used to the technique, you'll be able to pick up a small amount of paint and apply it directly without the risk of bleeding.

2 Without moving the stencil, apply accent colors (here, red and green) over the gold to selected parts of the design. Color over as much or as little of the gold as you wish.

3 If you want to use complementary colors—for example, purple over metallic gold—then let the gold dry completely before adding the purple.

4 If you finish a repeat and find you have colored over more of the gold than you want, just reapply the gold paint.

5 Lift the stencil, and move on to the next repeat.

■ Don't expect the painted parts to have the same really soft feel as the unpainted parts, because they will have absorbed a fair amount of paint. But the look is stunning—it reminds me of a microscopic view of a butterfly's wing, which reveals the individual iridescent scales that make up the jeweled surface.

Stenciling Yardage

SPREAD CLOTH SMOOTHLY OVER TACKY WORK SURFACE

POSITION, AND ROLL A PRINT; NOTE REGISTRATION LINES AND CUTOUTS

AFTER ONE AREA IS PAINTED, SHIFT FABRIC TO DO A FRESH SECTION

DRAPE OR LOOSELY PILE STENCILED CLOTH TO THE SIDE TO FINISH DRYING

It's all very well to make a single meticulous stencil print for the front of a T-shirt, but what if you want to put ladybugs all over a huge curtain? Do you really want to spend a hundred hours on it? My personal approach to volume stenciling relies on using rollers and acrylic paint and working on a large, smooth surface, such as a countertop or table.

1 The first step is to spray the work surface lightly with stencil adhesive and let it dry thoroughly. It will clean off afterward with rubbing alcohol, but if you can't bear the thought of doing this to your dining room table, cover the surface first with freezer paper (plastic side up), tape it down well, and spray adhesive onto the freezer paper.

NOTE: When I need to work on large surfaces of fabric, it's typically for curtains, and for these, I don't really care whether the stenciled parts remain soft to the touch—in fact, if they're stiff, it saves on starch. I can therefore avoid using the more expensive fabric paints and stick to liquid acrylics, which have the added advantage of air-curing, rather

than heat-setting. On more than one occasion, I've even used house paint. To make the acrylics somewhat softer, add fabric medium. Just be sure you don't end up having to heat-set each motif with an iron, a process that will take far longer than the stenciling itself.

2 To begin, spread the first section of cloth smoothly

STENCILED YARDAGE GIVES THE LOOK OF LACE FOR THE PRICE OF MUSLIN

over the tacky work surface. Make sure there's enough area clean and clear on both ends of the work surface to accommodate the unstenciled cloth and the finished portion.

3 Position the stencil, and make the first print with a roller-stenciling method (see Chapter 2). Move the stencil over, and make the second print. It goes faster if you just hold the stencil in place with your hand. If you need guidelines, use a chalk pencil or temporary fabric marker or press a grid of creases into the fabric before starting.

4 Keep going until the entire first section has been stenciled. Give the paint a minute or two to get surface-dry. Then lift the cloth off the work surface, and shift it over to the "done" side of the table, pulling the next section of unpainted cloth onto the work surface.

5 Smooth the cloth, and continue as for the first section. Keep processing section after section until the entire piece has been stenciled. If acrylic paints are used, it shouldn't require heat-setting; just give it a long cure time.

6 When working with sheer fabrics, some paint will pass through to the work surface underneath. As you lift each stenciled section, wipe the work surface with a damp cloth so that the paint residue won't adhere to the reverse side of the next section of cloth.

Devoré

Devoré is a French word that means eaten up or consumed. In the world of fabric artistry, devoré refers to the removal, or "eating up," of fibers in a decorative pattern. In England, the same process is called burnout, in reference to the chemical burning away of the fibers.

Two types of fibers can be burned away: wool and cellulose. The process for wool, however, uses highly caustic lye, so most studio work focuses on cellulose burnout, which uses the less toxic sodium bisulfate as the chemical agent. This chemical, in the form of a gel or paste, is applied to the surface of the fabric, either freehand with a brush or piping tool or through a stencil. When the material is then heated (or ironed), the sodium bisulfate creates sulfuric acid, which eats away at any threads or fibers made of cellulose. This includes organic fibers of plant origin, such as cotton, rayon, linen and viscose, but not synthetic fibers, such as polyester, or fibers of animal origin, such as silk or wool.

Fabrics suitable for devoré are blends of cellulose and either polyester or silk. The treatment burns away the cellulose, leaving the noncellulose part unaffected. With silk/rayon velvet, for example, the woven base of the fabric is silk, while the pile is rayon, a cellulose fiber. During the devoré treatment, the pile is selectively removed, leaving a richly embossed pattern in the cloth. With silk/viscose satin, the process removes the viscose satin, leaving the flat silk backing and creating a matte embossed pattern. In polyester/cotton blends, the two fibers are wound together in the threads. When the cotton is removed, the threads are left much thinner, rendering the fabric translucent. There is also a silk/linen blend with a silk warp and a linen (cellulose) weft. Removal of the cellulose gives the look of "pulled threads."

■ Many decorative effects are possible with the devoré process, depending on the type of fabric used. Buy a variety of devoré fabrics from sources that specialize in fabric techniques, or experiment with fabrics of unknown fibers—you never know what interesting results you might discover.

■ For the examples in this book, I used a commercial gel called Fiber-Etch Fabric Remover™; it's convenient and ready to use. If I were going to be processing large volumes of fabric, however, this could get expensive, and I would then consider looking up some recipes to make my own paste.

■ There are a couple of points to keep in mind with all variations of this process. Always clean the back of the stencil between repeats, just in case there was a bleed. Otherwise, an invisible deposit of gel will be left on the next print. If the repeats are positioned such that the margin of the stencil overlaps them, dry each section with a hair dryer before doing the next repeat. This will prevent the back of the stencil from picking up gel from the previous repeat.

■ When working on a large piece (such as a long scarf), which means moving the cloth along on the work surface, be careful not to transfer any residual gel to the new section of cloth via the work surface. Whenever the fabric is moved, wipe the work surface with a damp cloth (or, even better, a cloth dampened with baking soda and water, but rinse off *all* traces of baking soda). Dry thoroughly before proceeding.

■ During the activation stage, work in a well-ventilated area. Activation produces very small quantities of sulfuric acid—something you want to avoid breathing. This is *not* a process for children to use.

DEVORÉ FOR VELVET

This process produces a luscious, sculpted pattern on velvet by removing selected areas of the nap. Depending on the type of stencil used, varying amounts of nap can be removed. With a reverse stencil, for example, there may be large areas of burnout, leaving a very transparent piece of fabric.

Remember, this process will work only with silk/rayon velvet, so check the fiber content before buying. As yard goods, silk/rayon velvet is generally available only in white and occasionally in black. For any other color, buy the white and dye it. I prefer to do this before the devoré process, because it makes it easier to see where the gel has been applied.

Dyeing doesn't have to be intimidating. I've used ordinary Rit™ dye (available in supermarkets), either the stovetop or the sink method. It's very easy —I just followed the enclosed directions, and it gave me good results. You may want to experiment with different concentrations to find the right strength. If you want to try more specialized dyes, consider taking a workshop to get you started.

■ Follow all safety cautions on the Fiber-Etch™ label. Wear protective glasses and gloves.

ROLLER STENCIL DEVORÉ GEL

ACTIVATE DRIED GEL BY IRONING

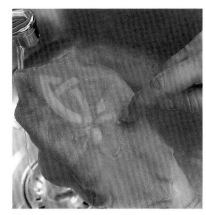

RUB OFF TREATED PILE UNDER WATER

FINISHED SAMPLE AFTER DRYING

STENCILING

Choose a work surface that is resistant to chemical damage and will hold the fabric flat and still. A remnant piece of countertop laminate material, lightly sprayed with stencil adhesive, works well. So does freezer paper (see page 240).

1 Smooth and secure the velvet face down onto the work surface. I find it easier to work from the back of the velvet, laying it pile side down and applying Fiber-Etch™ to the wrong side. Others do the opposite and work on the pile side.

2 Position the stencil (lightly sprayed with adhesive) on the wrong side of the velvet.

3 My method differs somewhat from the instructions that come with Fiber-Etch™, but it's what I've found easiest. Instead of a brush applicator, I use a high-density foam roller and proceed as though roller stenciling. The challenge here is that the gel is transparent, so it's hard to see exactly what you are doing.

4 Scrape a thin layer of gel onto your palette. Pull the roller through the gel, loading it in the same way as for roller stenciling. Work the roller back and forth to distribute the gel evenly. Don't overload the roller—then you won't have to offload (you don't want to waste this stuff, since it's a lot more expensive than paint).

5 Start rolling the gel through the stencil onto the back of the velvet with a really light touch, to prevent bleeding. As the roller deposits the gel and the gel gets absorbed, gradually increase the pressure. Lift up a corner of the stencil to make sure it's evenly covered, then remove the stencil. Dry the gel with a hair dryer.

ACTIVATION

The gel is actually an acid salt; it turns into an acid through heat activation, which can be done with an iron. However, you must be careful not to overheat the velvet, because the silk backing is delicate.

1 Put a thick terrycloth towel on the ironing board, and lay the velvet face down, so as not to flatten the pile. (This also protects the ironing board from the chemicals.)

2 With low, dry heat, move the iron around for a few minutes, until the treated pile becomes stiff. To protect the silk backing, cover the back of the velvet with a pressing cloth.

3 Test frequently for doneness by turning the piece over and scratching the pile with your fingernail. It should become stiff and scratch off easily. At this point, rinse the fabric under water, rubbing gently to remove the treated pile. If you prefer, lay a cookie sheet flat in the bottom of the sink and spread the fabric on top. Then rub gently with a terry facecloth or your fingers to remove the fibers.

NOTE: If doing a lot of velvet at one time, place a fine strainer over the drain or work in a separate container so that the plumbing won't get clogged with velvet fuzz.

4 Wash with soap and water. Rinse well. Roll in a towel, then let dry.

Devoré

GEL IS COLORLESS, SO APPLY IT SYSTEMATICALLY TO AVOID MISSING A SPOT

IRON REVERSE SIDE TO ACTIVATE GEL

RUB LIGHTLY TO REMOVE SATIN FINISH

DEVORÉ FOR SATIN

1 Most of the remarks and instructions for velvet also apply to silk/rayon satin, except that the satin has no pile. In this case, you should work on the right (shiny) side of the fabric, so lay it out on the work surface right side up. Use freezer paper or adhesive to hold it still (see page 240).

NOTE: With satin, I find it easier to work with a brush. Because the satin is so fine, it takes very little chemical, so it is easy to apply too much if a roller load is slightly uneven. A soft stencil brush works better.

2 Squeeze a small amount of Fiber-Etch™ onto a plastic or glass palette. Pick up a *little* on the end of the brush, and work it into the bristles. Tap the brush on a paper towel to make sure it's not overloaded. The gel is essentially colorless, so it is difficult to tell how much is on the brush and where it's been applied to the stencil. Therefore, work very systematically in covering the stencil cutouts. Be careful not to apply too much gel at once, because this fabric bleeds easily. I usually go over the stencil twice, with a thin coat each time, just to make sure I've applied enough gel to produce a good burnout but not enough to bleed.

3 Let the gel dry, then activate it by ironing on the reverse side of the satin, using a dry iron on the "wool" setting or lower. When the treated areas become brittle (test with your finger), it's ready. Do not overheat or over-iron, or the fabric will become scorched.

4 Rinse under water, as with velvet, and rub the surface of the piece with terrycloth or a soft surgical brush to remove the satin finish. Wash with liquid soap, rinse and dry.

NOTE: You can keep iron and ironing board free of chemicals by putting devoré pieces between two pressing cloths or paper towels during the heat-activation process.

ROLL GEL OVER STENCIL

IRON UNTIL MEDIUM BROWN

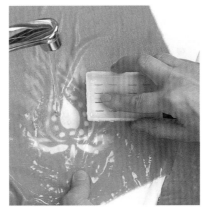

RINSE AWAY TREATED FIBERS

TRANSLUCENT PAISLEY

DEVORÉ FOR POLY/COTTON

This is my favorite fabric to work with because it is so easy, fast and inexpensive. All the threads in the cloth are made of a poly/cotton mix, so when the cotton gets removed, you're left with thin, translucent polyester threads. It's the same effect as when sheets get old and worn out, except that with devoré, there is a nice pattern to the worn parts.

The higher the cotton content of the fabric, the more pronounced the burnout. The standard content for poly/cotton yard goods is only 35 percent cotton, although occasionally, you may find some with 55 percent. Some brands of sheets are a 50/50 blend, making them a very cheap source of yardage. If you get enthusiastic about this treatment, buy white poly/cotton sheets on sale, cut them up and dye them to suit. You'll save a bundle. Personally, I love the effect when the fabric is left white. It's an elegant, lacy white-on-white look.

1 Working with cotton is similar to working with satin, except it doesn't bleed as easily. Wash and dry the fabric before starting, then spread it on the "tacky" work surface, or iron it to the plastic side of freezer paper (iron from the paper side).

2 Use the roller method for fast, even gel application.

3 Let the piece dry, then iron on the reverse side to activate. Here's where the term burnout comes from, because the treated area starts to turn color when heated. When it's at about "medium toast" level, it's done. Be careful not to burn it.

4 As with the other fabrics, rinse and rub away the treated fibers. I use a surgical brush to do this. The brown color disappears as the cotton is washed away. The final step is to wash, rinse and dry.

WHITE-ON-WHITE NAPKINS ARE AN ELEGANT PROJECT

Discharge Dyeing

What this process lacks in terms of a poetic name, it makes up for in its ease of application and its exciting, creative unpredictability. In this context, "discharge" means the chemical removal of color from cloth. This can be done uniformly to an entire piece in a patterned resist fashion (using tie-dye or batik) or in a completely controlled manner (using stencils, block printing or screen printing).

In this section, I look at a narrow subset of options: creating designs by removing color, rather than adding it, using stencils with a bleach paste as the discharging agent. It's also possible to elaborate on these effects by overdyeing or layering patterns of discharge and dye.

Where the uncertainty of the process lies—as well as some need for experimentation—is that it's impossible to predict how the original dyes will discharge or what the resultant color will be. For example, black cloth is often used in discharge printing because the effect is so striking. But the original black may have been created with any number of dyes, whose identities are unknown to you. There may be blues, reds, browns or yellows in there, and you won't find out which until you've discharged a spot.

NOTE: A word of caution: I must emphasize that this process is not exact. There are no rules that will guarantee identical results with each use. Remember, too, that although bleach is a household product, it is still a potentially harmful chemical. This is *not* a process for children to attempt. Anyone who has heart or respiratory problems or who might be pregnant should not work with discharging agents. Use basic good sense when working around chemicals, including wearing a vapor mask and safety goggles. I like to do this outside, with a little breeze to keep the air fresh.

Dark fabrics (especially black) yield the most dramatic discharging. It can be very surprising to see what colors remain under black as the dye is removed. This makes it tricky choosing cloth to buy, particularly when you have a specific palette in mind. You can solve the problem by taking along a bleach-dampened cloth sealed in a plastic bag when shopping for fabric. Ask the clerk for small swatches of potential candidates, then go out to the parking lot and wet them with the bleach to see the resulting colors.

TYPES OF FIBER

Discharge processes work best on natural fibers. Since polyester is usually colorfast, blends containing polyester may not discharge very well. For cellulose fibers, such as cotton, linen and rayon, bleach is an effective color remover; for animal fibers, such as silk or wool, thiourea dioxide is probably the safest discharging agent. I will describe only the bleach process for cellulose, as adverse reactions to the fumes from thiourea dioxide are not uncommon. To learn more about that process, try to find a course to take.

NOTE: Another approach is to start with undyed cloth that you dye in your own colors, then discharge using stencils. As with the other fabrics, this will take some experimentation, because the discharge color will vary with the type of cloth and the dye color.

STENCIL FABRIC WITH BLEACH GEL

REPEAT UNTIL COLOR STARTS TO CHANGE

BLEACH AS A DISCHARGING AGENT

I use ordinary liquid household bleach, which typically contains 5.25 to 6 percent sodium hypochlorite in water. This is the standard discharge chemical used for stripping color from dyed cellulose fibers. Never use it on protein fibers (silk or wool), as it will damage or destroy them. Fresh bleach works best.

■ Liquid bleach, slightly diluted, can be used with a mister for a fine-spray application, but for use with a stencil brush or roller, the bleach must be thickened into a paste. Do this with sodium alginate (see recipe and instructions below).

■ Bleach is a caustic solution, which can burn or corrode organic tissue, so always wear protective gloves. You should also wear an organic vapor mask (although if you work outside with some wind blowing, you may be able to get away without one) and safety goggles, in case of splashing.

Scour the fabrics properly beforehand, because formaldehyde is sometimes used in sizing textiles, and it may react with bleach to create toxic fumes.

Scouring removes grease, sizing, starch, pectin and detergent residues from cloth. These substances can prevent even and wash-fast dyeing.

1 To scour cellulose fibers, mix one teaspoon synthrapol and three tablespoons soda ash for every pound of dry fabric in enough warm water to cover fabric. Stir to dissolve the soda ash. Wash the cloth in this, and rinse well.

2 After rinsing the fabric, let it dry, then iron it flat. While it's drying, mix up the stenciling medium. Pour one cup water into a studio blender. ("Studio" tools are those used only for art and craft work and never for food preparation.) Add half a teaspoon sodium alginate, and blend until smooth. Let stand 5 to 10 minutes. If you want it thicker, add a little more sodium alginate, and repeat.

3 Put a few spoonfuls of the sodium-alginate mixture in a palette cup or small container. Slowly add undiluted household bleach, stirring constantly until it reaches a good consistency for stenciling. Ideally, the mixture will have diluted the bleach by no more than about half.

4 Secure the fabric right side up (see page 240). Position the stencil, and apply the thickened bleach with a stencil brush or roller, loading and offloading in the usual way. Repeat until the color begins to change. This should start to happen soon.

5 Remove the stencil, and let the bleach work for a few minutes, then rinse the cloth well in water. Neutralize the bleach by soaking the cloth in a bucket containing one tablespoon metabisulfite for every gallon of water. Rinse again in clean water, and wash well in warm, soapy water. There should be no smell of bleach remaining.

Discharge Dyeing

1 To create an all-over pattern, shown here on cotton velveteen, use a large piece of lace (made stiff and water-resistant with several coats of shellac) as a stencil.

2 Apply spray adhesive to the back of the lace so that it can be pressed into close contact with the fabric.

3 Spray slightly diluted bleach from a fine-spray bottle over the lace, making an effort to get uniform distribution. Wear safety goggles, rubber gloves and, if indoors, a safety mask.

4 Let the piece sit until the desired amount of color change has been effected. Peel off the lace, and neutralize the bleach (see page 253), then wash the velveteen, and let it dry.

5 To iron, place the fabric nap side down on a thick, folded terrycloth towel, and steam-iron it lightly from the reverse side.

Sun Printing

This really simple process is frequently used in the South Pacific to decorate pareos. I bought the one pictured here years ago during an extended stay on the French island of New Caledonia. The market was full of shops hung with lengths of brightly colored cotton decorated with obviously stenciled motifs. They were irresistible to this novice stenciler.

1 To make a sun print, use a photo-sensitive paint such as Setacolor Soleil™. The first step is to color the background. Dilute the paint with water: one part paint to two parts water.

2 Moisten the cloth with water, and stretch it on a frame or spread it out on a work surface.

3 Cover the fabric with the diluted paint mixture, using a sponge or large brush. You can use more than one color. Or simply dip the cloth into a pot of the color, and wring it out.

4 Immediately arrange opaque stencils and masks on top of the painted fabric, and leave it flat in the sun to dry. When dry, the masked areas will have lost color, appearing as pale motifs in a sea of color.

NOTE: All sorts of objects can be used as masks: feathers, flowers, leaves, shapes cut from cardboard, even lace. Fall-outs from opaque stencils are ideal, especially if you cut details into them. Turn the stencils themselves into interesting masks by giving the outside edges a decorative trim. More than one color can be used for the background. Typically, background colors are bright, wild and loosely intermingled. An interesting effect can be obtained by sprinkling the still wet painted surface with dry, coarse salt. When the surface is dry, brush off the salt. Scattered frostlike spots remain.

Katazome

Sometimes slow and traditional is the only way to go, because part of the pleasure of the result is in getting there. The fine Japanese craft of katazome is steeped in the rituals of a 1,000-year history. The process bears little resemblance to Western notions of stenciling and does not lend itself to shortcuts. In fact, in Japan, each step of the process was once a profession in itself.

The Japanese have long decorated textiles, particularly kimono textiles, by applying a rice-flour-based paste to the fabric so that dye can penetrate only those areas not covered by the paste. Called *norizome*, this technique, or rather collection of techniques, is what we would call paste-resist dyeing. Katazome, one of the methods for applying the paste, uses stencils, or *katagami*.

Exactly when the Japanese began using stencils for dyeing patterns is not known. There are many examples of heavily stenciled leather armor dating from around 800 A.D. By the 15th century, stencil-dyed patterns were the standard decoration for the armor and clothing of the samurai class. Produced by highly specialized artisans, the design and craftsmanship of these stencils reached exquisite levels of artistry during the 17th, 18th and 19th centuries.

Katagami are made from layers of special mulberry paper laminated together with fermented persimmon juice (*kakishibu*), sun-dried, then smoked. After months of repeated treatments, the paper becomes waterproof and very strong.

Unlike Western stencils, which often try to eliminate bridges through the use of multiple overlays, the Japanese incorporate both bridges and cut areas as equal and essential parts of the design, thus creating strongly graphic images. Nor do they rely on bridges to hold the stencil together or to provide stabilization. If necessary, a sheet of silk gauze is glued to the finished stencil to provide backing and support for islands and fragile areas, much in the manner of stencils used for Western silk-screen printing. Of course, the original Japanese method was not quite so simple. It involved inserting and gluing fine silk threads between two identically cut stencils, a very tedious process.

Stylistically, Japanese stencil designs fall into several types of pattern, each requiring specialized cutting tools and cutting techniques. For examples of these, refer to *Carved Paper* by Susanna Campbell Kuo (see Further Reading).

Since traditional *katagami* were used to print kimono cloth, they were usually all a standard width—about 14 inches, which was the width of the cloth looms. The length could vary according to the pattern, which would be created in such a way that the repeats of the pattern formed a continuous design when printed down the length of the bolt of fabric.

NOTE: Katazome is not well known in North America. In Japan, it is becoming a lost art, with few masters of the craft still living. It is a detailed process and very distinct from Western stenciling. Even the tools and materials are different, so it is not something a Western stenciler can simply try out with standard equipment. The process is merely outlined here in an abbreviated form (and with a few Western influences) and is meant only as an overview. If you want to try katazome yourself, consult one of the titles listed in Further Reading for complete instructions and recipes. I highly recommend you take a course or workshop as a first step before investing in the specialized tools and materials.

Katazome

CUT STENCIL FROM MULBERRY PAPER

SHELLAC GAUZE INTO PLACE

SPREAD PASTE THROUGH SCREEN

REMOVE STENCIL

WHEN PASTE DRIES, APPLY PAINT

RINSE PASTE OFF FABRIC

THIS PROCESS PRODUCES STRONG GRAPHIC IMAGES

STENCIL CUTTING

1 First, transfer the design to the stencil paper. This can be done directly or by affixing a tracing-paper pattern to the stencil paper.

2 Cut the pattern lines with a very sharp knife. Each cut must be done with the blade perpendicular to the surface so that the size of the cutout is the same, front and back. If the pattern has many small identical shapes (dots, petals, and so on), specially shaped cutting tools can be used instead of a knife.

3 Glue a sheet of silk gauze over the entire stencil using lacquer or shellac.

NOTE: Customarily, several sheets of mulberry paper would be stacked together and as many as 6 to 12 stencils cut at the same time, especially for the more intricate designs.

4 Carefully cut away any temporary bridges.

5 Immediately before the stencil is used, soak it in water to make it pliable.

PASTE APPLICATION

Nori paste is made from rice flour, rice bran, water, salt and calcium hydroxide. The process, which involves mixing, kneading, steaming and mashing, takes several hours. The paste is then spread through the stencil with a wooden spatula. It adheres extremely well to fabric and can be used with very fine stencils. When dry, it resists color applied by brush or brief dips in a dye bath, so the areas covered by the paste remain undyed.

PAINTING

Once the nori paste has dried, color can be applied to the cloth with paint or certain dyes. With paints, multiple colors can be used, either blended or kept separate. Apply them with brushes. If heat-setting is needed, do it without burning the resist. Otherwise, allow to air-cure.

DYEING

Not all dyes can be used with this process, since nori paste is a water-soluble resist. Any product that requires hot water, long submersion or stirring will not work. Traditional methods favored natural dyes that could be applied either by brush or by immersion at cool or lukewarm temperatures. Indigo was particularly popular as an immersion dye, since it does not require a mordant. After the discovery of aniline dyes in the 19th century, dyers began mixing synthetic dyes right into the nori paste, which meant that color could be applied through the stencil itself.

PASTE REMOVAL

After the dyeing (or painting) and fixing steps, the nori paste is softened by soaking in water. The fabric can then be stretched on the bias, which usually lifts the paste right off, revealing the dyed pattern. This is followed with a final wash in warm water.

Embroidered Stenciling

This interesting variation on fabric stenciling can be viewed as the textile equivalent of adding penned details to a print. In other words, instead of using pen strokes to create the shading on a pear or the veins on a leaf, these details are added with embroidery. This works best with fairly simple stenciled images, so there's no need for more than a beginner's expertise in stenciling. In addition, some basic needlecraft skill is required (two or three simple embroidery stitches).

START WITH SIMPLE IMAGES AND SIMPLE SHADING STENCILED ONTO CLOTH

USE EMBROIDERY THREAD AND SIMPLE STITCHES FOR EXTRA SHADING OR DETAIL

Chapter 16

LETTERING

To anyone not involved with decorative painting, the word stencil often conjures an image of packing-crate lettering. This is the stencil we all met in grade school, indispensable for the title pages of all those social studies projects: Mesopotamia, Roman Emperors, The Pyramids.

Today's creative stencilers wouldn't voluntarily use such letters unless they really *were* labeling crates for an overseas freighter or had some particular artistic reason for choosing that style. If you are prepared to cut your own stencils, the possibilities are endless. Printers, sign writers and art-supply stores carry catalogs of lettering styles available on CD-ROM. Libraries and bookstores stock books featuring a wide range of fonts, including historical styles and embellished initials. Letter sets are also available free on the Internet. Many of these fonts can be adapted to a stencil format—usually, it's simply a question of how to handle the "doughnut" letters (i.e., those letters whose centers fall out when cut directly as a stencil).

If you prefer a ready-to-use stencil, you can buy precut stencils in a variety of fonts and sizes. Some stencil companies offer custom-cutting services as well.

Stenciled lettering can be used for a variety of applications besides the one-off production of school cover pages and posters. On a small scale, you can put titles or monograms on stationery, journals, memory books, glassware and linen. On a larger scale, you can transfer memorable quotes, nursery rhymes or lines of poetry to walls, floors and furniture.

Many of the techniques described in earlier chapters can be used with letter stencils. It is a straightforward application of those methods to stencil words in plain paint, gold leaf or plaster or to emboss them on paper or metal. Patterns, outlines or drop shadows can also be added. It all depends on how much work you're prepared to do. This chapter summarizes different overall approaches to lettering with the help of stencils, but it doesn't repeat step-by-step instructions that have been covered elsewhere.

ABCDEFGHI
1234567890

Composition

When choosing a font, try to capture the spirit of the message you want to stencil. Whether it's a statement of whimsy, *passion* or **ERUDITION**, the right style of lettering will complement the words. The way the letters are laid out is also important. Should they march primly and evenly along a straight line, dance up and down an imaginary wave or wander across the wall, expanding in size as they go? Or should they be arranged to cover an entire surface?

Once you've chosen a style and layout, the next step is to determine the placement of each letter. Some commercial stencils have registration marks that position each letter with respect to its neighbors, but that won't help fit the words exactly across a 10-foot stretch of wall, for instance, or onto the lid of a toy box. That usually requires a dry run on a long strip of paper, adjusting the spacing to fit; then the strip can be used as a template for positioning.

Theoretically, this could all be done by measuring and calculating, but in practice, I always get the calculations wrong. As a mathematician once said, "In theory, there is no difference between theory and practice. But in practice, there is." Besides, it's a lot easier to let a computer position the letters.

1 Type your phrase on a computer, and print it out. Make any adjustments in size and position by photocopy enlargement and cutting and pasting.

2 If you're working with a lettering stencil, you can use this paper printout as a guide for placing each stenciled letter. Tape the printout above your work guideline so that you can mimic the spacing as you stencil each letter.

3 If you want to cut a stencil for the whole phrase, use the photocopy as your pattern. Before cutting it, insert bridges wherever necessary to hold the doughnut letters together. Mark the bridges on the pattern with some whiteout and a black pen.

4 The stenciling part of the process is the same as stenciling a linear border, whether across a chest of drawers or along a wall. Mark a guideline for the path that the letters are to follow, then stencil them, either one at a time or all at once.

◼ For a simple monogram, a set of initials or a single word, you don't need much planning at all. Just plunk the stencil in the corner of a napkin, rub some paint over it, and *voilà!*

Wall lettering doesn't have to be a border or a linear phrase. You can create all-over patterns with words. These kanji characters were stenciled in a diamond layout, using a translucent glaze over a faux-linen background.

Letter Stencils

BRIDGE PROBLEM

Stenciled lettering would be a no-brainer if it weren't for the fact that the alphabet has a half-dozen or so doughnut letters. These letters must have bridges to keep the stencils intact. Bridged fonts usually portray most of the letters with bridges, even if they don't all need them. Depending on the style of lettering and the medium used, these bridges can be more or less intrusive. The next section presents various ways of incorporating or eliminating the bridges.

STENCIL METHOD BRIDGE STYLE

The only real disadvantage to stencils with bridges is that the gaps within the letters seem to broadcast "stencil!" However, some fonts incorporate these gaps more gracefully than others. The names on the laundry bags shown here were done with commercial stencils, as was the embellished initial on page 265. The combination of decorative motifs and metal leafing make the bridges less noticeable—they seem more like a deliberate component of the design.

TWO OVERLAYS

Overlays can be used to make the components of individual letters touch without gaps, as shown with this "A." Or they can provide a motif that breaks up the doughnut topology, as with this "Q." The main disadvantage to using overlays is the extra time and effort required.

Letter Stencils

STICKERS AND STENCILS

This approach to letters was mentioned in Chapter 2. It is suitable only for the well-organized artist, because it requires holding on to and keeping track of *all* the pieces produced when a letter stencil is cut. For example, with an uppercase "B," there's the piece that looks like a "B" sticker, the two little pieces that fall out of the middle and the big outer-stencil piece. Whenever you want to stencil "B" without a bridge, you must have all four pieces at hand, and all the pieces must have stencil adhesive on the back.

1 Cut a stencil for each letter needed. As you finish each letter, draw a set of crosshairs over the entire piece of stencil film, crossing cutouts and stencil parts alike. Apply stencil adhesive to all the pieces and save all of them.

2 Now, place sticker letters along the guideline, spacing them according to your plan. In this case, I've photocopied my phrase on strips of paper that I've taped along the wall, just above the guideline for my stenciled words. The copy acts as a spacing guide, as described on page 262.

3 Place the matching stencil over the first sticker letter, adjusting it for a perfect fit by lining up the crosshairs. Also lay down any little doughnut-hole pieces, such as the center of the "O." Smooth out all the pieces so that they are firmly attached.

4 Now lift up and remove the sticker letter. A bridgeless stencil of the letter remains on the surface. Paint it, using either a dry-brush (stippling or swirling) or roller-stenciling method.

5 Remove all pieces for that letter, and go on to the next one. If using solid oil paint or a plaster medium, skip every other letter to avoid smudging with an overlapping stencil. Once the first set of letters is dry, go back and fill in the remaining ones.

LINE UP STICKER LETTERS USING PRINTOUT AS A GUIDE

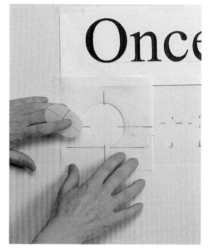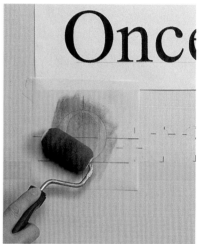

POSITION STENCIL AND CENTER OF "O"; REMOVE STICKER LETTER; STENCIL LETTER

HAND-FINISHING

This may be the most efficient approach to large stenciled letters, especially if they are placed where they won't be seen up close—say, along the top of a wall. In this case, any bridges can be made quite small compared with the overall dimensions of the letters. They are easy to fill in afterward with an artist's brush. Freehand paint touch-ups always look a little different from stenciled paint, but if the touch-ups are relatively small and far enough away to avoid close inspection, they won't be noticed.

APPLY SIZE TO BRIDGES

LAY DOWN GOLD LEAF, AND GENTLY RUB AWAY EXCESS

Letters done with metallic leaf can be touched up invisibly, because there are no brush strokes to be seen. Use a fine brush to apply size to the gaps, then lay down the leaf. Most leaf-supply companies also sell adhesive size pens, which can be used to apply even layers of size in lines of various thicknesses. They work really well for touch-ups.

Letter Stencils

SHADOW FONT

Shadow fonts are the only stencil style that makes any letter of the alphabet look bridgeless, even though the stencils have plenty of bridges. If it's appropriate to the project, this is an easy way to apply elegant lettering.

REVERSE STENCIL

Another way to represent letters without bridges is to stencil the *background* instead of the letters themselves. This approach can be used with any style of font. Here, it's shown with a hand-drawn font, printed with the same hand-cut stencil that was used to emboss the plate for the travel journal shown on page 260.

PEEL STENCIL OFF BACKING

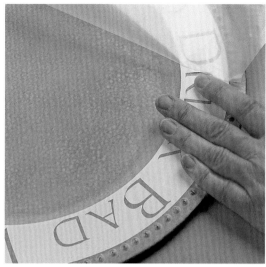

POSITION STENCIL, THEN REMOVE TOP SHEET

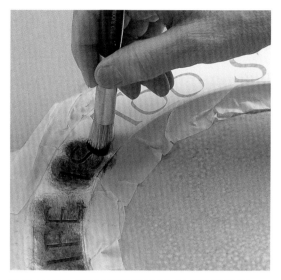

TAPE MASKS REST OF TRAY DURING STENCILING

SINGLE-USE CUSTOM VINYL STENCIL

For the ultimate approach to perfect bridgeless lettering, you can order custom stencils with the entire text cut from a sheet of adhesive-backed vinyl. These stencils come adhered to a top sheet that keeps all the pieces in place for positioning on the surface to be painted. It is a single-use method that produces completely bridgeless letters. There are many fonts from which to choose, and they can be cut in any size.

The text can be set up in any format, so all that's required is to position the stencil, paint the whole thing and peel off the stencil. For this circular tray, it saved me hours of fiddling.

A custom stencil is an expensive treatment for a mere tray; I've done it here mainly to show its versatility. It is far more cost-effective for larger projects, especially for putting text on walls. If you don't have much time or don't feel up to the planning needed but want a perfect result, this is the way to go.

Letter Stencils

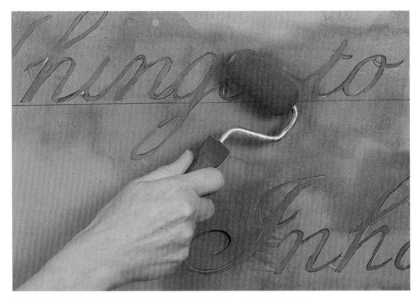

CUT LETTERS FROM FREEZER PAPER ON WALL, THEN STENCIL

PROJECTION

The projection stenciling method is a kind of homemade version of the custom stencil. Just one note of caution: Any projected image will be totally accurate only directly in front of the projector; the farther the image spreads from the center, the more it will be distorted. This doesn't matter much for most images, as the distortion is usually quite small, but for lettering, even small changes in either size or alignment may be noticeable.

In many cases, a projector still works just fine for lettering purposes, especially with text that's rather freeform in style or layout or with an old-fashioned handwritten style, such as the example shown here. Before starting to trace the text, I drew straight lines on the freezer paper where I wanted the text to go. This allowed me to reposition the projected image whenever necessary to maintain proper alignment.

For very precisely structured fonts, transfer the text to the freezer paper by drafting it onto strips of tracing paper first. Then affix the tracing paper to the freezer paper as a pattern, and cut through both tracing paper and freezer paper to form the letters.

The important feature of the projection method in this case is not the projection but, rather, the fact that the letters' doughnut holes stay in place, creating a bridgeless-style stencil.

The rest of this method is described in Chapter 8. In summary: Simply cut out the letters in situ, peel off the cut pieces, and stencil the revealed gaps.

EMBOSSED LETTERS

Embossing letters works best when it's done in one step, using a one-piece stencil. This method is particularly suited for monograms, initials and short graphic phrases. The basic instructions for embossing paper and metal foil are covered in Chapters 17 and 4, respectively, so this section discusses only the aspects that relate to lettering.

PAPER EMBOSSING

This is a really easy way to personalize stationery with a monogram or a set of initials. There's no paint involved and thus no brushes or stencils to clean afterward. It takes just a few seconds to complete a simple monogram. Because the letters are shaped only by contours in the paper, rather than by color, the bridges are pretty much inconspicuous.

1 If you're doing a number of sheets at one time, it's worthwhile to mark the relative positions of paper and stencil on either the stencil or the light table to facilitate placement of the stencil.

2 Don't forget to turn the stencil over so that the letters are backward when you work. Paper is embossed from the back, which means everything looks like a mirror image. When the paper is turned over to the right side, the letters will be correct. While you're at it, put monograms on the envelope flaps too.

A LOVELY WAY TO PERSONALIZE STATIONERY

METAL-FOIL EMBOSSING

EMBOSSED LETTERING WITH REVERSE STENCIL

Metal-foil pieces can make striking accents on journal covers and small home accessories, such as frames and trays. Because the foil is quite heavy, you should avoid tiny letter stencils when embossing.

Metal embossing may be started with the design right or wrong side up, depending on whether the final lettering will be inverted or protruding. You should try out the options on pieces of scrap foil first. This will help you decide which style you want and also which way the stencil needs to be placed so that the writing is right side up when finished.

1 For the travel journal shown here, I combined a reverse stencil for the title with a silhouette of one of the animals seen on safari. After embossing along the stencil edges, I rubbed as much protrusion as possible into the shapes with a smooth wood embossing tool.

2 I filled the back of the rhino and letters with hot glue to prevent the shapes from becoming dented whenever the journal was handled.

3 Then I glue-gunned the piece to the center of the cover (which I had previously paint-stenciled in a leopard pattern).

Chapter 17

PAPER

Most novice stencilers begin by working on paper. Cheap and disposable or recyclable, it's the ideal surface for practice and trial and error. But with the right paper and the right approach, stenciling on paper can also be an end in itself.

Paper surfaces are less forgiving than walls, wood, canvas or glass. They are not sealed and, depending on the finish and composition, have varying reactions to water-based paint. They can stretch and buckle or even disintegrate. If you are too aggressive in your application, you'll end up with colored patches of damp pulp. And a mistake cannot simply be washed away.

When starting to work on a good paper project, as opposed to a practice one, keep a few things in mind. The work surface must be meticulously clean, because paper is easily soiled. If dampened, the paper will warp. Try to avoid using adhesives on the stencils, because they cause some types of paper to tear when the stencil is removed.

Painted Paper

BRUSH-STENCILED TISSUE PAPER

HEAVY PAPER STENCILED AND FRAMED BY CUTOUTS

STENCIL BRUSH

Stenciling on paper with a brush is no different than stenciling on a wall with a brush, except that paper is not nearly as tough as a wall. The lighter the paper, the lighter your touch should be. It is very easy to damage the surface of paper once it becomes damp, especially when brushing with a circular motion instead of stippling.

 I love to use fabric paint for brush stenciling on paper. Until it has been air-cured or heat-set, it tends to be a more or less reversible paint, which means that it goes on very smoothly, blends well and doesn't set up as hard and fast as do acrylics. Solid oil paint also works well because it doesn't contain water.

■ Even the flimsiest paper can be stenciled as long as all the excess paint is offloaded and a gentle touch is applied. One example above shows random blossoms stenciled onto tissue paper. I used a soft brush and held the stencil in place by hand (no adhesive). Stamens were added freehand.

■ There are many ways to play around with color and pattern when working on tissue paper. To obtain a very delicate watercolor look, for example, cover one of the stenciled tissue sheets with plain white tissue. For a different effect, put a sheet of colored tissue underneath a white one that has been stenciled.

■ With heavier, more absorbent papers, you needn't be as concerned about extreme offloading, and you can layer more prints, working into freeform stenciling, if you wish. One worry-free way to make cards is to stencil clusters of

STENCILED GIFT BOX BEFORE FOLDING; FINISHED BOX AND TAG ON PAGE 270

freeform motifs on loose paper, then pick out some favorites and frame them into cards by means of small cutout windows. That way, expensive card stock won't be wasted on trial-and-error compositions.

■ Poster board is a forgiving surface for stenciling. It is both smooth and absorbent, so just about any kind of paint can be used. It's a good material for stenciled gift boxes. A number of companies manufacture templates for a variety of box shapes; use these as patterns to cut and score the stock. Stencil the pieces before folding them, as it's much easier to work on a flat surface.

STENCIL ROLLER

For speed or for printing large motifs, it's usually worthwhile to exchange a brush for a stencil roller. This method even works with tissue paper (as shown with the gold koi on black below), as long as enough paint is offloaded from the roller. Tissue is very sensitive to moisture, and it's easy for excess paint to pass right through the paper and stick to the work surface.

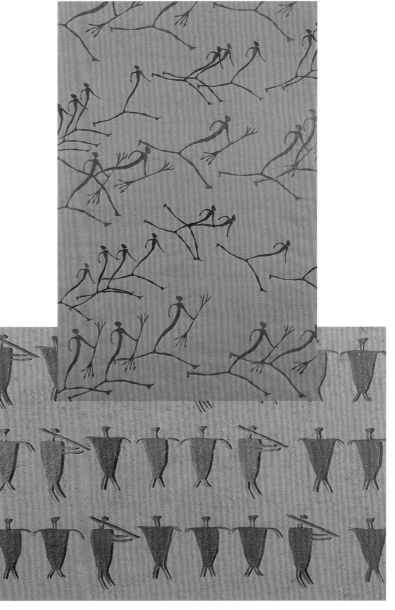

For tougher papers, it isn't necessary to be so careful. You can use almost any paint, including latex house paint. The two examples shown above were done on brown kraft and handmade paper, both roller stenciled with metallic paints.

NOTE: With heavy papers and for impasto stencil work (see Chapter 4), you may find it easier to use a little spray adhesive on the back of the stencil. If this leaves any sticky residue on the paper, it can be removed easily with an art eraser.

Painted Paper

SPATULA

Mediums that are applied with a spatula or a trowel are not usually suitable for most types of paper, because they allow too much moisture to stay in contact with the paper for too long, causing the paper to buckle. This problem can be minimized by sealing the surface first with a painted print and stenciling the impasto medium as an overlay. With a little experimentation, you may find one or two products that work well here. The basic method used is described in Chapter 4.

For the petroglyph characters stenciled on the stationery sheets, I first created a silhouette with black acrylic paint. This sealed the surface enough that I could safely use a spatula to apply gold gel through an overlay stencil. This is not so much to get some tactile relief as it is to get a very opaque gold layer in one pass, even though it was applied over black.

A thick medium can often be used with small motifs by simply choosing a thicker stock of paper. I used ornamental gesso on these small blue note cards.

WATERCOLOR

Here's a technique that breaks all the rules for stenciling. I water-misted heavy watercolor paper on both sides until it was thoroughly wet. Holding the stencil in place by hand, I brushed fabric paint sparingly over the cutouts with a soft stencil brush, using long, gentle sweeps. After removing the stencil, I accented facial details with a sharp watercolor pencil. Then I alternated water misting and pencil touch-ups until I was satisfied with the color dispersal. This uses the same stencil shown on page 112.

Leafed Paper

1 Motifs stenciled with metal leaf or leaf flakes look stunning on paper. Water-based adhesive size works well if it is applied carefully by pouncing with a fine-textured makeup sponge. Try to find a thick brand of adhesive, as the thin ones bleed very easily and warp the paper. Do not use stencil adhesive on the back of the stencil.

2 Remove the stencil. As soon as the adhesive is dry (i.e., clear but still tacky), apply the leaf or leaf flakes. Tamp into place with a soft brush.

3 Burnish it flat with a soft cloth. This should dislodge most of the excess leaf. Continue rubbing gently with the cloth or with a soft stencil brush until all the excess leaf has been brushed away.

4 Add relief to the leafed image by making dots, swirls or outlines with very viscous size or with a glue gun. Let these embellishments dry until clear (it takes a while), then lay bits of leaf on top, and rub with a soft cloth or brush.

Embossed Paper

One of the easiest techniques for adding a little decorative zip to paper is embossing. All it requires is a stencil, a simple embossing tool and a light table (or some kind of lighted work surface) to sculpt a low-relief motif into a sheet of paper or card stock.

■ The stencil should be fairly simple, ideally one piece, without excruciating detail. It should have a palpable thickness. Metal stencils work well for this, as do Mylar stencils of 7-mil thickness or greater. Stencils that are any thinner don't create enough relief in the paper for an effective image. Laser-cut stencils are best because they produce very clean, sharp edges.

■ Many stencil companies offer small stencils specifically for embossing. They also sell embossing tools, as do stores that specialize in paper crafts. About the size of a pencil, the standard embossing tool has a small metal ball at each end, one slightly bigger than the other. A knitting needle can also be used, although it isn't as comfortable to hold.

■ A fancy light table is not necessary. The one used here is small and inexpensive, meant for working with embossed cards. You can improvise with a lamp set under a glass table.

■ This process works best with good-quality heavy paper or light-to-medium-weight card stock. Very thick or heavily colored paper is not suitable, because the outline of the stencil must be visible through the paper when it is placed on the light table.

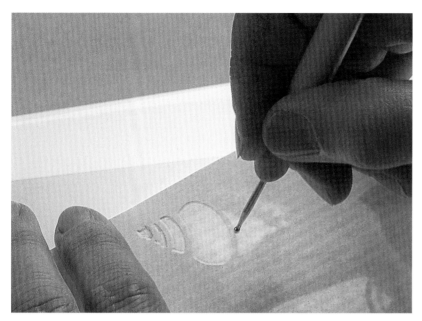

PLACE STENCIL UNDERNEATH PAPER BEING EMBOSSED

BASIC METHOD

1 Begin by attaching the stencil to the right side of the paper, using low-tack tape.

2 Then turn the paper over, and place it on the light table. The stencil should be backlit through the paper.

3 Using the larger end of the embossing tool, trace the inside edge of the motif. Press hard enough to make an impression but not so hard as to tear the paper.

4 Now use the smaller end of the tool to trace again, this time pressing a little harder; again, be careful not to tear the paper.

NOTE: If the embossing tool has just one tip size, then use it to trace the design twice—lightly the first time and harder the second.

5 Remove the stencil, and turn the paper over to see the finished impression.

■ Emboss a single motif like this one in the corner of a note card, or if you're up for a little more work, do a small border across the top of notepaper sheets. Either way, it makes a quiet, elegant statement.

NOTE: Embossed images can also be stencil-painted. Some people stencil the paint first, then emboss, while others do it in the reverse order. I prefer the paint-first approach, because then I don't risk flattening the embossed edges when applying the color.

An overlay can also be embossed on the motif, as long as both pieces of the stencil are simple and the backlit stencil can be seen well enough to line up the overlay. The star on this card was done with a two-piece stencil.

Etched Paper

STIPPLE ETCHING GEL

IRON TO ACTIVATE THE ACID IN THE GEL

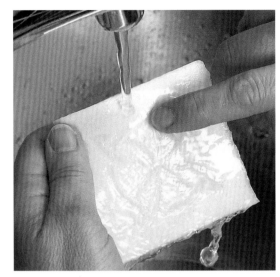

RINSE AND GENTLY RUB AWAY DARK PARTS

This is similar to the devoré technique for fabric (see page 248). Stencil a paper-dissolving gel (called Paper-Etch™) onto the surface of thick paper stock, heat-activate the gel, then rinse away the treated parts to leave a low-relief pattern on the paper.

Not all types of paper are suitable for this technique. Paper-Etch™ works with cotton-rag watercolor paper without fillers, finishes or plasticizers. You can also use Velvet Paper™ (a specialty paper with a velvetlike nap) or Carving Paper™, which is a very soft, thick, 100 percent cotton paper sold by the makers of Paper-Etch™. I used the latter for the examples shown here.

1 Paper-Etch™ bleeds very easily, so use it carefully with a stencil. Use a stencil brush or makeup sponge and a stippling technique to apply several light coats. Because the gel is colorless, it is extremely hard to see what has and has not been covered. Therefore, work systematically from one side of the stencil to the other. Do not move the stencil between coats, because you won't be able to reposition it correctly.

2 When finished, remove the stencil and let the gel dry. A hair dryer will speed things up.

3 Now heat-activate the gel. There are two ways to do this. The first is to cover the paper with a sheet of tracing paper and iron it with medium heat until the treated area becomes very dark. (The exact color depends on the type of paper and may be gray, brown or almost black.) The second way is to put the paper in a 200-degree-F oven for about 10 minutes, or until the same color change has occurred.

4 Rinse the paper under a gentle stream of running water, and brush away the darkened bits until the original color is revealed.

NOTE: When rinsing Carving Paper™, use a finger or very soft artist's brush as a removal tool, because the paper is quite fragile. It helps to have a flat support under the paper, such as a cookie sheet, while rinsing it. For Velvet Paper™ or watercolor paper, use a soft bristle brush or a plastic surgeon's brush.

FINISHED MOTIF SCULPTED INTO PAPER

5 Blot the paper with a towel, and allow it to dry flat. The stenciled parts should be visible as a design carved into the paper. The depth of the relief depends on the composition of the paper and how far the gel penetrated from the surface.

SAFETY NOTE: Follow label instructions carefully when using Paper-Etch™. Be sure to heat-activate in a well-ventilated area.

STENCILED PROTECTANT COVERS RAISED AREA WHILE REST OF PAPER IS ETCHED

Cut Paper

Sometimes you need go no further than the stencil itself for a combination of function and decoration. This Japanese bookmark is essentially a simple mulberry-paper stencil. These don't take much longer to make than their painted counterparts, because the paper is thin enough that it can be stacked for easy multiple-copy cutting.

You can reverse the etched relief to create a protruding design and a receding background by stenciling the pattern with a resist material that won't discolor under heat. One material that works this way is Scotch Gard™ fabric protector (not carpet protector). However, it's very difficult to keep this product from bleeding, so the resulting image always looks a little more aged than perfect. I get better results applying the Scotch Gard™ with a makeup sponge (after spraying a puddle of it onto my palette) than I do by spraying it over the stencil.

Let the Scotch Gard™ dry, then apply Paper-Etch™ over the entire piece of paper. Let dry, then heat-activate and rinse as described on facing page. This is an unpredictable process, so be prepared for mixed results.

Sources

The following material is divided into three main sections. The first section, General Product Information, includes general information on products for stenciling. The second section, Specific Products Used in This Book, provides a detailed listing of products and manufacturers. It is subdivided by type of project and corresponds approximately to the chapters in this book. The final section, Companies Whose Products Were Used in This Book, is an alphabetical list that includes contact information.

GENERAL PRODUCT INFORMATION

PAINTS, GLAZES AND FAUX-FINISHING PRODUCTS

Various brands of paints, glazes and faux-finishing products are available at paint, hardware and building-supply stores. If a particular brand is not sold in your area, you can usually order it online. Art and craft brands can be found in stores that carry craft supplies and fine-art materials as well as online. Fabric paints are sold in craft and fabric stores and in stores that sell quilting or silk-painting supplies.

STENCIL FILM FOR HAND-CUT STENCILS

■ Freezer paper: sold under various brand names in supermarkets
■ Plastic shelf liners: sold in rolls in hardware stores under various brand names; look for the kind labeled "repositionable," as it has a low-tack adhesive on one side
■ Overhead transparency film: sold in sheets and rolls in office-supply stores
■ Mylar (polyester) and other transparent films: sold in sheets and rolls in various thicknesses; available in art-supply stores and in quantity from G.E. Polymer Shapes and Grafix Plastics
■ Adhesive-backed 7-mil transparent stencil film: available from StenSource International
■ E-Z Cut transparent stencil film: from PJ's Decorative Stencils

COMMERCIAL STENCILS

Many companies now produce laser- and die-cut stencils. Each has a particular style, so it's worthwhile looking around to see what's available. Some brands are available in paint, hardware and craft stores; others are sold only by mail order or on the Internet. Almost all companies have websites with online catalogs.

There are too many stencil companies to provide a complete listing, but you can find most of them, including their mail-order addresses and websites, through the Stencil Artisans League, Inc. (SALI). This is an international nonprofit organization dedicated to promoting and preserving the art of stenciling and related decorative painting. Membership (not expensive) is open to amateurs, hobbyists and professionals and comes with a subscription to the quarterly magazine *The Artistic Stenciler*. SALI also hosts an annual convention, complete with classes and trade show. If you're serious about stenciling, either professionally or just for fun, consider joining SALI. Find out more at www.sali.org, or write to SALI at Box 3109, Las Lunas, NM 87031. Telephone and fax: (505) 865-9119.

SPECIFIC PRODUCTS USED IN THIS BOOK

STENCILS AND GENERAL TOOLS

Except for a few of the lettering stencils, all stencils used in this book were either designed and hand-cut specifically for the book or taken from the commercial collection produced by Buckingham Stencils Inc. These can be seen at www.buckinghamstencils.com. Other stencils and general products used in this book:
■ Fishermen stencil used with the crackle finish background in Chapter 4: adapted from a Moses Eaton stencil found in Janet Waring's book *Early American Stencils* (Dover Publications)
■ Commercial alphabet and monogram stencils: Delta Technical Coatings and American Traditional Stencils
■ Custom-cut and -formatted lettering stencil in Chapter 16: Say What? division of The Mad Stencilist
■ Stencil adhesive: Buckingham Stencils Inc.; many other brands in craft, art-supply, paint and hardware stores
■ Stencil-cutting knife: small Olfa utility knife, with snap-off blades, sold in craft, art-supply, paint and hardware stores; X-acto knives and other brands of craft knife are also suitable
■ Heat cutter for stencils: available from some craft stores, also from American Traditional Stencils and PJ's Decorative Stencils
■ Stencil brushes and rollers: Buckingham Stencils Inc.; other brands and other applicators sold in craft, art-supply, paint and hardware stores, as well as online through commercial stencil companies
■ Surgical brushes: Lee Valley Tools
■ Palette trays: Buckingham Stencils Inc.
■ Self-healing cutting mats: craft and fabric stores
■ Fine-tipped paint-liner bottles: Maiwa Handprints
■ AirPen®: Silkpaint Corporation
■ Tape: Painters Mate® Green and Painters Mate® Delicate from Tape Specialties Ltd.; sold in paint and hardware stores
■ Paint pens: Painters® opaque paint markers, from Hunt Corporation, sold in craft-supply stores

FINISHING AND FAUX-FINISHING PRODUCTS AND TOOLS

■ Glazes, clear finishes, specialty finish products, primers: from Adicolor, Briste Group, Ritins, General Paint, Zinsser and Polyvine, sold in selected paint stores; other brands are sold in paint stores everywhere
■ Floetrol flow enhancer (Flood Company): sold in paint and hardware stores
■ Shellac (Zinsser): sold in paint and hardware stores
■ Clear water-based finishes for use over painted surfaces: Clear Gloss and Matte Mediums (Liquitex), J.W. etc. Right Step, Varnishing Wax (Polyvine), Dead Flat Varnish (Adicolor)
■ Oil-based varnishes for wood: Varathane (Flecto), Marine Spar Varnish (General Paint)

PAINT FOR STENCILING

■ Latex house paint: various brands sold in paint stores
■ Water-based faux-finishing glazes: Adicolor, Briste Group, Polyvine, Ritins; other glazes by makers of most brand-name house paints in paint, hardware and craft-supply stores
■ Acrylic hobby paints: Ceramcoat (Delta Technical Coatings), Americana (DecoArt); other brands may be available from craft stores in your area
■ Fabric paints: Setacolor (Pébéo), Jacquard Textile Colors
■ Artist's acrylic paint: Liquitex, Golden, Winsor & Newton, JoSonja, Permalba (Martin F. Weber)
■ Solid oil paints: Oil Bar® (Winsor & Newton), Paintstik® (Shiva), Stencil Magic Stencil Creme (Delta Technical Coatings), Easy Blend Stencil Paint (DecoArt)
■ Wood stains: DecoArt Gel Stain, Old Masters Gel Stain and other brands are available at paint and hardware stores and Lee Valley Tools
■ Interference colors: Liquitex

IMPASTO STENCIL MEDIUMS

Available in paint and hardware stores, craft-supply stores and on the Internet.
- Generic drywall compound, joint compound
- Patching compounds: Spackle™ (interior and exterior)
- Venetian plaster or polished plaster products: Adicolor, Briste Group, Ritins
- Textured aggregate coating: Briste Group
- Sandstones: DecoArt
- Ornamental gesso: Ritins
- Liquitex Gel medium: Liquitex

METALLIC MEDIUMS

All sold in art-, craft- or sign writers' supply stores or on the Internet.
- Gold, composition gold- and silver-leaf products: GrafTek, Le-Franc & Bourgeois, Old World Art
- Oil-based size: Rolco
- Water-based size: Old World Art, Delta Technical Coatings
- Metallic powder: Gold Leaf and Metallic Powders
- Foil: Renaissance Foil™, adhesive and sealer by Delta Technical Coatings
- Metallic gel: Metal Series (Adicolor), MT900 Topcoat (Briste Group)
- Metal paint/patina finish: Magic Metallics (Mayco Colors), Metal Effects® (Modern Masters)
- Metallic paints: available in most brand-name hobby and artist's paint lines
- Embossing foil and embossing tools: LeFranc & Bourgeois

DISTRESSING MEDIUMS

- Crackle paint finish: Lee Valley Fish Glue
- Craquelure: Polyvine Craquelure

OUTLINING

- Silk-resist squeeze bottles with needle tips: Maiwa Handprints
- AirPen®: Silkpaint Corporation

MASKING

- White Mask Liquid Frisket: Grafix Plastics
- Incredible Nib frisket applicator: Grafix Plastics

PROJECTION STENCILING

- Overhead projector: borrow or rent from school or library
- Opaque overhead projector: Artograph Inc., sold in art- and craft-supply stores
- Freezer paper: various brands, available in supermarkets
- TransferRite™: stores selling sign-writing supplies
- Low-tack shelf paper: hardware and kitchen-supply stores

ARCHITECTURAL ELEMENTS

- Watercolor crayons: Staedtler, sold in art-supply stores
- Watercolor pencils: Staedtler, sold in art-supply stores
- Groundstone coating and blocking tape: Briste Group

FAUX MARQUETRY

- Water-based gel stains: DecoArt Gel Stains, sold in craft-supply stores
- Water-based stain/sealer: Liquitex Acrylic Wood Stains, sold in art- and craft-supply stores
- Oil-based stains: Old Masters Gel Stain, available from Lee Valley Tools
- Solid oil paints: Oil Bar® (Winsor & Newton), sold in art-supply stores
- Freezer paper: grocery stores
- Maple veneer bundle cut to business-card size: Lee Valley Tools
- Citristrip® paint stripper: paint and hardware stores
- Oil-based varnish: Flecto's Varathane oil-based wood finish, General Paint's Marine Spar Varnish, available in paint stores

FAUX TILES

- Craquelure kit: Polyvine, sold in selected paint stores or on the Internet

- Makeup sponges: pharmacies
- Sea sponges: paint stores
- Spattering tool: Loew-Cornell, sold in art-supply stores
- Watercolor crayons: Staedtler, sold in art-supply stores
- Impasto medium: see Impasto Stencil Mediums at left

GLASS AND CERAMIC STENCILING

Sold in art- and craft-supply stores.
- Nonbake glass and tile paints: PermEnamel (Delta Technical Coatings), Ultra Gloss (DecoArt)
- Bake-on glass and tile paints: Porcelaine 150 (Pébéo), Vitrea 160 (Pébéo)
- Impasto glass medium: Gel Crystal (Pébéo)
- Fake-etching medium: White Frost (PermEnamel by Delta Technical Coatings)
- True-etching medium: Armour Etch, Etchall
- Cloisonné: Pébéo; Delta Technical Coatings and DecoArt produce similar products
- Self-adhesive vinyl such as MacTac™ or Rubbermaid Con-Tact Ultra™: hardware stores
- Makeup sponges: pharmacies

UNDER FOOT

- Porch and floor latex enamel paints: many brands, sold in paint and hardware stores
- Wood stains: different brands, sold in paint and hardware stores
- Clear sealers: different brands, sold in paint and hardware stores (make sure it's the right product for going over stain or paint, whichever you need)
- Primers: choose according to floor material (wood, vinyl, concrete, etc.)
- Floorcloth canvas: sold by art-supply stores, tent and awning makers and marine suppliers, as well as mail-order and Internet sources: available primed or unprimed
- Acrylic gesso: Liquitex; this and other brands sold in art-supply stores

STENCILING ON FABRICS

Sold in fabric, art-supply and textile-art stores or on the Internet.
- Fabric paints: Pébéo Setacolor, Jacquard Textile Colors
- Devoré medium (Fiber-Etch™) and devoré fabrics: Silkpaint Corporation, Maiwa Handprints, Farthingales Fabrics by Mail, Dharma Trading
- Prehemmed silk scarves and other paintable silk items: Silkpaint Corporation, Arty's
- Sun-printing medium: Setacolor and Setacolor Soleil by Pébéo
- Discharge chemicals (sodium alginate, Synthrapol, soda ash, metabisulfite): Maiwa Handprints
- Katazome materials, tools and courses: Maiwa Handprints, John Marshall Ltd.

LETTERING

- Metal alphabet stencil: American Traditional Stencils
- Plastic alphabet and monogram stencils: Delta Technical Coatings
- Custom-shaped and -cut stencils: Say What? division of The Mad Stencilist
- Alphabet pattern books: Dover Publications
- Metal foil, wooden embossing tools: LeFranc & Bourgeois
- Miniature light table, metal embossing tool: American Traditional Stencils
- Metal-leafing flakes: LeFranc & Bourgeois, GrafTek

STENCILING ON PAPER

- Acrylic paint, solid oil paint, fabric paint: see above sources
- Paper-Etch™: Silkpaint Corporation
- Miniature light table, embossing tools: American Traditional Stencils
- Paper-box templates: Draggin It, American Traditional Stencils
- Acrylic ink: art-supply stores
- Velvet paper, carving paper: Silkpaint Corporation
- Mulberry paper: Maiwa Handprints
- Impasto glass medium: Gel Crystal (Pébéo)
- Ornamental gesso: Ritins

Sources COMPANIES WHOSE PRODUCTS WERE USED IN THIS BOOK

ADICOLOR, 572 Millway Ave., Concord, ON L4K 3V5 Canada www.adicolor.com Faux-finishing products: Wet Edge Plus®, Stucco Antico, DFV® sealer, Natural Stone FX, Metal Series gel

AMERICAN TRADITIONAL STENCILS INC., www.amtrad-stencil.com Mylar and brass stencils, embossing tools, miniature light table

ARMOUR PRODUCTS, Box 128, 210 Lawlins Park, Wyckoff, NJ 07481 www.armourproducts.com Armour Etch glass-etching cream, sold in craft stores

ARTY'S, The Janlynn Corporation, 34 Front St, Indian Orchard, MA 01151-5848, www.artys.ch Products for silk, textile arts and crafts

B&B ETCHING PRODUCTS INC., 19721 N. 98th Ave., Peoria, AZ 85382 www.etchall.com Etchall glass-etching cream

BRISTE GROUP INTERNATIONAL, 4019 Chesswood Dr., Toronto, ON M3J 2R8 Canada, www.bristegroup.com Faux-finishing products, including polished plasters, aggregate coatings, clear polishing topcoats, Groundstone and blocking tape

BUCKINGHAM STENCILS INC., 1710 Morello Road, Nanoose Bay, BC V9P 9B1 Canada www.Buckinghamstencils.com Stencils, stencil rollers, palette trays, stencil brushes, paints, video

DECOART INC., www.decoart.com Products for decorative artists, including Americana acrylic paints, Ultra Gloss glass paint, fabric paint, sealer, Gel stain, impasto mediums

DELTA TECHNICAL COATINGS INC., www.deltacrafts.com Products for decorative artists, including Ceramcoat acrylic paints, PermEnamel glass paints, fabric paints, sealers, glazes, retarders, stains, impasto mediums

EASY LEAF PRODUCTS, 6001 Santa Monica Blvd., Los Angeles, CA 90038 www.easyleaf.com Bronze powders, gold leafing materials

FARTHINGALES FABRICS BY MAIL, 309 Lorne Ave. East, RR#3, Stratford, ON N5A 6S4 Canada www.farthingales.on.ca Fabrics for devoré and discharge treatments

FLOOD CO., Box 2535, Hudson, OH 44236-0035, www.floodco.com Floetrol paint conditioner and flow enhancer

G.E. POLYMER SHAPES, www.gepolymershapes.com Transparent plastic films, including polyester, for stencil blanks

GOLDEN ARTIST COLORS, 188 Bell Rd., New Berlin, NY 13411-9527 www.goldenpaints.com Artist's paints and mediums

GRAFIX PLASTICS, 19499 Miles Rd., Cleveland, OH 44128 www.grafixplastics.com Liquid frisket and applicator, transparent plastic films, including polyester, for stencil blanks

GRAFTEK, A Division of S&Z Assoc., Box 23260, Knoxville, TN 37933 Gold-leafing products, gilding kits

HUNT CORPORATION, www.hunt-corp.com Painters® paint markers, art products

JACQUARD PRODUCTS, Rupert, Gibbon & Spider, Box 425, Healdsburg, CA 95448 www.jacquardproducts.com Products for painting and dyeing textiles

J.W. ETC., 2205 First St., Ste. 103, Simi Valley, CA 93065, www.jwetc.com Right Step water-based clear coat

LEE VALLEY TOOLS, Box 6295, Station J, Ottawa, ON K2A 1T4 Canada

www.leevalley.com Surgical brushes, wood-finishing products and tools, glues

LEFRANC & BOURGEOIS, COLART AMERICAS INC., Box 1396, Piscataway, NJ 08855-1396 Gold-leafing products, heavy foils for embossing

LIQUITEX, www.liquitex.com Professional and student-grade artist's paints and mediums

THE MAD STENCILIST, Box 5497, Dept. N, El Dorado Hills, CA 95762 www.madstencilist.com Stencils, custom-lettering stencils

MAIWA HANDPRINTS LTD., #6-1666 Johnston St., Granville Island, Vancouver, BC V6H 3S2 Canada, www.maiwa.com Fabric dyes and paints, devoré supplies, stencils, floorcloth supplies, katazome supplies, books, workshops

MARTIN F. WEBER, 2727 Southampton Rd., Philadelphia, PA 19154-1293 www.weberart.com Permalba artist acrylic paint

MAYCO COLORS, www.maycocolors.com Magic Metallics metal paint and patina finishes

MODERN MASTERS INC., 7340 Greenbush Ave., North Hollywood, CA 91605 www.modernmastersinc.com Metal Effects® (metal paint and patina finishes)

OLD WORLD ART, DIVISION OF CALDEX CRAFT PRODUCTS, INC,, 1953 South Lake Place, Ontario, CA 91761, www.caldexcrafts.com Gold-leafing products

PÉBÉO www.pebeo.com Paints and other mediums for use on glass and ceramic surfaces, Setacolor fabric paints

PJ'S DECORATIVE STENCILS, Box 5774, Albany, NY 12205 www.pjstencils.com E-Z Cut transparent stencil film

POLYVINE INC., 27825 Avenue Hopkins, Unit 1, Valencia, CA 91355-4577 www.polyvine.com Faux-finishing products

RITINS STUDIO INC., 170 Wicksteed Ave., Toronto, ON M4G 2B6 Canada www.ritins.com Faux-finishing products, classes

SHIVA PAINTSTIKS, James Richeson & Co. Inc., Box 160, Kimberly, WI 54136, www.richesonart.com Shiva Paintstiks®, art supplies

SILKPAINT CORPORATION, 18220 Waldron Dr., Box 18 INT, Waldron, MO 64092, www.silkpaint.com Paper-Etch™ (paper-dissolving gel), Fiber-Etch™ (cellulose-fiber-dissolving gel), Velvet Paper™, Carving Paper™, AirPen®

STAEDTLER INC. www.staedtler-usa.com Art, craft and drafting supplies, including watercolor pencils and crayons; sold in art- and craft-supply stores

STENSOURCE INTERNATIONAL INC., 18971 Hess Ave., Sonora, CA 95370, www.stensource.com Sta-Put 7-mil adhesive-backed transparent plastic stencil film

TAPE SPECIALTIES LTD., 615 Bowes Rd., Concord, ON L4K 1J5 Canada www.thegreentape.com Painters Mate® Green and Painters Mate® Delicate tapes

WINSOR & NEWTON, Box 1396, Piscataway, NJ 08855 www.winsornewton.com Oil Bar® (artist's quality solid oil color in stick form)

ZINSSER, 173 Belmont Dr., Somerset, NJ 08875 www.zinsser.com Shellac, BIN®

Further Reading

PAINTING AND FAUX FINISHING

The Art of Faux, by Pierre Finkelstein, Watson-Guptill, 1997.

Classic Paints & Faux Finishes, by Annie Sloan and Kate Gwynn, Reader's Digest, 1993.

The Complete Book of Floorcloths, by Kathy Cooper and Jan Hersey, Lark Books, 1997.

Decorative Gilding: A Practical Guide, by Annie Sloan, Reader's Digest, 1996.

Decorative Style, by Kevin McCloud, Simon and Schuster, 1990.

Decorative Wood Finishes: A Practical Guide, by Annie Sloan, Reader's Digest, 1997.

Exploring Color (revised edition), by Nita Leland, North Light Books, 1998.

The Handbook of Painted Decoration, by Yannick Guégan and Roger Le Puil, English translation by Josh Heuman, W.W. Norton & Company, 1996.

Light: How to See It, How to Paint It, by Lucy Willis, North Light Books, 1988.

Master Strokes, by Jennifer Bennell, Hutchinson Australia, 1988.

Understanding Wood Finishing: How to Select and Apply the Right Finish, by Bob Flexner, Rodale Press, 1994.

GENERAL AND TRADITIONAL STENCILING

The Art of Decorative Stenciling, by Adele Bishop and Cile Lord, Penguin Books, 1976.

Decorative Stenciling and Stamping: A Practical Guide, by Annie Sloan, Reader's Digest, 1997.

Decorative Stencils for Interior Design, by Maggie M. Maule, Angus & Robertson, 1991.

Early American Stencils on Walls and Furniture, by Janet Waring, Dover, 1968.

Stencil It! by Sandra Buckingham, Firefly Books, 1993.

The Stenciled House, by Lyn Le Grice, Simon and Schuster, 1988.

Stenciling, by Katrina Hall and Laurence Llewelyn-Bowen, Friedman/Fairfax, 1995.

Stenciling Techniques, by Jane Gauss and the Stencil Artisans League Inc., Watson-Guptill, 1995.

Stencilling, by Joanne Malone, Penguin Books Australia, 1991.

Stencilling, by Lynne Robinson and Richard Lowther, Conran Octopus, 1995.

Stencilling: A Harrowsmith Guide, by Sandra Buckingham, Firefly Books, 1989.

Ultimate Stencils, by Althea Wilson, Harmony Books, 1990.

PROJECTION STENCILING

Projection Art for Kids, by Linda Buckingham, Hartley & Marks, 2002.

Projection Stenciling, by Linda Buckingham and Leslie Bird, Hartley & Marks, 1999.

FLOORCLOTHS

The Complete Book of Floorcloths, by Kathy Cooper and Jan Hersey, Lark Books, 1997.

Fabulous Floorcloths: Create Contemporary Floor Coverings from an Old World Art, by Caroline O'Neill Kuchinsky, Krause Publications, 1998.

Painting Floorcloths: 20 Canvas Rugs to Stamp, Stencil, Sponge and Spatter in a Weekend (The Weekend Crafter), by Kathy Cooper and Deborah Morgenthal (editor), Lark Books, 1999.

FREEFORM TROMPE L'OEIL STENCILING

Stencilling on a Grand Scale, by Sandra Buckingham, Firefly Books, 1997.

Trompe l'Oeil Murals Using Stencils, by Melanie Royals, North Light Books, 2001.

JAPANESE STENCILING

Carved Paper: The Art of the Japanese Stencil, by Susanna Campbell Kuo, Santa Barbara Museum of Art, 1998.

Katazome: Japanese Paste-Resist Dyeing for Contemporary Use, by Kumiko Murashima, Lark Books, 1993.

Katazome Manual, Maiwa Handprints, 1993.

PAINTED MURALS

Decorative Designs, by Graham Rust, Bullfinch Press, 1996.

Grand Illusions, by Caroline Cass, Phaidon, 1988.

The Painted House, by Graham Rust, Knopf, 1988.

Painting Murals, by Patricia Seligman, Macdonald Orbis, 1987.

Trompe l'Oeil: Creating Decorative Illusions in Paint, by Roberta Gordon-Smith, North Light Books, 1998.

Trompe l'Oeil: Murals and Decorative Wall Painting, by Lynette Wrigley, Rizzoli, 1997.

TEXTILE ARTS

"Dyeing with Bleach," by Lois Ericson, *Threads* magazine, August/September 1997.

DESIGN SOURCES

Dover Pictorial Archive Series, by various authors (Dover Publications). This series is the best historical and ethnic design source for those wanting to create their own stencils. Some volumes include stencil patterns; others have many designs that can be modified to create stencil patterns. There are too many books in this series to list by title, and new titles are added every year.

Index

Index

A SPECIAL THANKS TO:

Laurel Aziz
Tiki Barber Aziz and Tiger Woods Aziz
Jean Bruce
Susan and Terry Dickinson
Michael Gemmell
Linda J. Menyes
Adrienne and Jody Morgan
Wendy Reynolds and Sean Philp